The Best of Bacon

The
Best
of
Bacon

Select Cuts

JOHN U. BACON

University of Michigan Press
Ann Arbor

To Teddy,
Truly, the best of Bacon

Published in the United States of America by the
University of Michigan Press
Manufactured in the United States of America
Printed on acid-free paper
First published May 2018

A CIP catalog record for this book is available from the British Library.

Library of Congress Cataloging-in-Publication Data

Names: Bacon, John U., 1964– author.
Title: Best of Bacon : select cuts / John U. Bacon.
Description: Ann Arbor : University of Michigan Press, [2018]
Identifiers: LCCN 2017060912 | ISBN 9780472130818 (hardcover : acid-free paper) | ISBN 9780472123858 (e-book)
Subjects: LCSH: Sports—Michigan—History—Miscellanea.
Classification: LCC GV584.M5 B34 2018 | DDC 796.09774—dc23
LC record available at https://lccn.loc.gov/2017060912

Cover photo courtesy of Eric Upchurch.

Contents

Preface

I wrote these stories between 1992 and 2018. They cover a dozen different sports for a dozen different media outlets, from the *Ann Arbor News* to National Public Radio, and they stretch from a couple pages to a dozen. But they have one thing in common: they all meant a lot to me when I wrote them, and they still do today. That's why I'm thrilled to see them together in one place, as well-preserved as anything in the increasingly ephemeral world of journalism can be.

It took more than a decade to bring this idea to life. Back in 2001, I published my first book, *Blue Ice: The Story of Michigan Hockey*, with the University of Michigan Press. A few years later I started talking with my friends at U-M Press about creating this book, but the timing never seemed right—until now.

Once I sat down with editor Scott Ham to start building this book, we decided pretty quickly we didn't want to produce a mere "greatest hits" collection, a random sampling of my favorite pieces. Instead, we sought to select and shape these stories to tell a bigger story about sports, and our relationship to them.

With that in mind, we discarded the idea of organizing these stories by superficial categories like geography, or chronology, or the sport or team I was writing about. In sifting through more than a hundred pieces, we whittled the list down to 40, and were pleasantly surprised to see they fell very nicely into themes, including sections on how we get hooked on sports; why we love playing them (despite frequent failures); the stars, the leaders, and the legends we admire; and how our love of sports is threatened by greed, in ways both obvious and subtle.

Once we framed the pieces along those lines, we could see that this collection has little to do with wins and losses. Instead, the stories here use sports as a prism to take a closer look at the character of the people who play, coach, and watch them. The subjects face conflicts over our most cherished values, and they work to resolve them—or exploit them. Because these stories address such universal themes, I hope they have retained a certain timeless quality.

That's why we've included stories from across the sports spectrum, including profiles of big names like Magic Johnson, Bo Schembechler, and Joe Louis, to profit-mongers determined to suck the fun out of our sports, to unsung heroes whose passion drives them to coach Little League baseball teams and run summer camps for peanuts—and die with no regrets.

These stories speak to the value of sports, but also *our* values. I don't think I'm the only one who's less interested in last night's box scores than the stories behind them: the untold personal struggles that transform even our best-known sports figures from two-dimensional caricatures into full human beings we can appreciate for reasons that go deeper than their win-loss record, and introducing the people who work off-stage to a broader audience.

While we gave ourselves a wide berth in picking these stories, we decided to stick to those that are tied to the state of Michigan. That wasn't too hard, because the Great Lake State has been home to major league baseball, football, hockey, and basketball since those leagues started—something only New York, Boston, and Chicago can also claim—not to mention the University of Michigan and Michigan State, plus countless amateur squads competing in everything from high school hockey to intramural softball.

Michigan is one of the nation's best sports states, a place where we define ourselves as much by our teams as our professions. When we get together for a game, we all wear the same colors. Sports build a bond so strong they often allow us to transcend our many differences.

I care deeply about all of the people in these stories, and I loved writing about them. I gave these pieces everything I had, often hammering out a dozen drafts during all-night writing sessions, and it felt good to see every one of these stories come out in print. If you know any writers, you know we don't always feel that way.

I've been reporting, writing, and commenting about Michigan sports for a quarter century now, from my days freelancing for the *Ann Arbor News*, writing Sunday features for the *Detroit News* and longer pieces for *Sports Illustrated, ESPN Magazine, Men's Journal, Fortune, Time*, the *Wall Street Journal*, and National Public Radio. What got me dreaming about this collection, however, was my experience telling sports stories every week on Michigan Radio, for sports fans and non-fans alike, who often say, "I don't care about sports, but I liked this."

Whether you're a sports fan or not, I hope you enjoy these stories, and the spirit that inspired them.

Kid Stuff

Sports are a passion usually sparked in childhood and, like most of our enthusiasms, fanned by our parents. That was certainly true for me. My father instilled my love of sports, and in the process created a bond that kept us connected even during my insolent adolescent years, when little else did. He believed that sports could teach bedrock values, a simple but powerful idea that has been the foundation of just about everything I've done since, as an athlete, coach, and commentator.

For my generation, our love of sports didn't grow only during organized games on official fields, courts, and rinks, where adults taught us how to play by the rules, but also on our driveways and streets, backyards and basements, where we lost track of time playing games we made up ourselves. Here we learned to pick teams, play fair, and settle disputes ourselves, with no parental supervision—and we kept it up, running an intramural softball league and putting together our own pond-hockey teams.

Of course, playing without parents also generated a lot of mayhem, but that was part of the fun—even if most of us don't allow our children to do the same things today. Call us hypocrites if you like, but when you read my stories about the crazy stunts we did, you'll understand.

As a coach and a sports writer, it's been gratifying to see that my experience falling in love with sports, and what they can do for us, has been shared by so many others, from Huron hockey's unforgettable assistant coach, to the kids on the Potawatomi reservation in the Upper Peninsula, to the friends of Wes Leonard in tiny Fennville, Michigan.

This section focuses on the games we play when the world isn't watching, yet matter as much to us as anything that happens in the big leagues.

A FATHER'S DAY GIFT

June 17, 2011
The Detroit News

My dad grew up in Scarsdale, N.Y.—but, as he's quick to point out, that was before it became "Scahhhsdahle." His father told him always to root for the underdog, and my dad took that seriously.

All his friends were Yankees fans, but dad loved the Brooklyn Dodgers. A perfect Friday night for him, when he was a young teen, was to go up to his room with a Faygo Redpop, a *Boy's Life* magazine—he was on his way to becoming an Eagle Scout—and listen to Red Barber reporting on the Dodgers' game. Instead of saying something prosaic like, "The bases are loaded," Barber would intone, "And the bases are *saturated* with *humanity*."

Dad was a decent athlete, but after the first day of his high school baseball tryouts, he didn't think he had much of a chance to make the team, so he skipped the second day—only to find out later the coach asked his friends where he was. A few years later, he redeemed himself by starring at shortstop for his fraternity softball team, which won the title when he pulled off a perfect squeeze play. You never forget those moments.

My parents raised three kids, and spent most of their weekends schlepping us to swim meets and hockey games. My dad had to wake me up at five in the morning, then pile me and my hockey bag into our 1965 Volkswagen Beetle—which had no radio and a heater only in theory. I'm sure I complained every time he woke me up. He didn't complain once.

My dad never played hockey, but he taught me the important things: Play hard. Play fair. Losing is okay. Loafing is not. And hot-dogging after a goal is simply unacceptable. You're better off not scoring than acting like you've never done it before.

My dad and I spent countless hours together watching George Kell broadcast the Detroit Tigers' games on TV, and listening to Ernie Harwell deliver them through the car radio.

In high school my brother and I both made the varsity hockey team, and played together for one season. My dad is not one to brag, but he gushed about how proud he was to see his two boys standing together on the blue line for the national anthem. It didn't matter to him that that was all the ice time we usually got.

When I became a sullen teen—at least at home—we didn't have a lot to talk about. Still, like Daniel Stern's character said in *City Slickers*, we always had baseball. That kept us connected, when it seemed like few things did.

After I left home, we started becoming good friends. As Mark Twain said, "It was amazing how much my father had changed."

We formed another bond when I took over my old high school hockey team, Ann Arbor Huron, which had not won a game in a year and a half. Assessing my team's situation, my dad said, "Well, when you're on the floor, you can't fall out of bed."

I gave my parents a schedule, but I didn't expect them to come to any games. I wasn't a teenage player, after all, but a 35-year-old coach. But they came to every one of our home games, and even our away games in Trenton, Muskegon, Traverse City, and Culver, Indiana, becoming valued members of the hockey parents' gang.

When we won our first game, they were there. When we finally beat our arch-rival, Ann Arbor Pioneer, in my third season, they were there. The lobby crowd was loud, but not my dad. He didn't say a word—he was too choked up to speak—but I'll never forget his glassy eyes as he reached out his hand to grasp mine, and he held it, firmly.

He knew how much it meant to me. And I saw how much it meant to him.

When I asked him a couple months ago what I could possibly get him for his birthday, he said, "Just your friendship."

Consider it done.

And that's what he's getting for Father's Day, too.

DON'T TRY THIS AT HOME

When I decided to write a column describing all the stupid, dangerous games we invented as kids, I assumed I was writing for an audience solely of my childhood friends, because who else would care? Well, I was wrong about that. The response was overwhelming, with readers chiming in about all the silly things they did as kids, with all of us marveling that we're still alive. It turns out making up ill-advised endeavors is a surprisingly universal experience—just one more way "sports," broadly defined, binds us.

June 16, 1992
The Ann Arbor News

I want to discuss the smallest sports of all—the games no one seems to play anymore: the games we used to make up.

You see, when I was a kid, we didn't spend our summers in a van going to travel team soccer games. The only rule our parents gave us was to get home when the streetlights came on. We took full advantage of this lack of parental supervision by inventing an array of unapproved entertainments.

Take the Baloney Game. This became popular when my friend's mom started working. We would go to Dave's house for lunch, where each of us would grab a slab of Oscar Meyer and whip it toward the kitchen ceiling. Whoever's slice stayed stuck the longest was declared the winner of Phase One.

But even the best tosses had to fall to earth sooner or later, which brings us to Phase Two of this lunch-meat biathlon: The Catch. As the baloney peeled off the ceiling, we craned our little necks skyward and opened our mouths to take a bite out of the falling pink disc. If we failed to sink our teeth into the baloney, our ceiling time, no matter how long, was disqualified. That's why all the kids whose baloney had already fallen would surround the last player still standing, and scream at him to miss his slice of baloney before it came down. We were not there to learn sportsmanship.

We played this game for months, until Dave's mom noticed a constellation of dark circles on her newly painted ceiling.

Fortunately, at about the same time, Scotty's folks bought an automatic garage door opener. It was amazing! You just pushed a button, and voilà—the garage door went up by itself! Can you believe it? We couldn't. Our little nostrils flared with the possibilities of something far more dangerous and parentally unacceptable: The Garage Door Game.

The rules were simple. See how far away from the open garage door you could push the remote control, take off running, and still make it under before the massive metal sheet cut you in half.

No cheating, no ties, no crying. As we moved farther from the door, we thought we had reached the limits of our abilities until Scotty himself pulled off a James Bond under-the-door roll on the concrete driveway. We were very impressed—certainly more so than Scotty's mom. The Garage Door Game was also short-lived.

But not long after that, Scotty's parents thought it was a great idea to give him a few BB guns. They must have been on drugs.

The catch was, none of us could shoot accurately enough to do any real damage, so we did what any twelve-year-old boys would do: invent the Triangle of Death, which entailed taking turns shooting the kid to our right. It went like this:

"Ready?"

"Ready."

Bang! "Ow!"

"Ready?"

"Ready."

Bang! "Ow!"

And so forth.

Incredibly, three decades later, two of us have jobs. Or all three, if you count whatever it is I do as a job.

Next came the Sour Milk Game, the Evel Knievel Game, and the Let's Make a Towering Inferno Out of the Oreo Package On the Coffee Table Game. But the Triangle of Death pretty much marked the zenith of this golden era.

Today these same friends put fruit in their beer, use "gift" as a verb, and insist their four-year-old sons wear OSHA-approved protective helmets to ride their tricycles up and down the driveways of their gated communities.

Yes, our games were totally unorganized and unsafe. But here's a stat for you: We all survived.

So, as for me, Give Me the Baloney Game, or Give Me the Triangle of Death.

HOW COACH MACK CHANGED MY LIFE

June 2013 and July 2014
The PostGame

I loved baseball from the start—but it didn't love me.

When I started in T-ball, I was so short that if the catcher put the tallest tee on the far corner of the plate, I couldn't reach the ball, only the middle part of the tee. Yes, I struck out—in T-ball.

Our first year of live pitching didn't go any better. One game we were beating the other team so badly, we were about to trigger the "Mercy Rule," and end the game. Coach Van pulled me in from my post in right field—where I kept company with the dandelions—and told me to pitch. I wasn't a pitcher—I wanted to be a catcher, like my hero Bill Freehan—but I'm thinking, "This is my chance." I walked three batters, but miraculously got three outs before they scored any runs. We won—and I figured that was my stepping stone to greater things.

I was surprised my dad wasn't as happy as I was. He knew better—but he didn't tell me until years later: Coach Van was not putting me in at pitcher to finish the game. He was putting me in to get shelled, so the game would keep going. He was hoping I would fail.

The next game, I went back to right field with my friends the dandelions, never to return to the infield the rest of the season. But when Coach Van and his family moved, our assistant coach, Mac Mackenzie, moved up to head coach—and my world changed almost overnight.

Coach Mack wore a baseball cap on his big, square head, with his big, square glasses. He looked tough, with a permanent squint and the underbite of a bulldog. When he was smashing ground ball after ground ball, sweat dripped off his pointy nose. He occasionally said the "s-word," which was novel then. We thought that was pretty cool.

He thought I was feisty, and funny. I can't say exactly why, but I could tell he wanted me to do well, and that he believed I would. Trust me, I was

7

no bigger, faster, or stronger than I was the previous season. But I had one thing I didn't have the year before: confidence. The effect was immediate, dramatic, and lifelong.

From the very first practice under Coach Mack, I started smacking the ball as if I'd been waiting years to do it—which I had been. Instead of playing back on my heels, hoping not to fail, I was up on my toes, swinging for the fences, eager to succeed.

Our first game that season he started me at catcher, and had me batting leadoff. I got two hits—the first of my life—and my teammates voted me captain.

I was on fire for baseball, playing some form of it every chance I had, whether it was a backyard game of "Pickle," "500," or home run derby. Didn't matter. I didn't *want* to play. I *needed* to play.

One Saturday morning practice was rained out. But, this being Michigan, the sun soon came out, so I biked down to our schoolyard to check it out. There were a few puddles here and there, but the biggest one was behind the plate, where I would be crouched, and it didn't look that bad to me.

I rushed home and called Coach Mack with my report. He told me if I made the phone calls, we'd have practice. After I convinced enough of my teammates to come down, I called Coach Mack, and his promise was good. We practiced, and I was in heaven.

After he'd hit ground balls to our third baseman, shortstop, second baseman, and first baseman, I'd say, "C'mon, Coach Mack—gimme one!" Meaning, bunt the ball, so I could scoop it up and throw the imaginary runner out at first.

He'd stare at me, break into a small, sidelong grin, and say, "There ya go," and tap one out just for me.

My newfound confidence proved to be transferrable. The next year I became a much better hockey player, too, and I don't need to tell you the central role sports have played in my life. But it all started with Coach Mack.

I've always been too dependent on my teachers, coaches, and bosses. When they don't believe in me, I don't go very far, but when they do, I'm capable of—well, more. And sometimes, much more. I'm sure this is why I've spent most of my adult life coaching and teaching on the side. I know how much difference it can make when you feel someone believes in you.

A couple years later, the MacKenzies moved to California. I have no idea where they are now. I don't even know if Coach Mack is still with us. But he's still with me.

July 2014 (One Year Later)

A couple days after I published the piece above, I got a full-page thank you letter from Coach Mack himself. Just getting it thrilled me, but his message was even better. It was direct, honest, and funny—just like the man himself.

He told me about his family, about moving to Scottsdale back in 1976, about his two bypass surgeries. In 1990, he received a heart transplant. He said he'd read my books and had every intention of writing years ago. But that day, when his wife found my story online, he was moved to write:

"I was blown away to see my name and the wonderful things that you had to say about me and my influence on you. I have had a very good and successful life with a few plaques, awards, and complimentary speeches given to me, but none compare to what you said and how you have honored me. Thank you from the bottom of my heart."

I don't know if Coach Mack got choked up writing it, but I got choked up reading it. I promised him I'd write him a longer letter soon, and I fully intended to. But my fall filled up with a nationwide book tour, speeches, deadlines, and the class I was teaching on the side. I kept waiting to find enough time to write The Perfect Letter—and I kept waiting. I wrote down Coach Mack's name on my to-do list month after month.

On a Tuesday night in July 2014, a year after I wrote my story on Coach Mack, I was teaching my sports writing students at Northwestern University how to write a profile. I told them their subject doesn't have to be famous, it could even be a former little league coach. Then I spontaneously launched into my story of Coach Mack, right down to the sweat dripping off the tip of his nose while he smashed grounder after grounder to the infielders. I couldn't resist telling them how great it was to hear from Coach Mack—which provided just another reminder I still needed to write him. I scribbled his name down yet again that night.

The next day, I received an email from a friend of Coach Mack's, a man I'd never met before. He wrote, "We lost Mack yesterday."

This hit me harder than I had expected. After all, I didn't think he'd live forever, especially with a heart transplant. I was glad I'd written the story about him—and felt even better Coach Mack had read it and responded. But when I went back to read our correspondence, I was pained to realize I had never written him the longer letter I'd promised. I felt worse when I remembered he lived in Scottsdale. A couple months after he sent me his first letter, I was invited to give a speech in Scottsdale—and if I had kept in better touch, I would have put it together, invited Coach Mack to join us, and he and I would have gone out afterward for a beer and told stories I would remember the rest of my life.

We don't have time to do everything we want to do. I realize that. And I'm lucky to have gotten back in touch with Coach Mack. I know that, too. But my regret was hard to shake. When I went for a run that day, around a few Little League baseball diamonds in Chicago, I wasn't ready for the tears streaming down from under my sunglasses.

After I drove back to my home in Ann Arbor on a beautiful summer night, right around our usual game time, I swung by our old schoolyard, where Coach Mack smacked those ground balls all those years ago. I was surprised to find the ball field had been replaced by a garden, with a shed in the middle of it. But when I crouched down into my old position, where home plate used to be, I could see it all—right down to Coach Mack, sweat dripping off his nose, tapping me another bunt to throw to first base.

Thanks, Coach. Sorry it took me so long to write.

THE ALMIGHTY CLEAVERS

May 27, 2011
Michigan Radio

I went to Ann Arbor Huron High School, considered by every objective source to be the greatest high school in the history of the universe. And one of the things that made it so great when I was there was an intramural softball league.

Maybe your clearly inferior high school had one, too, but it couldn't have been as cool as the one we had at Huron, which was not only created and run entirely by students, but the burnouts, no less. That meant the adults, perhaps wisely, wanted nothing to do with it. No umpires, either.

So the burnouts got the park permits—God bless 'em—and every clique had a team, from the auto shop guys to the marching band dweebs. They gave their teams names like the Extra Burly Studs, the Master Batters, and—yes—the 'Nads. If you pause to think of their cheer, you'll get the joke.

During the spring of my senior year, most of my friends weren't playing varsity sports, so we came home every day after school to drink a few Stroh's Bohemian Style beers ("America's Only Fire-Brewed Beer") and watch "Leave It to Beaver" reruns on channel 20, on something called UHF. (Kids, go ask Grandpa.)

When softball season came around, we were inspired to build a team around that very name: The Cleavers. But if we were going to face battle-tested squads like the All-Star Rogues and the Ghetto Tigers, we knew we'd need an edgier name. And that's when we came up with—yes—the *Almighty* Cleavers. You know, to instill fear in our opponents.

You can imagine how well that worked.

Our next stroke of genius was our uniform: we each got one of our dads' undershirts, then used a laundry marker to write one of the TV show characters' names on the back: Ward, June, Wally, the Beav himself, even Eddie—we had 'em all. Now all we needed was ten more players.

No problem. Once word got out about our hardcore name and uniforms, people flocked to our team, including a half-dozen women. None of the other teams were coed, but there was no rule against it—because the league had almost no rules. That's what you get when you play in a league founded by burnouts.

We didn't just expect to lose. We were *built* to lose. But we didn't care. In fact, that was our team motto: "We Don't Care." Whenever someone caught one of our teammates running too hard or—God forbid—sliding into home plate, we would launch into our chant: "We Don't Care! We Don't Care!"

We had two other team rules: The girls could play wherever they wanted, and nobody was allowed to yell at anyone, no matter how badly they screwed up.

It probably helped that, like most teams, we brought cooling beverages to each game, be they "jumbos" of Goebel's, "torpedoes" of Colt 45, or, for big games, an actual quarter barrel of Stroh's. We'd set it up right at the corner of Huron Parkway and Fuller, with Lord knows how many teachers, parents, and police officers driving by. When I say no one cared, I mean it.

Yes, I know what we were doing was stupid and illegal, but you have to remember this was when Huron actually had a smoking lounge, *for students*, and the city had a five-dollar pot law, so the Almighty Cleavers were probably on the conservative side of things—though admittedly on a very relative scale. All of this might explain why I can't recall a single fight among the twelve teams that played in our league. (Take that any way you want.)

But what unfolded next defied explanation: playing against a bunch of guys who clearly wanted to beat us, our coed squad won our first game. And then our second. And then our third.

It was incredible. Our secret weapon: the girls. Once they realized no one was going to yell at them, their Inner Softball Demons came out—and before we knew it, we finished the regular season at 9–2, in second place.

Well, our magical season had to come to an end, and it did—with a playoff loss to the always-tough Junior Junkies. Even more heartbreaking, actor Hugh Beaumont, who played Ward Cleaver, died the week before, prompting all of us to draw black armbands on our sacred jerseys.

Then something even stranger happened. The mother of one of our team founders happened to be the president of the American Psychiatric Association, so reporters were always calling her up to get her expert opinion on this or that. When an Associated Press reporter asked her about violence on television, she made the usual points, but then said, "Well, it can't be *that* bad. My son watches 'Leave It to Beaver' every day with his friends."

As luck would have it, the reporter happened to be a big "Leave It to

Beaver" fan and wanted to interview her son and his teammates. Next thing we knew, our team's story ran on the Associated Press wire, in the *Detroit News*, and the *Detroit Free Press*, and we were even featured in *TV Guide*, for crying out loud.

My grandparents, who had just flown in from their small town in eastern Canada for a couple graduations, must have been completely confused. Or maybe they just assumed all American teenagers appeared in national stories for playing intramural softball as a rite of passage before graduating.

The unexpected attention was nice, but it wasn't the point. I don't know if I've ever had more fun playing anything than I did playing intramural softball that spring. No parents, no umpires, no rules except most runs wins—and win or lose, get over it. "No One Cares!"

It was low rent, small stakes, and big, big fun—because it was *ours*.

I'm not sure kids today have any idea what that feels like.

HOOPS THE POTAWATOMI WAY

Writing is hard for many reasons, but I've never had any difficulty coming up with ideas for stories and books, and my computer is clogged with lists of them. But some of these pieces were conceived by others, including this one. An editor at the Detroit News stumbled upon the Northern Lights Conference, with teams on Beaver Island and Mackinac Island, and thought it would be a hoot to run a story about it. We decided to focus on the Hannahville Reservation team, with the expectation that I would make fun of them and their tiny league. But when I got there, and met the players, coaches, and community leaders striving to make this work, I just couldn't do it, so I decided to turn a lark into a story about people struggling to find their way in the world.

It was about minus-10 degrees during my visit, so the team's plane trip to Mackinac Island was canceled. I came back a month later to finish the story. I've stayed in touch with tribal chairman Ken Meshigaud, one of the most interesting people I've met.

March 3, 1996
The Detroit News

HANNAHVILLE POTAWATOMI RESERVATION—Jeff Paupore coaches the Hannahville Indian School basketball team, and he's got a problem: how can he get his short, fast-break-loving players to beat the big, plodding Mackinac Island Lakers on their miniature court?

Tribal chairman Ken Meshigaud, thirty-seven, has never played or coached basketball, but he might have received the answer twenty-five years ago.

"I remember it very clearly," Meshigaud says today. An elderly medicine man named Stanley bent over and told young Meshigaud, "One thing you have to do is learn the white man's game. You don't need to beat them at it—you may not want to sometimes—but you must understand it."

If there's a secret to the Potawatomi's phenomenal revival the past decade, from their casino operations to their high school basketball team, it's their ability to create something new.

"That's *exactly* what we were trying to do," says Scott Brant, who started the Hannahville basketball team in 1990. "We were just out there to learn, and play the game."

To do so the Hannahville basketball and volleyball teams joined a conference with four other schools, all of which are situated on the Great Lakes, have less than forty students each, and are willing to travel four hours by bus, plane, and horse-drawn sleighs to play each other in gyms that are often no bigger than volleyball courts.

They call it the Northern Lights Conference, and the games are different up here.

Tom Murphy helped form the NLC before becoming principal at Houghton. He says the four tiny schools started their poetically named league in part because their Not-Ready-For-Class-D-Players at each school "could never beat anybody else at anything."

In 1987, Grand Marais and Paradise, both on the picturesque northern shore of the Upper Peninsula, formed their new league with Mackinac Island and Beaver Island, located right in the middle of Lake Michigan. It is probably the only league where you can get to all the member schools by sailboat.

One summer Murphy did just that, and concluded, "It has to be the most scenic athletic league in the nation."

In 1990, the Hannahville Indian School, located on the Hannahville Indian Reservation just thirteen miles west of Escanaba, became the fifth member of the circuit.

All five schools are near beautiful tourist areas that thrive in the summer and stagnate in the winter. The school leaders were desperate to offer a healthy alternative for mischief during the long winter months and create an incentive for studying in the bargain.

Despite the comfortable fit, the Hannahville basketball and volleyball teams had a hard time learning "the white man's game."

They lost every game their first year. During a practice near the end of the season, Brant passed a ball to one of his five remaining players and broke the kid's finger, forcing them to forfeit their last weekend.

They lost every game their second year, too—but at least they played them all.

In Jeff Paupore's second year as coach, Hannahville already has four league wins entering its final contest with Mackinac Island. Not bad for a team whose roster includes a ninth-grade boy, an eighth-grade girl and just five other players. In the miniature Northern Lights gyms the overaggressive Eagles often foul out, forcing them to finish their games with only three or four players left on the court.

Fouls are a bitch.

The Mackinac Island team has three advantages: more experience, fifteen basketball players, and a quaint colonial gym that's less than half the area of Hannahville's full-sized hardwood. A half-court shot on the Island is equivalent to an NBA "three."

It was not surprising when the Lakers drubbed the Hannahville Soaring Eagles in their first game six years ago, 113–26. Last year, the Eagles lost both games on Mackinac Island's quirky court, 116–41 and 117–67. But eyebrows rose earlier this year when Hannahville went into the fourth quarter at home against the Lakers tied 32–32, before self-destructing.

To beat the Lakers, Hannahville will have to understand their opponents' game, while sticking to their own.

When you see the Nah-Tah-Wahsh ("Soaring Eagles") team play ball in their state-of-the-art gym, wearing their expensive Russell uniforms, it's hard to believe that just fifteen years ago some houses on the reservation still had dirt floors; that ten years ago the school was just a ragtag collection of leaky-roofed sheds that were so cold students wore coats during class and so rickety some were condemned; and that just five years ago only 10 percent of the 104 Hannahville homes had phones.

Today, 19 percent of those homes have computers.

To get to where they are, the Potawatomi have had to struggle for two hundred years against the dual forces of "Chimokomin" (white people) and alcohol.

Ken Meshigaud's Potawatomi ancestors were forced off their Lower Peninsula homeland in 1822. Michigan territorial governor Lewis Cass shamelessly exploited the Potawatomi's weakness for alcohol by putting the Potawatomi leaders and a huge store of whiskey in the same Chicago meeting room for "treaty negotiations."

For two weeks, the Anishnawbe ("original people") held onto their land and Cass held onto his liquor, until finally one leader broke down and pleaded: "We care not for the land, the money or the goods," he said. "It is the whiskey we want—give us the whiskey."

Though President Jackson ordered the Potawatomi to Kansas, about six thousand resilient souls slipped away to Wisconsin and Upper Michigan, as it was called then. The tribe wandered homeless until 1913, when Congress gave them the 3,359 acres they named "Hannahville," after a sympathetic missionary's wife.

Despite the government's concerted efforts, the Michigan Potawatomi survived.

Of course, surviving and thriving aren't the same thing. The reservation didn't get electricity until 1966, and their own one-room schoolhouse until 1975, but things didn't really take off until Ken Meshigaud and the casino transformed the tribe forever.

The Chip-In Casino sits on the edge of the reservation and brings in about $7 million a year. Unlike one Minnesota tribe that lines its members' pockets with $20,000 a month, the Potawatomi give only $1,000 a year to each full tribal member. The rest goes to projects like the new water tower, natural gas pipelines, three dozen new tract homes a year, a $1.2 million health center, and, not least, the $4.5 million new school.

Changing habits is even more important than changing the landscape. Of all the habits the Anishnawbe adopted from the white man, the most destructive by far is drinking. Nationally, Native Americans are four times more likely to suffer cirrhosis of the liver and fatal alcohol-related accidents than non-Natives, and three times more likely to commit suicide and homicide.

"My father would sometimes go a week or two without coming back to the house," Meshigaud says of his alcoholic father. "We'd have no food, no kerosene for the lamps. A lot of us [on the reservation] didn't grow up with the 'do-your-best' ethic, because of the substance abuse problem in those families."

If the rest of the nation is waging a war on drugs and alcohol, the Potawatomi have mounted a full-fledged blitzkrieg. According to Carol Bergquist, an independent researcher invited to study the tribe, since 1990 the percentage of active drinkers has dropped by 69 percent, and is still falling.

The tribe also offers programs on everything from job-seeking skills to parenting workshops to vocational training, and the results of their efforts are staggering: in the last twenty years the Potawatomi's graduation rate has grown from 15 percent to 75 percent. In the last five years, their unemployment rate dropped from 85 percent to 14 percent, while their average household income has almost doubled, from about $14,000 to $25,000.

The Potawatomi have made all these changes without losing their culture, their language, or their easygoing ways. "If I'm at a ten o'clock meeting and it's 10:10, I start stressing out," says Carol Bergquist. "They laugh and calm me down. 'Carol, the meeting starts when everyone who needs to be here is here.'

"It's the coolest place to work," she says.

In the same way casino jobs provide adults incentive to stay sober and graduate from high school, the Nah-Tah-Wahsh sports teams provide the kids incentive to study and behave.

"The whole idea was to use athletics to encourage better academics," says Scott Brant, the team's founder. "Winning meant nothing to us."

Sports also keep idle hands busy.

"If I haven't got anything else to do, I'll make trouble or play basketball," admits Joe "Red Cloud" Sagataw, their star point guard.

Fortunately, Joe and the other Potawatomi kids get plenty of opportunities to play ball, including "Rec Night" pickup games in the school gym from seven to nine.

Although the basketball game is fast and fluid, you notice a conspicuous lack of trash-talking, foul-calling, and post-basket celebrating. It's eerily peaceful, like a TV game with the sound turned off, which might be expected from the descendants of a chief named "He Who Sits Quietly."

But make no mistake: they love their hoops. There are so many baskets tacked onto the homes along Hannahville's grid of two-lane roads that the 3,359-acre reservation looks a lot more like the Indiana countryside than anything you've seen from Hollywood. About a third of the students at Hannahville wear NBA garb to school, and if you tell them you work for the *Detroit News*, they'll invariably ask if you've met the Pistons' Grant Hill.

The reservation's primary pastime is no longer drinking, but basketball.

Joe Sagataw, the grandson of the former tribal chairman Omar Sagataw, has over one hundred cousins, but he's starting to stick out from the pack.

The fifteen-year-old junior is the team's leading scorer heading into the season's last game, just like his cousin Kenny Wandahsega was three years ago. Kenny was everything Joe aspired to be: the star point guard, a promising student, and a popular young man with both adults and kids.

"I look at Joe and he reminds me of Kenny—a spittin' image," says Mike Philemon, who was Kenny Wandahsega's best friend. "They're both good athletes, naturals. They even look the same out there on the court. Joe looked up to Kenny—but a lot of people did."

On August 4, 1994, Wandahsega and his friends were drinking along the banks of the powerful Menominee River. When Wandahsega jumped in, the current pulled him under and trapped him under the bank, where the search team found him four days later. People in Hannahville have still not gotten over the loss of Kenny Wandahsega—especially Joe Sagataw.

"We were as close as we could have been," Sagataw says quietly, "but he screwed it all up himself."

With Kenny's tragedy as motivation, Joe Sagataw seems doubly determined to make the most of his opportunities. His classmates voted him the "brightest student" and president of the student council. A few years ago Joe skipped a grade as casually as some kids skip class.

"I was sitting in class one day," Sagataw recalls, "and they said, 'Here's your new class.'"

Joe Sagataw dreams of going to college and then law school, but he lives in a modest home with no phone. If Governor Engler cuts tuition aid to Native Americans, it's highly unlikely Sagataw will be able to afford it.

"I figure if I can just keep from endangering myself," Sagataw says, "maybe I can do some of the things Kenny couldn't."

The trip to Mackinac Island requires four hours and three vehicles. Normally they would sleep over and play another game the next morning, but this midweek makeup game won't allow for that.

For some of the kids the trip is a chance to go on their first plane ride. For others it's a rare opportunity to get off the reservation. But for seasoned travelers like Joe and his longtime girlfriend Rosie, who plays on the volleyball team, it's simply a good time to take a nap next to each other in the back seat.

The highlight of the journey is not the five-minute plane ride across Lake Michigan's frozen surface, but the thirty-minute trip from Mackinac Island's tiny airport to its tiny high school in a sleigh pulled by two Percheron horses. The dirt-free snow on the Mackinac Island roads is so white it looks bleached. The scene is akin to a Budweiser ad—except for the three players bumper-skiing off the back.

When the driver eases the packed cart down to the redbrick high school, the kids ignore the Grand Hotel nearby to point to the incredibly small gym. A young referee is already there, shaking his head. "My partner told me it was small, but . . ."

As the boys get dressed in a three-stall bathroom, some of them sitting on toilet seats to tie their shoes, the volleyball players try to learn how to carom their passes off the impossibly low ceiling, which is allowed in this gym. It's so small the volleyball players have to run in from an open doorway to serve the ball.

Coach Jeff Paupore seems caught in between the two worlds he lives in.

"It's a different game, coaching these kids," he says outside the bathroom which is serving as the team's locker room. "They don't see organized ball until high school, so the pick-and-roll, double-dribbling, even checking in at the scorer's table—it's all new to them."

He's had to learn a few things, too, starting with his players' mental approach to the game.

"They don't get all psyched up before games," he says. "They're not bothered by losing like I am—which I think is a positive. They're not caught up in our rat race."

Minutes before game time the basketball players listen to their coach's pregame talk in the hallway, sitting under the grade-schoolers' coat hooks and snowmobile helmets. In the Northern Lights Conference, teams spend as much time preparing for their opponents' gym as they do for their opponents' players.

"You can forget about fast-breaking there, because there's no place to fast-break to!" Paupore says, his throat muscles straining. "This is their court, they know how to frustrate you. Remember, there are no losers if you just play hard. Just keep your heads out there."

Basketball in this gym feels less like a sanctioned high school contest than a college dorm-room nerf-hoops game. But when the game starts, the Eagles snap out of their pregame trance and rebound, pass, and drive like they're late for the plane home.

In the first minute Joe Sagataw grabs the ball under his own bucket. He starts running low like a sprinter leaving the blocks, his tail of black hair flying behind him like a mustang's mane, when he suddenly cuts toward the hoop and uncoils for a graceful layup. A couple minutes later Joe feeds the ball into center James Larson, who fakes going up, turns around, and swishes a four-footer—and does it again a minute later.

When forward Tonto Wandahsega looks up at the scoreboard it reads: Home 6, Visitors 10.

"Hey man, we're ahead!" he says, pleasantly surprised.

In the first four minutes the Eagles combined the best of the two styles of play, fast and slow, but they forget Paupore's advice when play resumes. Sagataw repeatedly drives the lane, but once he's inside the paint, he has no room to stretch toward the bucket. Things usually come easily for the talented Joe Sagataw—and when they don't, he gets frustrated.

With the Lakers in the midst of a 22–8 third quarter run, Sagataw stubbornly tries to go to the bucket once more, only to find three big men waiting for him. After they knock the ball away, Sagataw watches helplessly as it rolls into Laker hands, then tries to trip the guy who picked it up on the way back up the court, getting a technical foul in the process.

Coach Paupore has seen this before, so he pulls Sagataw to cool off on the bench, while James Larson puts his basic block-and-tackle post moves to good use. His buckets keep the Soaring Eagles within forty points midway through the fourth quarter.

The effort is good enough for their pom-pom girls, who seem unable to finish a cheer without giggling at the end. Their spontaneous encouragement for every pass and shot, whether good or not, is touching. The Laker fans join their clapping when Jeannie Wandahsega, nursing two floor burns from the volleyball game earlier that day, checks in for Hannahville.

When she goes in, Joe Sagataw collects himself and returns to the court. Like his team, just when you think Joe's about to unravel, he comes back stronger. He calls a play at the top of the key, and patiently works the ball around until James Larson gets open down low. Sagataw gives him the ball for Larson's trademark turnaround jump shot. The Eagles do it again and keep doing it, forcing the Lakers to take fouls or let Hannahville make easy buckets. When the game ends the Lakers have more fouls than the Eagles.

No, it's not a victory—the Lakers win, 90–55—but no one fouled out this time, and it sure beats the wash-outs during last year's games here. After the game Joe talks to Rosie about the speech he will give at school the next day on the perils of drunk driving—a manifestation of Scott Brant's saying, "Our wins and losses happen off the court."

When they hop on the horse-drawn wagon waiting outside the gym to take them back to the airport, Tonto Wandahsega asks, "Who had fun?" then answers his own question. "I had fun. I had fun just playing."

And that's when it hits you: these kids don't hustle at the end of a 90–55 loss to cut the margin, to be martyrs, or to hear their coach's praise. They dive for loose balls with a minute left simply because the ball's in play.

When you've traveled as far as the Potawatomi have, the difference between winning and losing a basketball game is meaningless. As Stanley the medicine man once said, the important thing is not winning the game, but learning it.

For Hannahville, that's victory enough—for now.

OUR UNFORGETTABLE ASSISTANT COACH

June 21, 2013
Michigan Radio

I first met Mike Lapprich when I was an assistant hockey coach at Ann Arbor Huron High School, and he was just a ninth grader. He was a big kid with a baby face, a shy guy with an easy smile—an oversized puppy.

I returned to the Huron hockey program five years later as the team's head coach. Lapper, as we all called him, had just finished his first year under the previous head coach as an assistant, at the ripe age of eighteen.

The team I inherited had not won a game in over a year, so I invited the returning captain out for lunch to get a sense of what the problems were, and how we might bring the program back. He took the meeting very seriously, even bringing a list of five talking points.

The first: "You have no idea what you're getting into."

The second: "Lapper's our man. He's the guy we trust. Keep him, and treat him right."

The captain was not making a suggestion.

We had a lot of work to do. So, we went to work. I was the drill sergeant, the bad cop, but Lapper was their big brother. Whenever one of them felt like quitting—and it seemed like half the players did at some point or other—he was the one who kept them going.

By the end of our first summer together, I had to pick one official assistant coach, who would get a few thousand bucks from the school to coach. When the athletic director was filling out the form, she asked me for the name.

"Mike Lapprich," I said.

She looked up. "He's 18. You sure?"

"Trust me. I'm sure." The captain had been right, of course: Lapper was the key.

Day by day, little by little, we learned to stretch like a team, to practice like a team, to dress like a team—green shirts and gold ties. And we learned to play the game as a team.

Lapper worked with the defense, where he helped cut our goals-against in half. On game days, he made the locker room look like the Red Wings' room. When the players arrived, they saw their pants and jerseys hanging up in their stalls, their names and numbers facing out, and rolls of tape stacked in pyramids on the training table. He loved the players, and they loved him. The best part is, both sides knew it.

The players proved it after our second season, when they voted unanimously for Lapper to receive the Unsung Hero award—a reward that had always gone to a player, never a coach. I'd never seen anything like it. When we announced the award at the banquet, and handed Lapper the trophy, he was too choked up to speak, and too modest to look up, just staring at the trophy—which tells you just about all you need to know.

After our third season, which we finished ranked number five in the state, Lapper's world was opening up. He moved into his own place, he enrolled in nursing school, and he even appeared in the pages of *Car & Driver* magazine, where he worked on the side. But the highlight, for him, was seeing his little brother Kevin play on our spring team. The first night they were on the same bench for one of our summer games, Kevin notched two assists.

After the game, Lapper went back to his parents' house for dinner, and gushed about Kevin's play. For Lapper, life didn't get much better.

Early the next morning, June 25, 2003, I got a call from Lapper's mom. She told me Mike had been in a car accident the night before, and he had died.

I was in disbelief—and when I gathered the players later that day in our locker room, they were too. Lapper was their big brother—and for most of them, the first person they were close to who died.

So many people showed up for Lapper's funeral, the overflow crowd had to stand in the foyer. We named the Unsung Hero award, our locker room, and a scholarship in his honor. But there was nothing we could do to lessen our loss.

At his grave site, in the shadows of Huron High and the VA Hospital, where Lapper volunteered, the pastor said a few words. When he finished, I escorted Lapper's parents to their car, then walked back up the gentle slope, where I saw our players walking down, without their gold ties. This was not how we do it, I thought, on this day of all days. But I figured they'd been through enough, and kept my criticism to myself.

One of our captains walked up to me, red-eyed, put his arm around me, pinched the knot of my tie, and said, "Coach, we have a place for these." He walked me back to the grave site, where I saw five-dozen gold ties draped over Lapper's casket.

And that's when I knew: Lapper's legacy was not having his name on a locker room door or a trophy or a scholarship.

It was helping dozens of boys become men—something they carry with them to this day.

YOU SHOULD HAVE MET
FENNVILLE'S WES LEONARD

This story was also someone else's idea, coming from a sports editor at a national newspaper. But after I sent him the piece, he wanted me to add a couple paragraphs about March Madness, the NCAA basketball tournament that was just starting up that week. It struck me as inappropriate to tie this story of a tragic teenager with something so trivial that I ultimately decided to move the piece to the Detroit News, which eagerly accepted it as is. It might have cost the story an appearance in the "Best American Sports Writing" anthology, where it was listed as a finalist, but I've never regretted the decision. When I received an appreciative response from the family, I knew I'd made the right choice.

March 18, 2011
The Detroit News

FENNVILLE, MICHIGAN—On Monday, I drove across the state of Michigan to see a Class C regional semifinal basketball game, pitting tiny Schoolcraft High School against even tinier Fennville.

Both schools were undefeated—but that's not why I was going. I was going to see the impact of a young man who would not be there.

Before I drove back home, I learned how quickly a record-breaking basketball game can become utterly insignificant—and then, just a few days later, how the next game can matter so much.

Fennville is about two hundred miles from Detroit, but it might as well be two hundred light-years. When you approach Fennville, you pass a sign declaring, "Hometown of Richard 'Richie' Jordan, Member of the 2001 National High School Sports Hall of Fame."

You haven't heard of Richie Jordan, who graduated almost fifty years ago and stands only five-seven. But everyone around here has, and down at the Blue Goose Café, they still talk about all the records he set in football, basketball, and baseball. But the last few years, they've been talking about Wes Leonard.

When Wes's father, Gary Leonard, joined his brother's company in Holland, near Lake Michigan, the family could have moved to any number of nearby towns, but chose little Fennville, which has just 1,500 people, a third of them high school students. Here, the whole town comes out for football and basketball games—and musicals and graduations, too.

"I left Fennville for another place," Fennville High School English teacher Melissa Hoover recalled in the teachers' lounge, "and I kept saying, 'In Fennville they do this,' and 'In Fennville they do that.' Finally, one of the teachers said, 'Well, maybe you should go back to Fennville.' She was right. So I did."

The Leonards loved Fennville, too, and Fennville loved them back.

Their oldest son, Wes, often asked his teachers about their weekends, partly to avoid work but also because he was simply curious about people—all people.

Leonard, the most popular kid in school, would invite the special-ed kids to join him for lunch, and soon the other jocks were doing it, too. When English teacher Susan McEntyre read her students' journals last semester, "Just about all the kids wrote that Wes was their best friend. They always wrote about that."

No matter what you were like in high school, you'd want Wes Leonard to be your friend. And he would be.

As an athlete, Leonard was the best thing to come out of Fennville since Richie Jordan himself—something people around here don't say lightly. Leonard was the Blackhawks' star quarterback—he threw seven touchdowns in one game this past fall—but it was on the basketball court where the junior center really connected with the fans. Sitting so close, they could feel Leonard's energy and drive and passion—and see his trademark grin.

But even with Leonard leading the team, no one dared to imagine they'd enter their last regular season game with a perfect 19–0 mark.

When the Bridgman Bees jumped out to an eleven-point halftime lead, Leonard took over, pushing the game to overtime. Then, with about thirty seconds left, he drove the lane for a pretty layup—and the win. Fennville's fans rushed the court and hoisted their hero onto their shoulders.

It was the kind of ending that sends announcers into paroxysms of hyperbole: Incredible! Unbelievable! Unthinkable!

Then, just seconds later, the truly unthinkable actually happened: Wes Leonard's enlarged heart gave out, and he collapsed, right on the court.

His father ran down to him, yelling, "Breathe, Wes, breathe! Don't die on me!" The paramedics loaded Leonard into an ambulance, where they worked to get his heart pumping again. His parents could only look through the back window, helpless.

Before midnight, the town pastor emerged from the hospital to tell the crowd gathered outside that Wes Leonard had died.

When a small-town hero fulfills his fans' every dream, they put up signs about him on the city limits. What happens to that town when its hero falls right in front of them?

The next day the grade school kids clutched teddy bears and cried in the corner. Wes's classmates hugged and sobbed in the hallways. The older townspeople gathered at the Blue Goose, talking about him softly, with tears in their eyes.

"If I was twice as good as everyone else, I'd be arrogant," said Mike Peel, fifty-seven, a real estate agent in nearby Douglas. "But he never was. Never even argued bad calls. He was the kind of kid who could hug his mom in front of a thousand people and not feel embarrassed about it."

Letters and posters came from as far away as the Philippines and Cambodia. The NBA's Golden State Warriors asked what they could do to help, Michigan State basketball coach Tom Izzo cut practice short to drive to Fennville to talk to the family and the team, and Bo Kimble, whose Loyola Marymount teammate Hank Gathers died on the court from the same condition in 1990, drove all night from Philadelphia to be with them for four days, arriving as a famous stranger and leaving as a close friend. The Blackhawks' archrivals in Saugatuck hosted the luncheon after the funeral.

Fennville's coach had to ask his players if they wanted to play their first-round playoff game that Monday. They thought about it. They discussed it. Then they decided, yes. This is what we do.

They moved the games to Hope College, where the Blackhawks drew over three thousand fans. When the other teams playing that day took the court, they were all wearing the same black T-shirts that Fennville wore, with Leonard's name and number on the back, and "NEVER FORGOTTEN" on the front.

The Blackhawks struggled in their first game, caught fire in their second, then came back in the district finals Friday night from nine points down to win by three.

"If you weren't there," Mike Peel said, "you wouldn't believe it."

This Monday, when Fennville faced Schoolcraft, the Blackhawks finally ran out of gas in the second half and lost, 86–62. But if you didn't see the scoreboard, you'd have no idea Fennville was getting trounced. The players kept working just as hard, and the crowd kept cheering just as loud, to the very last second.

Harder days are ahead. They know that.

They also know people like Wes Leonard come along in a place like Fennville every fifty years or so, and they might not see another like him the rest of their lives. But the very qualities Wes Leonard brought out in them—pride, unity, and joy—are the very traits they'll rely on to get them through.

The people of Fennville will never be the same.

But they will be okay.

THE CAMP DIRECTOR PUTS OUT THE CANDLE

November 1998
Traverse Magazine

TORCH LAKE—Pat Rode has faithfully served Camp Hayo-Went-Ha for thirty of his sixty-nine years, but his tour of duty ends next week, when he will finally step down.

The problem is, there are several generations of campers, counselors, and parents who can't imagine Camp Hayo-Went-Ha without Rode. Since they heard the news, they've been sending him a steady stream of correspondence, reminding him of conversations they'd had with him years ago.

"You try to do things that make sense, to be a good role model," he says. "But you just never know how much you're getting through until you read those notes. It makes it all worthwhile."

For years, Rode spent his winters as a psychology professor at Central Michigan University, and his summers as the camp's assistant director before becoming Hayo-Went-Ha's sixth director in 1981.

Early in his tenure, he had to fight to keep this rustic, Outward Bound–style camp from being converted into a cheesy family resort, with pools, slides, and shuffleboard. He won, saving this unique experience for thousands of boys.

Running the state's largest YMCA camp entails maintaining two dozen cabins and a dozen vehicles, supervising seventy staff members, and, not least, looking after some four hundred campers every summer, many of whom come from suburban Detroit. During a typical sixteen-hour day, Rode functions as an accountant and a mechanic, an executive and a psychologist, a taskmaster and a friend.

When Rode retires, the state YMCA will replace him with one part-time and two full-time employees.

Many say three people won't be enough. "For us, Pat's been the spirit of Hayo-Went-Ha," said parent Linda Karr. "My god, what are we going to do when he leaves?"

The camp was born in 1904, near the tip of Torch Lake, and named after Chief Hiawatha. The cabins, staircases, and footbridges on the 640-acre campus have the kind of rustic but tidy look of the *Swiss Family Robinson* movie set.

But camp sessions play out more like *Fantasy Island*, with the anxious newcomers hoping this special place can help them find what they need before they depart. Hayo-Went-Ha is set up to give bored kids adventure, forgotten kids attention, and just about everyone—campers and counselors alike—a sense of belonging.

Each four-week session starts in Bonbright Lodge, a sixty-seven-year-old meeting hall made from logs, where Rode introduces himself and his staff. Then he describes the "spirit of Hayo-Went-Ha," which he defines as "honesty in dealing with people, respect for others, and an understanding of your place in a world that is greater than all of us."

It may sound corny to outsiders, but so many campers and alums talk about the "spirit of Hayo-Went-Ha," it's obviously real to them.

Before the opening ceremony two years ago, Rode learned that twelve-year-old Dana Burton was having a difficult time with his parents' divorce. Knowing Burton was in the audience, Rode tailored his opening speech accordingly.

"Whatever you're feeling, you can talk to someone here about it. It could be another camper, a counselor, the camp nurse, or me. You're safe here. You belong."

Rode's speech stirred feelings Burton had been suppressing for months. Walking back to their cabins, the two somehow bumped into each other, and started a casual conversation.

"I wasn't too comfortable telling people about the divorce, because I wasn't sure how they would react," Burton recalls. "But I felt comfortable talking to him about it. He kept reminding me that I'm safe here, everyone loves me here, and everything is going to work out."

Burton threw his arms around Rode, and let loose the tears he'd been holding back for so long. By the time their conversation ended, Burton had established a second home.

This is not to say Hayo-Went-Ha is some backwoods encounter group. It is, first and foremost, a place for kids to test themselves outdoors. The eight- to twelve-year-olds complete two short trips each session, while the thirteen- to sixteen-year-olds spend a couple weeks on more rigorous, exotic trips, including canoeing through northern Minnesota, hiking the Canadian Rockies, and sailing the Mediterranean Sea.

"Physically, nothing could be harder than these trips, and I've been through airborne training," Rode says. "When you finish, you can say, 'Hey, I did that, and I can probably do a lot of other things, too.'"

Linda Karr, mother of camper K.C., says "K.C.'s friends ask him why would he pay money to hike hundreds of miles with eighty pounds on his back. And his answer is always the same: because it's the greatest experience he's ever had.

"When we pick up our two boys from camp, they're at the top of their game. Camp makes them better people."

Of the many mantras Pat Rode recites, the most often repeated is this: None of us can do it alone, but there are a lot of people who are willing to help you.

He comes by this belief honestly. Rode's childhood had little in common with the happy ones he tries to create for the people at Hayo-Went-Ha each summer. Pat was sickly, his father was frequently absent, and his mother was buried on his twelfth birthday.

"But," he adds, "so many people went out of their way to help me that, well, you've got to give back."

He has. In addition to his time and energy, Rode has given money to pay former campers' rent, college tuition, plane tickets, and even, on a couple occasions, their bail. Only one has failed to pay him back.

"I believe in second chances," Rode says. "And third and fourth and fifth chances. However many it takes."

More than 70 percent of Hayo-Went-Ha's campers return each year; 80 percent of their counselors are former campers. For a job that pays only $150 to $190 a week, the turnover is amazingly low. Perhaps that's because the camp's main currency is not money but bonding, one thing Hayo-Went-Ha can offer in abundance.

When Rode's colleagues at Central Michigan University, where he taught during the school year, asked why he didn't teach one of the cushy summer school classes for four times what he could make at camp, he replied, "How many eleven-year-old friends do you have?"

As for me, I didn't want to go to summer camp. I spent my summers at our family cottage on Torch Lake, but the idea of going to a YMCA camp simply wasn't for me. I liked playing baseball, riding bikes, and going to hockey school with my best friend. I figured the kids who went to Hayo-Went-Ha either couldn't play baseball, or didn't have many friends.

But by my sixteenth birthday, thanks to the introduction of the curveball, I quit playing baseball. Far sadder, my best friend had been killed in a car accident.

With nothing else to do, I finally went to Camp Hayo-Went-Ha. To my surprise, I discovered the kids there were tougher than most of my hockey teammates, and got to go on exotic trips. It was life-changing—so much so, I stayed on two more summers as a counselor, and have stayed in touch with the friends I made, including Pat Rode, for decades.

My brother joined the HWH staff during my third summer, just a few months after he dropped out of college.

"Absolutely changed my life," he says. "Being responsible for the kids made me think about what's real. It made me realize the need to win was less important than the need to participate, and be a contributing member. It made me realize not just my physical abilities but my mental abilities. And I made my closest friendships there.

"That's what camp did for me."

After camp helped restore my brother's confidence, he climbed Mt. Rainier, returned to school, earned two degrees, and started a promising career. And when he got married four hours from camp, Pat Rode made the trip.

A former camper turned counselor recently left Rode a small note. "One of my best memories from camp is the day you sat down with me on the boathouse steps and we just talked—for half an hour. You often explain how counselors should make kids feel special. Well, that's the most special I've ever felt. Thank you for making this place so wonderful."

At Pat Rode's final farewell ceremony, a dozen alums flew in just to thank him.

As always, Rode lit his candle and those of his staff members, who then lit their campers' candles, too, until the once dark hall was bright enough to see the tears on the faces of Pat Rode's campers, his counselors, and even the old camp director himself.

Then everyone blew out their candles, returning the big room to its original darkness, and listened to Pat Rode say goodbye. My brother draped his right arm around his wife, and his left arm around me. After all those years, I still felt part of something special—and I still do.

That's what summer camp did for me.

Confessions of an Idiot

Probably no one popularized first-person sports journalism more than the great George Plimpton, author of classics like *Paper Lion*, *Out of My League*, and *The Bogey Man*, among others. Many have followed, but no one has surpassed him, in my opinion.

The problem is, when writers try, they don't try hard enough. They make a half-hearted effort at, say, the balance beam, chuckle at their incompetence, and quit. I find such stories unsatisfying, because they only tell us what we already know: laypeople with no training and no determination don't stand a chance. Further, they aren't risking anything, so there are no stakes to keep us interested.

The form, at its best, requires authors to have some reason to think they just might not embarrass themselves, to put their heart and soul into the effort. When they inevitably fail, it has to hurt their pride, if nothing else. But, as Teddy Roosevelt said, at least they fail while daring greatly.

I also believe if the author can't learn something about the sport and the athletes who've mastered it by going "inside," then it's all for giggles, and that's not enough. We have to get close enough to the experts to see something we couldn't see from the press box.

I hope you enjoy these, and appreciate anew just how good the pros really are.

PAPER VIPER

I was motivated to write one of this piece, "Paper Viper," when I was working in the Joe Louis press box, listening to my colleagues rip Steve Yzerman for failing to bury a one-timer with Chicago's Chris Chelios hanging all over him, after 50 minutes of working his tail off. These were the same colleagues who couldn't run down the street, let alone skate the length of the ice.

I was writing for the Detroit News when Detroit still had a top minor league hockey team called the Vipers playing at the Palace. I wanted to find out just how big the gap is between the weekend player and the professional athlete. I figured the Vipers would be a great team to test this theory, and I was just the man for the job. Why not go down there and see what I can do?

Why not, indeed.

November 11, 1995
The Detroit News

"Bet you lunch you don't survive the whole practice."

I looked up at the speaker, John Craighead, who happened to be the Vipers' all-time penalty-minutes leader. I was sitting in his stall in their luxurious Palace locker room, getting ready to take the ice for a Monday practice. Since Craighead's hands were too banged up from three fights in the previous night's game, I'd be taking his spot as the left-winger on the fourth line that day.

I looked Craighead square in the eye and said, with more brass than brains, "You're on."

I opened my big mouth too soon. I learned I was in for a ninety-minute practice run by the most demanding coach in pro hockey, Rick Dudley.

"No other team works this hard," said Alan May, 31, who's played in enough places to know, including 313 games with the Calgary Flames. "It's because our coach is a lunatic, but we like him."

And on no other day did the Hardest-Working Team in Hockey work harder than on Mondays—especially at the end of practice, when the players skated fifteen laps at top speed one way, then fifteen more the other.

"You're in for a helluva skate," captain Darryl Williams told me. "Monday's are a bitch."

Even before I heard such dire warnings I suspected I was biting off more than I could throw up. The apex of my career was a three-year stint on the Ann Arbor Huron varsity ice hockey team, which consisted of two phases: the first, "This kid's got a lot of potential," and the second, "This kid had a lot of potential." I sort of skipped the middle part, where I was supposed to realize all that potential. My short-lived career was about as successful as Rudy's at Notre Dame—minus the game-ending sack.

But, in the war of attrition that is adult hockey, I was still standing, and even played a significant role on the best men's team in Ann Arbor. Although I'd gotten smarter and my hands had improved, I was still slow, short, and weak—not a winning combination.

Fully aware of these shortcomings, if not the task in front of me, I did what I could the week before to get ready for battle. I went to the weight room a few times, I dropped in for a couple pickup games, and I even replaced my usual dinner of pepperoni pizza and Stroh's with mushroom pizza and Pepsi. I know it sounds extreme, but my attitude was, hey, whatever it takes, baby. I was playing to win. By the time I accepted Craighead's bet in the locker room that day, I had dropped down to a lean, mean 160 pounds of blue, twisted steel.

Fearing a full-contact practice, I girded my loins and everything else with new equipment, most notably shin guards and pants. My old equipment was made sometime during the Great War, and was so flimsy you could fold it up and put it in your back pocket, whereas this new stuff had all kinds of additional features, like padding.

The new equipment would prove a grave tactical mistake.

I put on the official sweater of the fourth line, a red practice jersey with the Vipers logo on the front, and walked through the dark tunnel toward the rink. And yes, looking up at the thousands of empty Palace seats did something to me.

Coach Rick Dudley, who's played and coached for the Buffalo Sabres, complimented his team for their 7–1 victory the previous night over the Kansas City Blades, then spelled out some of the drills we'd be doing before adding with a sinister grin, "And don't forget, we've got the laps at the end."

Don't bother worrying about the laps, I thought. From the get-go I knew I had my work cut out just to survive the "soft" stuff that led up to it.

I was able to keep up during the initial skating drills, but my new team-mates were cruising through it, barely breaking a sweat, while I was going full blast. Not a good sign.

From there we moved onto a drill with three lines of players at the far end, with each player leaving in sequence. To my surprise, on my half dozen trips down the ice I scored three times, one off the left post, another through the goalie's legs and a third—yes!—past his glove into the upper shelf.

The key was my change of pace. While everyone else was ripping slap shots, I was baffling the goalies with my off-speed wrist shots—which were, of course, intended to be full blast.

It was good that I enjoyed myself while I could.

In rec-league hockey, drills with pucks are usually much slower paced than skating drills, but at the pro level they go every bit as fast with the puck as without, which requires just as much huffing and puffing, and left me just as gassed.

Another difference: conventional drills usually involve a lot of starting and stopping, and focus on either the offensive or defensive end. Not so Dudley's drills, which had us constantly turning, weaving, and passing—almost always in the neutral zone—and usually required a few cycles before we were allowed to shoot. Despite playing and coaching the game for some twenty-five years, I was so thoroughly confused I didn't do a single drill correctly the first time.

Things got even more complicated when Coach Dudley had us skate with our linemates. Since I was already breathing hard a mere twenty minutes into practice, I was relieved to be on the fourth line—and even more relieved that my linemates were as patient as they were talented.

Like the majority of their Viper comrades, center Darryl Williams, twenty-seven, and winger Steve Junker, twenty-three, have both played in the NHL. They were undoubtedly tough, but they had the lumberjack kind of hardiness typical of Canadians, which is not at odds with being gener-ous. That last quality I would surely put to the test.

A typical drill would start with Williams and I on the boards near the blue line, with Junker at the far boards. The defenseman would give Wil-liams a breakout pass, cueing Junker and me to start skating toward the other end. Williams would pass to Junker then weave behind him, then Junker would dish to me and follow, and so on. We'd keep that passing up until we hit the other blue line and circle back, then reverse again at the first blue line, and then again, passing the puck as often as possible the whole way. After the fourth reverse, we'd come flying in 3-on-0 on the goalie.

At that point Williams and Junker almost always gave me the shot from the high slot—not because I was the go-to guy but because after all that skating and turning, I was invariably the last man to cross the blue line. One time I was so far behind that I received Williams's pass behind the blue line, offsides.

After each repetition I'd retreat to the bench, suck down as much water and air as I could, then bend over until our line was called out again. My heart was pumping so hard it felt like only one layer of skin kept it from popping out onto the ice, and my lungs were working so hard to push the thick air in and out it felt like I was breathing peanut butter.

I was dying, and I knew it.

I think my linemates did, too.

When it was our turn again, Williams turned to me and asked, half-grinning, "You ready to go? We can skip one, if you want."

Oh, how I would have loved to. But a bet was a bet, and I didn't much feel like ticking off John Craighead, the current heavyweight champ.

As I dragged my butt through each successive rush I could see my game fall apart. After just thirty minutes I couldn't even do the simple things right, as though I were drunk. When it became obvious we'd be doing a lot more skating than hitting, I cursed my new, clumsy equipment, which felt like I was wearing Sears catalogues for shin guards and an oak barrel for pants.

Once gassed, I started skating straight-legged instead of bent-kneed (a major hockey no-no), I fumbled the puck, I missed my linemates on easy passes, and I even began to dread Williams's drop passes to me in the high slot.

"Oh crap," I thought when his perfect dishes came toward my stick. "Now I have to shoot the damn thing." Shooting the puck—normally the dessert course of any drill, and the reason forwards play this game—became a joyless chore, and going upstairs on the goalie was out of the question. Hey, the goalie wants the damn puck, he can pick it up from the ice, just like the rest of us.

"Your skills deteriorate so much after thirty, forty-five seconds," defenseman Greg Andrusak told me. "Then you start giving up penalties, turnovers, goals."

Or worse, your lunch.

After I had soaked through my helmet, T-shirt, and shorts with sweat, I started looking for two things: a clock, and a bucket. Bill Murray, their head trainer, smiled when he showed me his watch.

"Only halfway," he said, doing a poor job of concealing his glee.

Keee-rrriiiips, I thought, forty-five minutes left. No way I'm going to make it.

That's when I asked Murray for the bucket.

He laughed at first.

I didn't.

"Haven't got one," he said apologetically.

And that's when Coach Dudley added defensemen to the drill. By then I was lathering sweat like a horse, my ears were popping from the pressure, and talking to others was as difficult as communicating underwater. My one attempt to carry on a conversation lasted just a few sentences before I realized the guy I was talking to had no idea what I was saying. Jozef Cierny is from Zvolen, Czechoslovakia, and doesn't speak a lick of English.

Right as I approached the Puke Line, Coach Dudley blew his whistle for a water break. I didn't need the water—I'd already swallowed about two bottles' worth (no exaggeration)—but the break from skating was a godsend. He followed it up by announcing—yes!—it was time for laps.

Oh joy. Oh rapture.

Coach Dudley divided us into three groups, with mine going last. (Coach Dudley, I think, had a soft spot for me.)

After seeing my fire-hydrant-red face, at least a half-dozen guys told me, "You don't have to do this." But none of those sympathetic souls happened to be John Craighead, who made the bet, so yes, yes I did have to do the laps.

And that's when something magical happened: In the eight minutes it took the first two groups to finish, I became human again, and was able to join my linemates for the fifteen laps.

I hung with them for the first four or so, but by the time they'd finished all fifteen they'd lapped me two and three times. Coach Dudley barked out each lap number to encourage us, and was nice enough to include my lap number, too.

"Eight!" he'd yell to his players, then mutter "*Seven!*" to me. And so it went. "Twelve! (Ten!)" "Fifteen! (Twelve!)." I was going 33 rpm in a 45 world.

But I finished. Okay, I finished dead last at four minutes and twenty seconds, far behind Peter Ciavaglia at 3:59, but I finished.

"Okayyyy, Junny!" Dudley yelled to me, in his Canadian accent.

Dudley gathered the team around him, and calmly implored them to skate harder.

"The whole idea," Coach continued, "is to hit the wall around lap eight or nine, and then keep going."

Lap eight or nine?! Hell, I hit that wall about half an hour ago, and my insides were now climbing the skyscraper behind it.

And that's when he announced that it was time to do it again. With my exhaustion-addled mind, I'd forgotten that little detail.

We did it again. The players' times ranged from 3:38 to 4:06 to . . . uh . . . well, on the second trial there's a blank spot on the sheet next to my name. I don't know when I finished. I just know I did.

I dragged my butt off the ice, done with my experiment. Or so I thought. John Craighead saw me and said, "Made it so far, eh?"

"So far?"

"Oh, yeah, the off-ice work's just begun," he said, with a devilish grin. "Hey, no bike, no lunch."

Would you argue with the best fighter in the locker room? I hopped on that bike and thought I was doing okay, but I had my bubble popped when the trainer said, "Go whatever speed you want on this thing. Just make sure you don't pass out."

After forty-five more minutes of pedaling, pull-downs, pull-ups, stick hops, and butterflies, I was finally—finally!—done, for real this time.

"Now all you need to do is get a beer and a cigar," Alan May said, "And you're finished."

I weighed myself: 154 pounds, 6 less than I weighed that morning. I returned to the locker room and watched the other players play ping-pong. I would have joined in, too, if I only could have raised my hands above my waist.

"You're gonna feel it tomorrow," Darryl Williams said to me.

"Tomorrow?!" I asked. "You mean . . . it gets worse?"

A day later I can tell you that, yes, it gets worse. I am trying to finish this story before the rigor mortis sets in.

While it's true I survived the practice, I'm not gloating. Any weekend athlete who thinks he can do what the pros can do had better think again.

"On TV the game looks pretty slow," Andrusak told me, "but it's a lot faster down here."

Amen.

And smarter and sharper and just plain better. I wasn't close to these guys—I couldn't even fake it plausibly—and I knew it. So next time you're tempted to yell at a player for missing a third-period one-timer in front of the net, just remember they're better than you are—or, more accurately, they're better than I am.

I took solace in Woody Allen's words: 90 percent of success is simply showing up. By that measure, I only had 10 percent left to go.

After it was all done, I collapsed in Craighead's stall, frozen like a prize-fighter after losing on a TKO. When Craighead saw me, he laughed. Then he said the words I longed to hear.

"How 'bout lunch?"

We went dutch.

MONSTER BITES MAN AT U.S. OPEN

June 23, 1996
The Detroit News

Jack Nicklaus stood under a big oak tree, talking to a half-dozen writers after his first round of the U.S. Open last week.

When one reporter asked him how he managed to knock a long iron out of the deep rough and stick it on the green, Nicklaus said, "It's not easy to do here." Then he added with a grin, "But that's why I'm on this side of the microphone, and you're on that side."

Monster, Schmonster, I thought. I was tired of hearing how impossible this course was. It's just *grass*, man. How tough can it be?

To find out, I agreed to take on the Monster under championship conditions. That meant playing from the U.S. Open tees with the fast greens, the stingy 70 par and, most importantly, the five-inch rough. And like the pros, I'd be allowed no mulligans, no gimmes, no winter rules, or hand-wedges, either.

Yo, Monster: You wanna piece of me? You got it.

Well, after suffering an injured wrist, a litany of humiliating strokes, and two blistered feet from hiking through five miles of rough, I'm not saying that anymore.

The Monster has earned my respect.

I'm no golfing die-hard, but on a good course I can usually play bogey golf. And during a few magical rounds over the years I've been so close to mediocrity, I could almost taste it.

On my quest I was accompanied by my attorney, a man known in college as "The Rhino" for his lean physique and gazelle-like speed in the 40. When I met him freshman year he was already famous for his ability to drink an entire beer simply by opening his throat and tilting the glass. That's right: he could down it at the speed of gravity, minus throat friction.

Since he joined a top law firm and became a member at Oakland Hills, those days are far behind him. He eats veggie-burgers now, and is smart enough to keep his name out of the paper. My attorney and I were joined by two highly capable caddies, Joe Wagner and Brandon Cassar, both high school students.

Since Wagner had never seen me play he naturally assumed I was a normal person, and would therefore want to hit a driver off the first tee. But the truth is I haven't used that club since the Reagan Administration, because all kinds of evil things happen when I have it in my hands. You could have glued the cover on it ten years ago as a prank, and I never would have discovered it.

So there I was, on the first tee of one of the grandest courses in the world with a dozen people standing by the pro shop watching me while Wagner held out the one-wood. I stared at it, motionless. Would I be man enough to admit my limitations and reject the driver for a three-wood, or would I succumb to the macho pressure?

I caved in like a house of cards in an earthquake. I grabbed that one-wood like I'd been hitting it all my life, teed the ball up high and swung the mother of all swings—only to smash a worm-burner three inches high.

Problem was, the rough at the end of the tee-box was five inches high. My ball traveled 200 mph for the first ten feet, then 2 mph for the next ten, then stopped cold in the high grass. I was just thankful that I could share my next shot in full view of the people watching outside the pro shop.

And the next shot.

And the next shot.

It took my fifth shot, my "bogey chip," to finally make it to the fairway, a mere 350 yards short of the pin.

From there, I didn't have any problem at all scoring my first ten.

Sure, maybe a lot of guys could notch a ten on the Monster's first hole, but how many could follow it up with *another ten* on the second hole?

While the peanut gallery could see the Monster was killing me, I slowly learned an important lesson about the rough: *stay out of it.*

When I met Nicklaus a few days earlier I was surprised by the thickness of his wrists, but suddenly it all made sense. I tell you the stuff alongside fairways groomed for a U.S. Open isn't rough, but a tropical rain forest. A typical hack from the rough produced a high-pitched thrashing sound, two fistfuls of tall grass thrown ten feet high, and a golf ball sent airborne for twenty feet before landing—you guessed it—right back in the jungle.

I lost one ball all day. Not in the water, in the woods, or out of bounds, but a mere twenty feet off the second fairway, in the deep rough.

Even when I could find the ball, my genetically inferior wrists didn't have a chance. I took over half of my many swings off the fairway. To get a feel for what my day was like, let your lawn grow for three weeks, then try mowing it with a three iron.

On those rare occasions I did get my ball back in the fairway, my swing was so screwed up from hacking in the tall grass that I'd rip my iron three inches too low, launching a strip of sod into the air ten yards farther than my ball.

My wrists hurt. I want to go home now.

On the bright side, I was a mere six strokes from playing pro-level golf—on hole number one. I cut the Monster's margin of victory down to five-over par on the second hole and a scant four-over on the third.

The pattern was obvious. At my current rate of improvement, I'd be firing a birdie on hole number eight and an eagle at nine. Everything was coming up roses.

My attorney felt compelled to advise me to use a long iron off the tee, and short irons from the rough. As Clint Eastwood once said, "A man's got to know his limitations." The Monster had exposed mine in the first five minutes.

On hole number seven I started off with a clean iron to the fairway, and followed it up with a solid second shot right in front of the green. My attorney, the caddies, and the photographer all dropped what they were doing to say, "Good shot!" They knew that might be the only chance they'd have to give me a compliment all day, and they didn't dare miss it.

I did have another flash of competence on number eight, a 474-yard hole that's a par 5 for members, but a par 4 for the pros—and on this day, me. I got on the green in three, ten feet from the pin, and tapped a slight right to left putt straight in the cup for par. The Monster may have been tearing me apart from limb to limb, but at least I got to poke him once in the eye.

I finished the front nine at 66, just one off the course record set by Tom Lehman, Jack Nicklaus, and others—for 18 holes. And hey, if I had just made *one* of those 20-foot triple bogey putts, I'd be right there, tied with the Bear himself.

Emboldened by these results, I was ready to attack the back nine.

As the round progressed I wizened up and settled down. Seeing this, my attorney stopped giving advice and started giving motivational pep talks, such as, "This is the hardest hole out here," "This green's impossible," and my favorite, delivered a nano-second before I started my backswing on the twelfth tee, "Watch out for the water way down there on the right, and the pick-up truck in front of it."

Before my attorney said this, I hadn't even seen those things, let alone worried about them. But, needless to say, just two seconds later my drive careened toward the pick-up truck as if it were a powerful electromagnet and my ball was lead. Worse luck, my ball fell short of the water, landing in the rough.

Now, a better player would have gotten upset, but by hole twelve I knew that I was not one of those better players.

I recalled a line from *Caddyshack*, where the judge hits a terrible shot and gets angry, saying, "I'm no slouch!"

Chevy Chase's character politely objects, "Ah, c'mon Judge. Don't be so hard on yourself. You're a tremendous slouch."

For me, getting mad at such shots would be the height of pretense.

On the back nine I approached the game less as a competition and more like Frisbee, taking simple satisfaction in watching the ball fly far away. I couldn't worry my pretty little head over such trivialities like where it landed.

Perhaps as a result, things went better on the back nine. At one point I actually confessed to my attorney that I was "playing fairly well."

What a crock.

I wasn't "playing fairly well," I was doing things I *never* do, like getting out of every sand-trap in one shot, averaging two putts per green, and playing the final three holes well under 10 (each).

Despite hitting into green-side bunkers on all three holes, I escaped number 16 with a bogey five. On number 17, after "laying up" ten yards past the ladies' tees, I salvaged another five, then finished number 18 with a six.

I wasn't "playing fairly well." I was playing the single best round of golf of my entire life. And that realization was more humbling than my back-to-back tens.

There I was playing out of my head to give the Monster everything I had, and all I had to show for it were a bunch of triple- and quadruple-bogeys. I made more snowmen that day than an Anchorage elementary school at recess. I was so befuddled I put the lit end of my "lucky cigar" to my lips. Twice.

My final tally was a heart-wrenching, mind-numbing, pride-swallowing 120.

That's right, folks. One hundred and twenty. Just 50 over par—for the first round. Imagine the leader board on Sunday if I had played with the pros. Steve Jones had finished at −2, Tom Lehman and Davis Love at −1, and—who's this?—some guy named Bacon came in at +200.

I had leapt as high as I could to look the Monster in the eye, only to discover I was staring at his knee-caps.

As for you, Mr. Nicklaus, I'll take your advice and go back to my side of the oak tree. And this time, I think I'll stay there, just so long as they keep the grass cut short.

SPINNER TAKES THE WHEEL

June 1997
The Detroit News

Your Driver's Ed teacher in high school was probably a humorless, hyper-critical guy who constantly badgered you to "slow down, slow down! Whaddaya wanna do, get us all killed?"

Not so our instructors at the Skip Barber Racing School. They spent three days at the Waterford Race Track preparing me and 23 other competitors for the Detroit Grand Prix Neon Challenge, a 30-minute race that runs Sunday morning, just a few hours before the real thing, on the same track.

Our instructors were energetic, highly skilled professional people who are so good at what they do, they once taught a blind man how to perform a high-speed stop on a test track.

"The guy was great," said Bob Dotson, a veteran driver and the leader of the instructor pack, who has more courage than your high school Driver's Ed teacher.

Initially, Dotson urged me to "accelerate, accelerate! Whaddaya wanna do, live forever?" But he quit saying that after the first day.

"It's good to be fearless," Dotson told me. "But not if you're brainless, too."

That deadly combination explains why, if you had polled my classmates at the end of the three-day course, I'm sure they would have elected me "Most Likely to Crash on Game Day."

Welcome to Satan's Driving Seminar.

My classmates included Channel 7's Mary Conway, WCSX's Steve Kostan, and *Auto Week* deputy editor Sam Moses, who once wrote a book about amateur racers titled, *Fast Guys, Rich Guys, and Idiots.*

Guess which category I'm in?

Although I had driven more than a quarter-million miles before entering the Skip Barber course, in just three days I was forced to rethink everything I thought I knew about driving. I also had to break a lifetime of lazy habits. I'm normally so distracted behind the wheel that some friends have taken to calling me "Mr. Magoo."

47

Other drivers keep their eyes on the road and their hands on the wheel. But my eyes wander aimlessly while my hands busy themselves with the radio, the wipers, and the ketchup I'm putting on my cheeseburger, while my right knee handles the steering. I keep track of my progress on the road by occasionally looking through the windshield for "updates" on where my car is headed, and what might be in its way. Sometimes it's really interesting, what you can see when you look up.

From day one of the school, all that changed—and fast. Before taking the course, I knew racing was dangerous, but I didn't realize how difficult it was to do well. Funny how spending three days screeching the tires around a racetrack, with disaster lurking around every turn, can heighten your appreciation for such things.

Dotson and his staff had to reteach us how to do everything, including braking, turning, and shifting gears. They also taught us how to get out of disaster once you've already gotten into it, but not all of us picked up the finer points of that lesson.

We started out learning how to brake, which isn't as simple as it sounds. They told us to forget about pumping the brakes in favor of consistent, hard braking, just short of locking them up. It's much more efficient—if you can do it.

Most of us couldn't. I tended to skid, then let up too much, then jump on the brakes too hard again. My car sounded like it was scratching out the Morse code for S-O-S in squealing rubber.

Seeing this, the ever-helpful Dotson gave me two tips: "One, stay cool. Two, buy golf clubs."

Before I could run off to the nearest golf course, they taught us about turning. Obviously, the goal here is to maximize speed through the turn without losing control. The Idiot (me) thinks you do this by diving into the turn as directly as you can, as quickly as you can.

Wrong on both counts. A good racer transforms a pointy 90-degree turn into a soft, wide arc. On a right-to-left turn, for example, the wise driver veers his car as far to the right as possible before the turn and keeps it there for as long as possible. While still in the straightaway, he gets all his braking done, and then hits the gas before turning the car left toward the inside of the curve.

If the goal is speed, it sounds counter-intuitive to slow down that much before turning, but Dotson told us not to worry about our speed *entering* the turn, but our speed *exiting* it. In this pay-me-now-or-pay-me-later bargain, it's better to sacrifice speed coming into the corner than coming out of it.

But just because your brain buys into it doesn't meet your guts will.

Turns out it takes a surprising amount of nerve to keep the car going straight that long before turning. It feels as if you're playing a game of chicken with the corner, waiting to see who'll be the first to turn.

But if you do it right, you'll come flying out of that corner like an inner-tuber being whipped around by a speed boat. As you start hurtling to the outside, toward the guardrail, it takes even more nerve to trust the car to stay on line. You feel as if you might be flung out of orbit.

This is what the pros call "using the whole road." Before the end of the course, I proved to be so good at using the whole road that I even reached a few sections of grass and dirt others somehow missed.

Once we got the hang of braking and high-speed turning, we moved on to downshifting, racing style. This entails hitting the brake, the clutch, and the gas simultaneously, to avoid lurching forward on the downshift.

My problem was simple: Like most standard cars, the Neon is equipped with three pedals to perform those functions. But like most standard humans, I am equipped with only two feet to press them.

The answer to this biological deficiency is found in the fancy heel-toe footwork professional drivers can do in their sleep, which allows your right foot to do two things at once, like so: When entering the turn, pivot your right foot so it's pointing to the driver's door, and hit the brakes with your right toe. Now press the clutch in with your *left* foot, then rev the gas pedal with your *right heel* (keeping your right *toe* on the brake) then shift gears. Once you complete the shift, pull your left foot off the clutch and your right hand off the stick shift and then smoothly pivot your right toe from the brake back to the gas—and do all that in about a second, without crashing.

If it's difficult to understand, it's much harder to do, like trying to rub your stomach while patting your head, playing hacky-sack, calling information, and filing your taxes without an extension. If you could have sat in the passenger seat while I attempted this high-speed feat of coordination, you would have thought I had given up racing altogether to perform some diabolical game of hokey-pokey, with the guard rail as the consolation prize.

After countless tries, I finally got through a turn without sending the rpm through the roof or my head through the windshield. But, instead of complimenting my Herculean effort, Dotson had the nerve to yell, "Relax your hands! You've got a gorilla grip on the steering wheel!"

I suppose he had a point. Looking down, I noticed my knuckles weren't merely white, my hands were welded shut. When I got out of the car, un-rolling my hands created so much cracking it sounded like I was making popcorn.

By the second day we were all starting to get it, even me. When I did it right—veer to the outside, keep it straight, brake-clutch-gas-shift, then get off the clutch, let go of the stick, hit the gas, dive into the corner—it created a satisfyingly seamless and quick run through the turns, as good as advertised.

At one point, Dotson was even moved to compliment my work—an uncharacteristic error he soon regretted. After hearing Dotson's kind words, I figured whatever I was doing right would be even better if I did it faster.

Despite a heavy rain, I was feeling good as I sped up to pass a fellow student heading into a tight right-hand turn. I didn't hear the voice in my head that was repeating all the things Dotson and the boys had been telling me all day, such as: "If all four wheels are on water, you're just a passenger; along for the ride," and "the biggest mistake is heading into a corner too soon or too fast."

When I saw that the guy in front of me wasn't slowing down enough for me to pass him, the smart thing to do would have been to slow down, ride behind him, and pass him on the next turn. But I wasn't out to do the smart thing. I was out to do the dumb thing, and do it as fast as possible.

I succeeded beyond my wildest dreams.

When I recognized that I was coming into the turn too fast and too deep, with no easy way out of this jam I'd created except to hit the car in front of me or try to pass him on the inside—where there was no room—I cranked the steering wheel even harder to the right, which put me in a vicious spin. Now, some guys can pull a 180, and a few might be good for a 360—but how many can pull a 720?

You're talking to one of the few, the proud. As my car whipped around in a circle, my life went before my eyes on the first rotation, then went before my eyes again on the second. Same life, two showings. As I watched my relatively boring life for the second time, it occurred to me that I needed to get out more.

Perhaps calmed by the mundane vision, I was surprisingly cool after my spinout. I put the car back in gear, got back on the track, and finished my laps.

Channel 7's Mary Conway thought my calm response was pretty cool, but after I spun out a second time she found the same reaction odd, and after I pulled the trick a third time you could tell she was getting a little alarmed.

Dotson must have agreed with her. After the most glorious spin, which I executed going about 60 mph into a 90-degree turn, he sent me out with another driver to examine the scene of the mishap, much the way you rub a dog's nose in his urine to get him to stop peeing all over your Persian rugs. It worked.

In the process, I've gained a new appreciation not only for the dangers of auto racing, but also how difficult it is to do well.

But the real test was coming Sunday morning.

In his send-off to the class, Dotson waved his arms over all his students and said, "Everyone here will be your best friends—at the start of the race. After that, everyone else in this room turns into monsters. Happens every year.

"Have fun!"

On the morning of our race, after we had put on our super cool fire suits and gotten into our customized Dodge Neons with our names on the sides, Dotson encouraged everyone to go as fast as they could, then pleaded with *me* to return my car in working condition. My editor, on the other hand, told me if I crashed, I could write more about it.

I split the difference.

Spinning on our wide-open practice course in Waterford simply puts you in the grass. Spinning on the Detroit Grand Prix course at Belle Isle will put you into a concrete wall, and out of the race. They didn't call it the Fisher-Price Grand Prix, after all. This was real racing.

When one of my peers asked one of our instructors how to avoid danger, she said: "I recommend driving between the walls."

Easier said than done. When one of my classmates returned from a warm-up lap around the Grand Prix course, I asked him what it looked like. He just rolled his eyes, shook his head, and said, "(*Bleep*)."

What looks like a long and languorous course on TV looked narrow, short, and scary to us. The difference between watching the race on TV and actually driving in it is the difference between watching a roller coaster from the ground and being thrashed about in one of the cars.

One of my compatriots said, "When I'm driving on this course, I feel like a mouse in a maze."

Eight of the 23 drivers had raced before, and it showed. They not only could go faster, they could do it without endangering themselves or others. One veteran had his name stitched onto his fire suit and a crash helmet with his blood-type printed on the back. It got my attention.

State Sen. Mike Bouchard, a fellow rookie, noticed that the course maps the veterans used listed the radii of all the turns, while his marked the locations of the hot dog stands.

We practiced at the Belle Isle track on Friday, qualified on Saturday, and raced on Sunday. Like most of the drivers, my times improved dramatically from Friday to Saturday. I started out running about 2 minutes, 30 seconds per lap on Friday and finished the day at 2:08. On Saturday's qualifying run, I was down to 2 minutes flat, a mere 1.5 seconds out of fifth place. Of course, in racing, 1.5 seconds can be measured on a calendar, which is why I started Sunday's race in 10th place in the 23-car field.

I learned three important things on race day. First, just because I could take a turn well at moderate speed didn't mean I could do it better by going faster. It was similar to my golf game: If I hit one shot nicely with a relaxed, easy swing, I assume my shot will go that much farther if I speed it up. In golf, that kind of thinking will send your ball veering into the woods. In racing, it will send your car careening toward the concrete wall—with you in it.

And that brings us to the second lesson: It turns out the walls really *are* made of concrete. Three cars proved that during our qualifying laps, and only two of them could be put back together by the crack pit crew in time to race on Sunday.

Lesson three: The hardest part about this race isn't driving for thirty straight minutes, it's *thinking* for that long. Just one mental lapse, and you're spinning out of control. Finishing our little 12-lap race required us to execute 168 turns, any one of which could knock us out of the race. It was like taking the Scholastic Aptitude Test at 60 mph—except that failing this test wouldn't get you rejected from a college, it would get you admitted to a hospital.

When the race started, I remembered a line from George Carlin: "No matter what speed you drive, anyone who drives faster than you is crazy, anyone who drives slower is stupid, and anyone who drives the same speed as you just can't be trusted."

Perhaps because I was working on three hours of sleep, thanks to the Detroit Red Wings winning their first Stanley Cup in 42 years the night before, I got caught napping on the first two laps when Bouchard and car dealer Joe Ricci passed me by.

"Crazy S.O.B.'s," I muttered.

I considered trying to pass them, until I saw another driver spin out right in front of me. Suddenly being stupid seemed better than being crazy.

Before long, Ricci and I settled into a nice dogfight, one we kept up the entire afternoon. I was the trailer for the first half-dozen laps. Along the way, I realized he was far from crazy, but he still couldn't be trusted, going the same speed as me.

With a few laps left, I decided the time to pass him was now or never.

It might have worked if I was actually ahead of him before the next turn. But I wasn't, which is why my left front fender and his right door were getting intimate until I backed off. I slammed over the striped curb and zipped over the grass corner. After trading paint, my side mirror dangled grotesquely from a few remaining wires, like the head from a decapitated robot.

My first impulse was to stop, apologize, inspect the damage, and exchange insurance information. Then I had a wonderful epiphany: *this isn't my car.*

With just two laps left, I saw Ricci had gotten himself trapped behind a slower driver, so I decided to take advantage of the situation, and pass them both. I finished 10th, right back where I started.

A few years ago, Ted Nugent won this race, then drove directly into a wall of tires, launching his car straight up in the air and into an impressive somersault—possibly the first time a driver celebrated his victory by spiking his car. Me, I was satisfied with the opportunity to race with Mr. Ricci, an amiable, sporting man, get out of my banged-up car unharmed, and return to my old life, limbs intact.

Apparently my driving mates were thinking the same thing. When we signed each other's souvenir posters, two drivers wrote on mine, "Keep your day job, Spinner."

Don't worry guys. I think I'll do just that.

WHAT COACHING WOMEN TAUGHT ME

When you write a commentary comparing how men and women do almost any-
thing, complete with generalizations and stereotypes, you're playing with fire. I
knew that when I wrote this piece and expected to get an earful of protests when
it ran—but a funny thing happened: nothing. We didn't get one email of protest,
but a lot of agreement from men and women alike. You never know.

February 16, 2012
Michigan Radio

I've coached high school boys' hockey teams for a total of nine seasons. But
in the late nineties, I spent two seasons helping the Michigan women's
hockey team—and I learned a lot more than they did.

My education started on day one. I skated onto the ice with a bucket of
pucks, dumped them at center ice, and picked one out for myself. I skated
around the rink, stickhandling and shooting on the open nets, but something seemed strange, and it took me a moment to figure out what it was: it
was *quiet*.

When you coach high school boys, it's never quiet. Ever. You can't even
finish dumping out all of the pucks before you hear the boys firing them all
over the rink. They shoot the pucks as high and hard as they can, trying to
break the glass. So what if smashing a pane of Plexiglas costs a few hundred bucks and ruins practice? You'll be a locker room hero the rest of the
season!

But at my first women's practice, I looked back at the pile of pucks I'd
dumped at center ice, and saw they were still sitting there. All the women
were skating around, without pucks, apparently waiting for me to say it
was okay to take the pucks.

This was weird. And it only got weirder.

When you blow the whistle to tell the boys what to do, they dive right
into the drill—and get it all wrong. When you tell the women what to do,
they huddle to discuss the whole thing for a minute or more among them-

54

selves, *trying to determine exactly what it is the coaches want them to get out of the drill*, then they do it exactly right the first time.

The women are always eager to please, and yelling at them is not only unnecessary, it's completely counterproductive. With the boys, you *have* to yell just to penetrate the inch of Styrofoam that lines their skulls.

The boys love showing up the goalies in practice by whizzing slap shots past their ears, and making the goalies look foolish with their best moves. The women shoot the puck right at the goalies' pads, because it makes the goalies happy, and that makes the shooters happy—even while it drives the coaches crazy.

The boys love shooting the puck, being the star, and beating anyone they can. Getting them to pass the puck is a constant challenge.

The women *love* passing the puck—and passing, and passing, and passing. And really, pretty much just the passing. They don't want to be the star, they don't want to stand out, and they'd be embarrassed if they made an opponent look bad. They just want everyone to get along. This is lovely— except the scoreboard keeps track only of total goals, which means, to win anything, *someone* has to score—and that means someone has to *shoot!*

Which brings me to a riddle I made up. How many women does it take to shoot the puck?

Five. One to shoot the puck, and four to say, "It's okay to shoot the puck!"

With the women, we had to convince them they were better than they thought they were, both individually and as a team.

"No, really, you're *better* than that team is. Honest!"

With the boys, we always had to convince them they were nowhere near as good as they thought they were. "No, really, you're not *that* good— honest!"

When a boy has a birthday, none of his teammates or coaches even know about it, because no one really cares about that. It's sort of weird to us when a teammate knows our birthday—and weirder when a coach does.

But women are different, and by mid-season, the other male coach and I knew at least that much. So when they told us one of our players was having a birthday, we surrounded her in a circle for a drill, and then surprised her by singing, "Happy Birthday" instead. We thought we were the most sensitive, new-age coaches who ever graced the ice.

Until we got to the locker room, that is, which they had decorated with streamers and posters and filled with cake and snacks and pop and the birthday girl's favorite music. The other coach and I gave each other the same look, which said: *We are in way over our heads.*

But there were a few times when coaching the boys was easier. If they had a conflict with each other, one guy might say, "Screw you!" The other might say, "Screw you!" back, and sometimes they even fought a little, but no one ever got hurt. And then it was over, they went back to being friends, just like that.

With the women, I was convinced they got along amazingly well, and I was gushing about this one day to the other assistant coach, a woman who had played at Harvard. She looked at me as if I had two heads.

"Are you kidding?" she said.

"No," I said. "Are *you?*"

She then proceeded to diagram the three major cliques that were actually running the team, drawing overlapping circles and arrows between players who liked each other and those who hated each other. I was dumbfounded.

"But no one ever argues," I protested.

She gave me a condescending look. "That's when they're *really* mad—and you have to watch out!"

I learned to watch out.

But since then I've noticed one thing about my male friends who coach women's sports: not one of them has gone back to coaching the boys.

A CRASH COURSE IN THE
BARWIS SCHOOL OF PUKE-ITUDE

September 16, 2016
Michigan Radio

When Rich Rodriguez became Michigan's head football coach in 2008, he did so on one condition: strength coach Mike Barwis and his staff were part of the package, and would need an unlimited budget to overhaul the weight room—right down to the floors. A million dollars later, the Wolverines' weight program was world class.

So it seemed fair to ask: What did Michigan get for its money? The only way to find out—I mean *really* find out—was to enroll in Professor Barwis's School of Puke-itude, and dive into the curriculum for six weeks.

Was I scared? Nah. I figured, how much harder could it be than what we weekend warriors put ourselves through just to avoid buying bigger pants?

But when I asked Barwis if I should prepare for my six-week tryout by doing bench presses or squats, he said, in his ridiculously raspy voice, "No. It's too late for all that."

Not good.

"Okay, what should I do?"

"Run."

"Why? We're not going to be running."

"Because," he explained, "we lift weights so fast your heart is going to give out before your muscles do."

Not good.

After a month of running, I ate a hearty breakfast, put on my workout clothes, then showed up at Michigan football's weight room Monday morning, March 16, 2009, for the first of eighteen scheduled two-hour workouts—"if you last that long," Barwis said.

Now before I could lift a single weight, I had to sign ten-pages of legal waivers, with each page describing some very specific ways I might die in the weight room.

"I will not sue if I am crushed by the free weights." Sign here.

"I will not sue if the bar falls back on my neck and kills me." Sign here

"I will not sue if I'm standing there and my heart explodes." Sign here.

After I finished signing my life away, Barwis announced the workout partners. "Bacon, you're working with Foote!"

That would be Larry Foote, the former Michigan All-American linebacker and two-time Super Bowl champion Pittsburgh Steeler. He's one of a dozen professional players who come back every year to work with Barwis, who refuses payment from those guys.

"Barwis is crazy," Foote told me, "but I love him. He will get you doing things you never dreamed of."

Just fifteen minutes into my first workout—in which I had to do more than six hundred reps of every lift I could name, plus a dozen I couldn't—I was sweating like a pig and panting like a dog. You could have taken my pulse by touching my hair.

A few minutes later, I already had the look of a man in deep trouble—slack jaw, head back, eyes half closed, mouth-breathing, knuckles dragging, body swaying—when I realized that big breakfast I just ate might not have been my best idea.

Recognizing my look of despair, Barwis pointed his thumb toward a big Rubbermaid trash can in the corner, barked, "Trash can's over there!" then calmly returned to spotting Foote doing his squats.

I started casually walking to the trash can, then started running—and made it just in time to stick my head in there and let loose my breakfast, and perhaps my dinner, repeatedly and loudly.

Well, I thought, *this is not exactly a career highlight. But just maybe, no one saw me.*

I pulled my head slowly out of the black abyss of the trash can. When my head emerged, the entire Michigan football team stopped what they were doing to give me a standing ovation.

"Yeahhhh!"

"Go, Bacon, go!"

"Get rid of the poison!"

"We have a winner!"

I had already written four books, including my first *New York Times* bestseller. But nothing I'd done impressed them—until this. Suddenly, I had street cred, and all my interviews went much better, because I'd become one of them.

Puking in that trash can was one of the smartest career moves I ever made.

I also gained some wisdom: There *is* a snobbism in the Michigan weight room, but it's not based on your stats or your weights, just how hard you're working.

I was the oldest, weakest, and fattest guy there by a long shot, and I was fully prepared to take a lot of crap the minute I walked through the door. But I never took a single shot for any of that. So long as I was sweating and breathing as hard as the players were, they would high-five, yell, and urge me on.

I now had the same status as every other guy who'd puked in that trash can—which is to say, everyone.

But I was a long way from finished. It was only 10:15. We still had 75 minutes left on the red digital clocks posted on every flat surface of the big room. I had never seen a clock move so slowly in my life. When I finally got through everything on the absurdly long list of sets, Barwis yelled, "Bacon, you're finished!"

I sat there sweating audibly on the end of a bench, as if my butt had been nailed to it.

"Bacon, you can go now!"

Not really, I thought. Because that would require both the getting up, and the going—neither of which seemed possible. After a few minutes, I gathered all my energy to stand up, and start shuffling across the floor. You could hear the sweat bubble up through the eyelets of my running shoes, while I made my way across the floor with all the grace of Frankenstein, as if I was trying to learn how to operate a new pair of prosthetic legs—with a remote control. Everyone laughed again, but I no longer cared. I just wanted to get home—if I could.

I had started going through something called "hypertrophy," which occurs when you push your body so far past its limits the muscles absorb much more water than normal, expanding them rapidly. That's the good news. The bad news is, "It's basically a catastrophic event to your body," Barwis explained. "Like a car accident."

When I left Schembechler Hall for the parking lot, I tried to wipe some sweat off my brow, which is when I discovered I could no longer raise my right arm. So I grabbed the sleeve with my other hand and whacked my face with the powerless limb. Eureka.

When I got home I tried to shower, forgetting that I could not lift my hands high enough to wash my hair. So I shot up the shampoo into the air, and hoped that some of it came down on my head, and turned around in a circle to wash it off.

If you think I'm exaggerating, ask anyone who's gone through hypertrophy. They'll tell you.

As I lay comatose on my couch, it occurred to me the players I had worked out with that morning had just finished their second class. How they do this is a mystery to me. I wasn't going anywhere.

After three weeks of this torture, I dared to think I might just make it. I was on my way to tripling my bench press and quadrupling my squat. I would only lose ten pounds, but reduce my body fat from 26 percent to 16 percent.

All this growing confidence was dashed the day Barwis announced I'd be joining the rest of the players after each workout for a half hour of laps, hundred-yard dashes, sprints, and suicides.

"If you're going to go around claiming you did this," Barwis said, poking me in the chest, "you have to do *all* of it."

We ran in two groups, the "fat boys" and the "speedsters." I was lumped with the fat boys, of course, but I couldn't even catch the long-snap center who was recovering from a broken toe. If we were a pack of predators in the Serengeti, I'd go hungry—or get eaten. At this level, even the so called "fat boys" are pretty fast.

I longed for the squat rack.

At the end of one of our dashes, I looked up to see a friend of mine, former Michigan All-American center George Lilja, standing in the end zone. I could barely speak, so I nodded and waved.

He couldn't resist. "What the hell have they got *you* doing?"

I sputtered, "Don't ask!"

After our workout, Foote got in my face. "Bacon, you're pushing yourself in *there*," he said, pointing to the weight room, "but you ain't pushing yourself out *here*. You're smiling and laughing and high-fiving all your damn friends. You gonna work with us, you gotta work!"

I didn't have to ask if he meant it.

As if on cue, Barwis told us we had to run the width of the field and back, three times. "Y'all got to finish in fifty seconds," he said, "Bacon in sixty. But Bacon, if you don't make it, *everyone else has to do the whole damn thing again.*"

Thanks, Coach.

The death stares I received from the same players who had just been cheering me on are something I will never forget. If this wasn't life or death, it seemed pretty close.

When Barwis blew his whistle, I took off like a man being chased by a tiger. But after five of the six widths, I had only kept pace at fifty seconds, and I was running out of gas.

By this time, the other players had all finished their sprints, under the required time, and turned back to yell at me. Foote's encouragement was the most memorable: "Move that white ass, Bacon!"

I figured one of two things were going to happen: I'd push myself so hard, I'd collapse at the finish line. Or I wouldn't, and the players would kill me. Either way I'd be dead, I concluded, so I might as well die with honor, and try to beat the time.

On my last width, I pulled and lurched and thrashed every limb of my body, throwing everything I had and then some, toward that finish line.

"Fifty-five!" Barwis bellowed. "Fifty-six! Fifty-seven! Fifty-eight—done!"

I had made it.

The guys cheered and raised their hands for some high fives, but I ran past them straight for the trash can, puked again, wiped my mouth, and got back on the line for our final sprints. Barwis and company had succeeded in turning me into something else.

After we finished we dropped on the field and gasped for air.

Barwis walked up to me, kneeled down, and said a few words I will never forget: "Bacon, that's the first time I saw you run that I didn't want to punch you in the jaw."

It doesn't get any better than that.

POND OF DREAMS: BUILD IT,
AND THEY WILL COME

January 22, 2010
Michigan Radio

Just over half a million kids play organized hockey in the United States, and it's a lot of fun, but not half as much fun as disorganized hockey.

We're deep in the dead of winter. And for most of us, there's not a lot to do, and not much to look forward to for the next couple months. But if you're a hockey player—scratch that, if you're a *pond* hockey player—this is the best time of year.

When I was growing up—not *that* long ago—we'd come home from school, slip our skates onto our sticks, throw the stick over our shoulders like hobos carrying their knapsacks, then trudge through the apple orchard behind our neighborhood to a pond in the middle of the woods. We'd lace 'em up and play until it was too dark to see, then put our boots back on and head home for dinner.

On weekends, we'd spend the whole day down there. Friends of mine who lived near Burns Park and Thurston Pond would skate all day, walk home to eat dinner with their skates on, then go back onto the ice for more.

We got more ice time in a single day on those ponds than we got in weeks of indoor practices and games. And it was more fun, too. No tryouts, no scoreboards, no whistles, no drills, no lines, no benches, no coaches, no refs—in fact, no adults at all—and no nets. Just a pair of boots at each end to mark the goals.

I don't recall once coming back from the pond upset that we'd lost. That's because we played about a dozen games a day, and whenever one team lost too many in a row, we'd just change teams. I also can't recall much about the hundreds of indoor practices I had, but I can remember those long, happy days on the pond like they were yesterday.

But when you drive by those very same ponds today, you won't see many kids. They're all packed in vans, being dragged to some travel team tournament two hours away. As soon as they get back, they'll run inside to play video games.

We're not only losing the spirit of the sport, and all the fun that goes with it, we're also losing our competitive edge. Herb Brooks, the mastermind behind the 1980 U.S. Olympic hockey team's upset over the Soviet Union, known as the Miracle on Ice, said it best: "I think we have too many elite [hockey] camps for the kids today, and as a result, we are creating a bunch of robots. We need to make it fun for the kids and let them learn to love the game the way we did."

When my old high school teammate, Pete Read, put together his third annual Michigan Pond Hockey Classic at Whitmore Lake last weekend, one of the nation's biggest outdoor tournaments, it was no surprise that almost all of the five hundred-some players who signed up were over thirty years old.

Read laid out fifteen rinks, separated only by snow banks. We played four-on-four, with no goalies or fancy nets—just a flat box of two-by-sixes. Everyone got dressed in one big tent, where hay bales were set up for benches. A hockey locker room is one of the few places on earth where the smell can be improved by fresh hay. The guys getting ready to play could see their breath, while the guys who'd just come back in the tent from their games could watch the steam coming off their pads as they stuffed them back into their bags.

My team, consisting of a bunch of former high school teammates, got our butts kicked in the first two games by margins like 21–14—football scores. In our last two games, however, we staged heroic rallies to lose by a little less.

But we all had a blast. Until our last game, that is, when the volunteer scorekeeper—God bless 'im—decided to play full-time ref, and rule on every out-of-bounds play and every goal. Before we realized what we were doing, we started sniping and hacking at each other, and the once-friendly match quickly devolved into—well, a little league hockey game. When we finally told the would-be ref we could officiate the game ourselves, we got back to playing pond hockey—and that's what we love.

One of my friends brought his son along, but he couldn't play with us because he had to play a travel team game later that day.

Poor kid doesn't know what he's missing.

Stars

Unlike most sports writers, I've never covered a single team for an entire season for one publication, what we call a "beat." Thanks to a few inspired editors at the *Detroit News* willing to take a chance, I was lucky to jump from freelancing to writing Sunday sports features. Writing weekly features is harder than covering a beat in some ways, because most Mondays I'd start researching and writing about a brand-new subject, whether it was the Kentucky basketball team, the Green Bay Packers, or bullfighters in Spain—then start over on a new subject the next week.

But the difficulties were far outweighed by the benefits, including the rare freedom to write about almost anything I wanted. The opportunity to choose my subjects meant I could usually avoid people I didn't like or admire, and focus on those I thought were worthy of more attention.

Wealth and fame don't impress me. It's not hard to find people who have one or both and are far from admirable. But talent and character do, and most people I've profiled have both.

The reason I admire Slava Fetisov, Jim Abbott, and others included here has nothing to do with their fortunes or their fans, but the uncommon talent and drive they developed to get where they are, and how they've handled the success.

JOE LOUIS, THE GENTLE GIANT

September / October 1997
Michigan History

On June 22, 1937, Joe Louis waited in the clubhouse of Chicago's Comiskey Park, anxious to take advantage of the opportunity of a lifetime. A year earlier, many experts thought Louis's young career was already finished when Nazi Germany's Max Schmeling knocked him out in twelve rounds. But there he was, just minutes away from the first heavyweight title bout any African American had been granted in twenty-two years.

Louis was determined not to make the same mistakes against heavyweight champ James Braddock as he had made against Schmeling. For his title shot he trained rigorously and took his trainer's advice.

Louis knew he was not just a boxer in this fight, but a symbol to millions of Americans. He resolved to make the most of it.

"We had to accomplish the biggest goal a black athlete had a chance at," Louis recalled years later.

In the course of his seventeen-year career, Louis entered the ring seventy-one times. He left it with sixty-eight victories, fifty-four by knockout. Two of Louis's three losses came well after his prime, and all three were at the hands of world champions. He didn't pad his card with tomato cans, either. Half of his opponents were top-ten contenders.

But Louis is still best known for two legendary fights: the Braddock bout and his rematch with Schmeling exactly one year later, in front of boxing's first global audience. Through his bravery, skill, and unfailing sportsmanship, Louis returned a sometimes suspect sport to respectability. He showed an entire nation it never had to back down to anyone, anytime, when it most needed to believe that. In the process, Joe Louis himself became one of the most heroic figures in American history.

Joe Louis was born into an Alabama sharecropper's family on May 13, 1914, the seventh of eight children. Although Louis had white and Native

American ancestors, he was always proud to consider himself first and foremost a black man.

When Joe's father was committed to the epileptic ward of Alabama's Hospital for the Negro Insane, his mother, a woman as tough and gentle as her seventh son, remarried and took her family north to Detroit in 1926. Young Joe would never be the same. When Louis visited the Ford plant where all of his older brothers worked, he was amazed.

"My God, it was bigger than a cotton field and a cornfield combined, bigger than some cities we had passed by on the train," he said. "I was impressed."

Louis was even more impressed by the city itself.

"I never saw so many people in one place, so many cars at one time," he wrote in his excellent autobiography, *My Life*. "I had never even seen a trolley car before [or] parks, libraries, brick school houses, movie theaters. . . . You can't imagine the impact that city had on me."

Life improved dramatically for the Louises when they moved north, but hard times soon followed when the Great Depression hit. Although prices dropped, Louis said, "Everything costs a lot of money when you don't have any."

The Louises resorted to soup lines to feed their children, a difficult concession for a proud family. When Joe searched for a way to help his family get out of poverty, he quickly eliminated education as a possibility. By his own admission, school overwhelmed him, so he transferred to Bronson High, an all-boys vocational school. Adding insult to injury, Louis's mom enrolled him in violin lessons, at fifty cents each, which represented a considerable sacrifice.

"Well here I was, six feet tall, big as a light heavyweight, going to Bronson Vocational School carrying this little bit of a violin," he said. "You can imagine the kidding I had to take. I remember one time some guy called me a sissy when he saw me with the violin, and I broke it over his head."

Classmate Thurston McKinney witnessed this and took note. McKinney, the 1932 Golden Gloves welterweight champion, invited Louis down to Brewster's East Side gymnasium. Louis was immediately smitten.

"I looked at the ring," he said, "the punching bag, pulleys, the exercise mat, and it was love at first sight."

He took the two quarters his mom had given him for his violin lesson to rent a locker at the gym and stuffed the violin in it. His old life, filled with frustration and disappointment, was over. His new life, bright with possibility, was just beginning.

A career in boxing doesn't hold much allure for most Americans today.

But in the 1930s boxing was at its peak. This was before a half-dozen boxing organizations started giving out titles, corruption consumed the sport, and boxing lost all but its cult followers. The NHL and NFL were only a few years old, and the NBA was still years away. When Joe Louis entered the ring for his first professional fight in 1934, boxing still enjoyed a prominent place among American sports, on a short list with baseball, college football, and horse racing.

Five months later, Louis defeated Charley Massera to win four hundred dollars—big money during the Depression, enough for Louis to return to the soup kitchen and pay back every cent his family had been given over the years. He often said paying off that debt was one of the proudest moments of his life.

Louis quickly boosted his boxing career from a paycheck to a calling. His power, technique, and aggressiveness were making short work of his opponents. By beating his first 21 opponents, 17 by knock-out, Louis earned a bout with former heavyweight champion Max Baer in 1935. During that fight, Baer's trainer tried to convince him that Louis hadn't really hit him yet.

"Then you'd better keep an eye on (referee) Arthur Donovan," Baer said, "because somebody out there is beating the hell out of me."

Louis finished the job with a fourth-round knock-out, for his 22nd straight win.

Tommy Farr was one of the few boxers able to go the distance with Louis, but not without some painful memories. Years later he said, "When I talk about that fight, my nose still bleeds."

No less than Ernest Hemingway, a true boxing aficionado, was moved to say, "Louis is too good to be true—and he is absolutely true."

Louis might have been a terrifying fighter, but he was never a terror. To avoid inciting racial incidents, Louis's managers urged him to fight clean and never smile when he knocked out a white opponent.

But such advice might have been unnecessary for Louis, a true sportsman.

Hall of Fame boxer Jack Sharkey fought both Louis and Jack Dempsey, and compared the two. "Every time Jack Dempsey hit me, he said, 'How come you're not dead yet?' Every time Joe Louis hit me, he said, 'Sorry.'"

When Louis fought Billy Conn, another Hall of Fame boxer, Conn slipped on the canvas but didn't fall. Although Louis could have finished him right there, he allowed Conn to recover his balance. Conn never forgot the gesture.

"He ain't gentle," he said, "but he's a real gentleman."

After twenty-seven straight victories, twenty-three by knockout, Louis earned a date with the great Max Schmeling, a former champion still in his prime, at Yankee Stadium on June 19, 1936. Although many Americans boycott the fight because of Schmeling's German citizenship, it was still the nation's biggest sporting event that spring.

But Louis didn't seem to get the message. From his lackadaisical training to his refusal to follow his trainer's advice, Louis was all hubris. Although married, he had countless affairs, including one with Sonja Henie. When he wasn't making time with a camp groupie, he was out playing golf, a sport Ed Sullivan introduced him to and Louis adopted as his own.

"I look back [at that time] and still get mad at myself," Louis wrote 42 years later. "I thought I could name the round that I could knock Schmeling out. Instead of training as I should have, I'd jump in the car and head for the golf course. Instead of boxing six rounds, I'd box three."

He also lost weight—something that is not rewarded in a heavyweight match, which has no weight limit.

"Those camp-following girls took too much out of me," he admitted.

Despite his poor preparation, Louis took the first three rounds from Schmeling, opening a gash above his right eye. Schmeling was so worried about taking Louis's jab to the face, he left his body open, but Louis was too undisciplined to take advantage of it. Instead, in the fourth round Louis went prematurely to his famous right hook and left his left hand down. He promptly got dropped by a Schmeling right to the jaw. "I never fully recovered from that blow," he said. "Everything was in a fog. I was fighting now on pure instinct."

Instinct alone wasn't enough. After Schmeling knocked Louis out cold in the twelfth round, Louis's trainers had to carry him to the dressing room.

"Next thing I know, I was crying like I don't think I ever did before," Louis said.

Millions shared Louis's sorrow. In Chicago's black neighborhood a riot broke out, and a girl in New York tried to kill herself by drinking poison. In Germany Adolf Hitler trumpeted Schmeling's triumph as proof of the superiority of the Aryan race.

If Louis could not stifle Hitler, he could still make history. Only one black man, Jack Johnson, had ever held the heavyweight title, and none had been given a title shot since Johnson lost the title in 1915. In the late 1920s African-American boxer Harry Wills was the number one heavyweight contender but could never get a fight with Jack Dempsey.

"They didn't want a black man to have that title," said Louis, who was especially incensed that the boxing powers deemed Max Schmeling a more fitting candidate for a championship bout than Louis. "Here I was," Louis said, "an American, and they were giving Nazi Germany a better shot at the title than me."

It was insulting, but not surprising. Louis's rise to prominence preceded Jackie Robinson's major league debut by a decade. When Louis's handlers finally managed to secure a commitment from heavyweight champ James Braddock to fight at Chicago's Comiskey Park on June 22, 1937, Louis knew he had to make the most of it.

On the first day of training camp, Louis's trainer, Jack "Chappie" Blackburn, read him the riot act. "All right, you SOB. When I finish with you, you're gonna be a fighting machine."

"This time, I listened," Louis said. "Chappie wasn't drinking, and I wasn't fooling around. He was completely devoted to his task and I was just as blindly devoted to mine."

This time Louis was ready, and had the confidence to wait until his opponent wasn't.

In the first round Louis's patient strategy seemed to backfire, when Braddock swung a short uppercut to Louis's chin, dropping him to the canvas. Kneeling down, Louis asked himself, "What the hell am I doing here?" He got right back up and, instead of panicking and going for a desperation knockout, he bided his time. Finally, when the bell rang for the eighth round, Louis knew Braddock's legs were gone, he couldn't keep his arms up, and he wasn't ready for what Louis was about to deliver.

This was the moment Louis had waited years for. When he saw his chance, he hit Braddock with a punch combination he called the DOA, "Dead On your Ass," which consisted of a left to the body and a right to the chin. The first punch knocked Braddock off balance. The second took him off his feet, sending him whirling in the air before he fell on his face.

Braddock said later Louis's final punch felt like "someone jammed an electric bulb in my face and busted it. I couldn't have got up if they offered me a million dollars."

While the referee counted Braddock out, Louis looked out across the heads of the crowd, dazed. The former cotton picker, reluctant violin player, and high school dropout was now the heavyweight champion of the world.

"Only one thing I remember saying, 'I don't want nobody to call me champ until I beat Schmeling,'" Louis said. "Bring on Max Schmeling. Bring 'im on."

The rest of the world wanted this fight as much as Louis did, but everyone had to wait exactly one year, until June 22, 1938. The fighters returned to the same place, Yankee Stadium, but the stakes were much higher. Before Louis and Schmeling met for that rematch, the Japanese had invaded China, the Italians had invaded Ethiopia, and the Germans had invaded Czechoslovakia. Americans feared the world was on the brink of disaster. "Schmeling represented everything that Americans disliked, and they wanted him beat, and beat good," Louis said. "Now here I was, a black man [who] had the burden of representing all America. White Americans, even while some of them still were lynching black people in the South, were depending on me to knock out Germany."

Jesse Owens, Joe DiMaggio, Babe Ruth, and Bill "Bojangles" Robinson, among many others, all stopped by Louis's camp to offer their encouragement. When President Franklin D. Roosevelt summoned Louis to the White House, he said. "These are the kind of muscles we're going to need to beat Germany."

Louis never felt better. When sportswriter Jimmy Cannon told Louis, "I'm betting a knockout in six rounds," Louis responded by holding up a single finger.

"It goes one," he said. This was not the cockiness he succumbed to before the first Schmeling bout. This was rock-solid confidence.

"I knew my body was in prime condition," he said. "I knew, I didn't think, I *knew*—I was going to beat Schmeling."

Just hours before the fight, Louis took a long walk with his trainers along the Harlem River.

"How you feel, Joe?" one asked.

"I'm scared," he confessed.

"Scared?"

"Yes. I'm scared I might kill Schmeling tonight."

But Louis knew Schmeling would be just as prepared and motivated to win as he was. Beating Schmeling, Louis believed, would require taking some risks. Against Braddock, Louis patiently waited for his chance. But against Schmeling, Louis felt he couldn't allow him to stick around that long before going for the knockout.

As Louis waited in the locker room for the fight to begin, he told his trainer, "If I don't have Schmeling knocked out in three rounds, you better come in and get me, because after that, I'm through."

"I had no intention of pacing myself," Louis said later. "It was going to be all or nothing, and I knew my whole career depended on this, right now. Before the bell rang, I felt like a race horse in the gate. I was rarin' to go."

Within the first five seconds Louis popped Schmeling with two left hooks to his face, snapping Schmeling's head back. He followed it up with a right to the German's jaw. Schmeling, knowing he had to respond immediately or he would never regain control of the contest, came back at Louis with his best stuff, a rapid right-left combination. Louis blocked the first punch and dodged the second.

Those were the only punches Schmeling threw all night. After each flurry from Louis's fists, Schmeling would stagger backward like a drunk, leaving himself open to more punishment. Louis pounced on Schmeling with another right to his jaw and sent him to the canvas for a three-count.

After Schmeling got up, Louis tore into him with more lefts and rights. Schmeling went down again. Louis waited just long enough for the referee to give Schmeling a two-count before he resumed his relentless attack. Schmeling dropped to the canvas for a third and final time. After a year of waiting for the fight of his life, Louis finished it off in just two minutes and four seconds—two-thirds of a round.

Legendary sportswriter Bob Considine summed it up this way: "The battery at Yankee Stadium last night was Louis pitching, Schmeling catching."

In virtually every major U.S. city, people flooded the streets to celebrate long into the night. In Detroit, confident residents had petitioned the city council two weeks in advance for the right to dance and sing in a large, roped-off block of streets. Police estimated the crowd near St. Antoine and Beacon Streets grew to about ten thousand fans, who partied under a banner proclaiming, "Joe Louis knocked out Hitler."

In Harlem the police commissioner ordered all traffic between 125th and 145th Streets shut off so the celebrants "could cut all the capers they wanted," according to the *New York Times*. "This is their night," the police commissioner said. "Let them have their fun."

The scenes looked a little different in Germany.

"When the Germans learned how badly I was beating Schmeling," Louis wrote, "they cut the radio wires to Germany. They didn't want their people to know that just a plain old [negro] was knocking the s— out of the Aryan Race." When Louis looked back on his career in 1978, he said, "I know now [the Schmeling rematch] was the top of my career."

The top, perhaps, but hardly the end. Louis stretched his string of title defenses to twenty-five over twelve years, records no heavyweight has approached since then.

In 1950, at age thirty-six, Louis went 15 rounds with Ezzard Charles, who won by a decision to take Louis's title. Louis won eight more times before his final fight against Rocky Marciano, who so idolized Louis he forever felt guilty about beating his hero.

Louis had no regrets. "I think the Marciano fight hurt him more than it did me," he said.

Louis endured financial setbacks the rest of his life, usually caused by his own free spending or his profound generosity, often to unworthy recipients. But Louis's troubles probably pained his fans more than they did him. He could always joke about his situation and himself.

"They say that money talks, but the only thing it ever said to me was goodbye."

He ended his autobiography with this paragraph: "Like the man said, 'If you dance you got to pay the piper.' Believe me, I danced, I paid the piper, and I left him a big fat tip."

In 1981, three years after he finished his life story, Louis died of a heart attack.

Today he is remembered as much more than a boxer. When someone asked Jesse Jackson how important Louis was to his family, he said only this: "I was born in 1941, and my name is Jesse Louis Jackson."

When Jimmy Cannon overheard a few writers condescendingly describe Louis as a "credit to his race," Cannon replied, "Yes, he's a credit to his race. The human race."

After World War II ended, Louis befriended his once bitter opponent, Max Schmeling. As the two former champions grew into old age, they often called each other and embraced whenever they reunited. For Louis's fifty-sixth birthday party, Schmeling flew from Germany to Las Vegas to surprise his old friend.

For all the things Louis is known for, that glorious rematch with Schmeling still looms largest. The classic duel was more than a boxing match. It was two warriors representing their countries in battle. At a time when Americans' fears were at their peak and their confidence at the bottom, the Germans seemed unbeatable—but Detroit's Joe Louis showed the world how it could be done.

REMEMBERING MR. HOCKEY

June 15, 2016
National Public Radio

Gordie Howe lived so long that most Americans don't realize his central role in helping the NHL expand from just six teams and getting millions of American kids playing hockey, including a dozen members of the 2016 Stanley Cup champion Pittsburgh Penguins.

Howe was one of nine kids born in a farmhouse in Floral, Saskatchewan—a town so tiny, its post office closed in 1923. During the Great Depression, a neighbor brought over a gunnysack full of leftover goods, including a beat-up pair of skates. Howe's mom gave her a few bucks, and gave Gordie the skates.

"I put those on," Howe recalled, "and I never took 'em off."

Howe was skilled, smart, and tough—the most complete player the sport has ever produced. He was even ambidextrous, with the ability to switch from a right-handed shot to a left-handed shot while barreling down on the goalie. Put it all together, and you get what they called "The Gordie Howe Hat Trick," consisting of a goal, an assist, and a fight, all in the same game.

During Howe's twenty-six-year career, he set records for most goals, most points, most games, and most—well, almost everything. He finished in the top ten in scoring for twenty-one straight years, which is impossible.

But his impact was greater than a bunch of records. What Arnold Palmer and Pelé did for their sports, Gordie Howe did for hockey: he served as his sport's greatest ambassador, the man they literally called "Mr. Hockey."

Gordie Howe was the first breakout hockey star in the States, followed by Chicago's Bobby Hull and Boston's Bobby Orr. That trio gave the NHL the boost it needed to double from the "Original Six" to a dozen teams in 1967, on the way to its current total of thirty teams.

In Howe's adopted state, his hockey heroics inspired dozens of Michigan towns to build ice rinks. The Pittsburgh Penguins just won the Stanley

Cup with seven players who played on those Michigan rinks, in little league, high school, or college.

In 1958, Red Berenson decided to leave his home province of Saskatchewan to attend the University of Michigan. He picked Michigan for the academics, the hockey program, and the chance to see Gordie Howe play, thirty-eight miles away. After a seventeen-year NHL career, Berenson returned to coach his alma mater in 1984. Among many others, Berenson's program produced Carl Hagelin and Hobey Baker winner Kevin Porter, both of whom now play for Pittsburgh. That is the long arm of Gordie Howe.

But what about Howe, the person? Usually it's a mistake to meet your heroes, but not Howe. He remained humble, and always took the time for his fans. As fellow Hall of Famer Bill Gadsby said, "The only guy in the locker room who didn't know Mr. Hockey was Mr. Hockey, was Mr. Hockey."

When Wayne Gretzky was only eleven, Howe attended a banquet to celebrate the budding star. But when Gretzky got to the podium, he couldn't speak. Howe rescued him by saying, "When someone has done what this kid has done, he doesn't have to say anything."

Gretzky never forgot Howe's graciousness when he needed it most, and the two became great friends.

If Gretzky was the alpha, I was the omega: a third-line right-winger for the Ann Arbor Huron High School River Rats. When I was a junior, in November of 1980, I was about to hop on a plane to Hartford when I recognized Howe at the counter. I couldn't resist: "Excuse me, but you're Gordie Howe, aren't you?"

"Yes, I am," he said softly, and thanked me for not making a scene. I quietly praised him, then blurted out—for reasons I still cannot fathom—that my favorite player was his longtime linemate, Alex Delvecchio, an amazing passer who set up hundreds of Howe's goals. When Howe stared at me for what seemed like a month, I concluded that might have been the stupidest thing I'd ever said.

But then Howe gave me a wink and a nod, and said, "Mine, too, sonny. Mine, too."

This week we learned Howe generated a few thousand stories like that. Here's another. The Penguins' stable of twelve American players includes defenseman Ian Cole. His father, Doug, plays in a beer league with me here in Ann Arbor. Doug grew up playing hockey in town, idolizing Howe like the rest of us, which sparked a love for the game that he passed on to his son.

When Ian was just eight years old, his dad took him down to a local rink to meet Gordie Howe. When Ian finally got to the front of the line, he bravely asked the legend, "Mr. Howe, what can I do to be a great player like you?"

Howe said, "Sonny, I'm gonna tell you the same thing I told Wayne Gretzky: you have two ears and one mouth. Keep two open and one shut."

Howe signed Ian's book, ruffled his hair, and said, "Good luck, kid."

Two days after Gordie Howe died, Ian Cole raised the Stanley Cup over his head.

And that was Mr. Hockey.

MAGIC'S JOURNEY

September 1997
The Detroit News

When you tell people you've just spent a day with NBA legend Earvin "Magic" Johnson, everyone asks the same question: "How's he doing?"

Very well, thank you very much. His health is excellent, his wife and three kids are happy, and he's driving his businesses in the fast lane.

In fact, by his own account, his life is better today in almost every way than it was before he announced he had contracted the HIV virus in 1991.

"I don't know if another athlete could have handled this," he says. "When I tested positive for HIV, my life was already in order. I could handle it."

Johnson is like the third little pig who built his home of brick and mortar; when the storm hit, his home could withstand it. Everything he needed to survive and ultimately triumph was already in place.

Despite Johnson's "Showtime" persona, his wild social life, and happy-go-lucky demeanor, from his childhood on Johnson built his life on a solid foundation of family, friends, an old-fashioned work ethic, and a strong sense of who he is—and who he isn't.

The sad stories of athletes blowing their fortunes after leaving their sports are too numerous to count. To avoid this fate, some former athletes get good advisors to manage their money, others get cushy, lucrative jobs as company representatives, but only a handful become bona fide business-men, controlling their own destiny.

Johnson is one of the few—and arguably the best.

He runs three companies, and more are on the way. He has a nice tenth-floor office on Wilshire Boulevard in Beverly Hills, with a highly profes-sional staff to help direct traffic.

"A lot of times an athlete plays his sport, and that's it," Johnson told me. "But I *always* wanted to be in business. I knew what I wanted."

Knowing what he wanted early in life set Johnson apart; knowing what it took to get there made it happen. His coaches from Little Leagues to the Lakers all say the same thing: Earvin Johnson was the quickest study and the hardest worker they ever coached. Show him a new play, and he not only would get it immediately, he would teach the others. Instead of complaining about extra work, he inspired his teammates to join him.

Translating that to business, however, required one other trait, developed long ago: the willingness to do the homework necessary to succeed. He acquired that trait not from business school, the *Wall Street Journal*, or corporate experience, but his fifth-grade teacher, Greta Dart.

In 1969, her first year as a teacher, Dart quickly established her high expectations for her students, but also her deep concern for them. Although she stands only five feet tall, shorter than ten-year-old Earvin Johnson, her presence loomed large over the magnetic class leader and his friends.

Although the teacher and student hit it off immediately, they shared one bad week in late winter, 1970, when Johnson put off his assignments. Because Dart had the cooperation of Johnson's YMCA coach, she told Johnson if he didn't get his homework done he wouldn't play in the championship game that Saturday.

"Well, she stuck to it," Johnson recalls with a grin. "I had to sit on the sidelines for the game, against a team we had already beaten once. It was close, but [teammate] Stevie Silvertooth hit two free throws near the end. We thought we had it won! We were going crazy!"

But, with just a few seconds remaining, one of the opposing players ran down the court and threw up a miracle shot, defeating Johnson's team by a single point.

"I was mad at her for a few days," Johnson says, "but then I realized what she was doing. She taught me a valuable lesson."

Johnson retained that lesson seventeen years later, in 1987, when he asked super-agent Michael Ovitz out for lunch.

"I walk into the restaurant like a big NBA star, and he looks me dead in the eye and says, 'Why should I represent you? The majority of athletes can play their sport, and nothing else. That's why I don't do athletes.' After Johnson pointed out that he was not like other athletes, that he always wanted to get into business and wasn't afraid to roll his sleeves up, Ovitz relented—a little.

"I'll think about it," he said, "and call you back."

"I was shocked!" Johnson says. "He set me down the first day! Man, you walk in six-eight, and you walk out feeling five-eight!"

Ovitz eventually agreed to a second lunch. He asked Johnson about his family, his values, his work experience as a kid. Johnson had no trouble answering any of those questions. He had delivered papers. He'd hauled pop on a Vernors truck. He'd scooped ice cream at the Quality Dairy.

Ovitz was also impressed that Johnson had obviously done some background reading on him between their two meetings. Finally, Ovitz said, "Okay, I'll take you on. Why? Because of all those reasons. But," Ovitz said, grabbing the sports page, "You gotta stop reading this, and start reading the business sections, the *Wall Street Journal*, the financial magazines. If you really want to be in business, you've got to do your homework."

Johnson couldn't help grinning at that. He knew the lesson well.

The association paid off handsomely. Before Johnson joined with Ovitz, he made less than $1 million a year in endorsements. Four years later, he was making more than $10 million—and he was getting more than money. Johnson always insisted on two things: that he get equity in the companies he worked for, and two, that they teach him about the companies and the businesses he supported.

By the time Ovitz left his agency for Walt Disney, Johnson was ready to fly by himself.

"Most guys don't take the time to get to know the CEO, to *learn* about the company," he says. "Look at the [Los Angeles] Forum: a lot of those season ticket holders are CEOs, presidents. They're right there, but a lot of guys never took advantage of that. Those guys want the good life, they want the limelight—and quick!—but they don't want to work for it.

"I know nothing but work. I get that from my dad. These days I don't finish until six or seven at night, all in a day's work. I've got more to do now than I did when I was playing.

"But I enjoy it. I enjoy working. I want to set an example, especially for the kids back home. I'm involved, I make the deals, I go to the meetings. That's why I'm where I am."

In business, as in life, Johnson is not merely a passenger. He's the conductor, in charge of his own fate.

Of course, money can't buy you love—or even support. Johnson needed lots of both when he sat down for that infamous press conference to announce that he had HIV. He knew he wouldn't make it through without a little help from his friends.

When most stars hit troubled times, they learn the hard way that many of their "friends" were merely opportunists, along for the ride while it lasted. Not Johnson. His old friends—his real friends—were right there when the storm hit, because they had never left him.

"I know thousands of people here, but only thirty people have been to my home," he says. Most of his friends go back to Johnson's high school or college days, people like Kenny Turner from Johnson's old neighborhood, and Darwin Peyton, Michigan State's former basketball team manager.

"I tell people this all the time: He really hasn't changed," Turner says. "Here's a kid who was born on the west side of Lansing, of modest means. You're *supposed* to change, but he really hasn't. I'm not just saying that—it's the truth. That's what sustains those relationships back here."

"I have the same friends," Johnson says. "I like having those friends around. I still run with the same people; in my office I have the same eight people. They don't leave, and I don't want them to leave.

"Coming from Michigan, you get to know people, what they're about. In Michigan, people work, everyone's direct. People are for real there. Out here, whoa!"

"As far as phonies go, he can spot them a mile away," says Jud Heathcote, Johnson's coach at Michigan State. "But he's very tolerant. Sometimes he plays games where they think they're leading him on, when in reality he's leading them on. You don't fool Earvin very often."

When Johnson was still playing in the NBA, he said, "It's really great being Magic Johnson the basketball player nine months of the year and just plain Earvin Johnson the other three."

Today he says, "Back home I'm still Earvin, or E, or EJ, or June-bug. I love home."

On November 7, 1991, Johnson announced to the world that he had contracted the HIV virus, which usually precludes the onset of AIDS. Observers noted that Johnson seemed calm—almost inhumanly so, given the seriousness of the situation. Many suspected that he was still in denial.

But Johnson's calm persisted, despite countless cheap shots from strangers and friends, despite suddenly being thrust into the role of symbol, then leader, of a cause he hadn't asked to join, despite the obvious threat the virus posed. He showed no fear, only optimism.

The skeptics probably didn't know that Johnson had stared down fear in many forms years earlier.

As soon as the news was out, Johnson—who had enjoyed tremendous popularity among virtually all Americans—was suddenly fair game. Many Americans took him to task for his hedonistic lifestyle, others questioned his sexual preference, and even NBA friends and teammates like A. C. Green and Byron Scott said he should not be allowed to play in the 1992 NBA All-Star game.

Like all Johnson's close friends, his former grade school teacher Greta

Dart remembers that time well. "It did cost him a certain amount of fan support, when it all came out," she says, "but I never heard him complain or bemoan the fact that he had HIV."

"I took some shots," Johnson says today, "but I'm strong. I knew it wouldn't bother me."

What most people probably forgot was that Johnson had not always been universally loved; he had taken shots before. Ten years earlier, when Laker owner Jerry Buss fired coach Paul Westhead, the media and fans blamed Johnson for the change. The *LA Times* called him a "glory hog," while the *New York Daily News* said he was a "spoiled punk." For the first time in his career, Johnson was booed at home and on the road—for months. How did he respond? His team went on to win the NBA crown in the spring of 1982, with Johnson earning his second playoff MVP crown.

Two years later, in the first meeting between Johnson and Larry Bird in the NBA finals, Johnson laid an egg. He misunderstood coach Pat Riley's instructions, he called time-outs erroneously, he missed crucial free throws, and he threw errant passes. In short, he stunk.

The Celtics won in seven games. Bird earned playoff MVP honors, while Johnson earned the title of scapegoat. The Celtics' Kevin McHale dubbed the Laker guard "Tragic Johnson." The press hung the loss on him for the entire summer, knighting Bird the superior of the two.

"I sat back when it was over," Johnson said. "And I thought, man, did we just lose one of the great playoff series of all time, or didn't we? Yet all you read was how bad I was."

The following spring, the Lakers won game six from the Celtics in Boston, clinching the NBA title and earning redemption. Abdul-Jabbar, not Johnson, won the playoff MVP, but Johnson didn't care about that.

"You wait so long to get back," he said after the game. "That's the hard part. [But] it's made me stronger. You have to deal with the different situations and see if you can come back."

He could not know how prophetic that would be.

Adjusting to his new status as an HIV carrier did not simply entail looking out for himself. Other celebrities with HIV, like Rock Hudson and Freddie Mercury, went underground after contracting the virus. But given Johnson's unique station in life, he had the potential to inspire others who had the disease and win over those who didn't to the cause.

Would he do so? Anyone who knew him knew the answer.

As a center for Lansing Everett, Johnson once played against Battle Creek. One of their players, Leon Guydon, wanted badly to get the better of his star opponent, but Johnson dominated him. In the third quarter, Guydon spat on Johnson—an act of disrespect that would cause most high school stars to retaliate, probably with fists.

Not Johnson. Since Greta Dart met Johnson in grade school, she says she can count on one hand the number of times she's seen him angry.

"I just wiped it off," Johnson says, "and told Guydon, 'Don't worry about it. Look at the scoreboard. It's gonna be over soon.'

"They tried to rattle me, get into my head, but it wasn't going to happen. I'm not a person who loses control a lot. I call that wasted energy and emotion. He was frustrated, but I have to take it in stride. Everyone's looking for me to lead them. The whole team structure breaks down if I collapse, so I gotta be the leader."

Johnson's awareness of his special role helped his team later that season when they played Detroit Northwestern for the first time. Both teams were highly rated, and Johnson was already the state's premier player, so the Northwestern student body had been anticipating the game for some time.

Because of forced busing Everett had a large number of white players, who were a bit skittish about the game to begin with. When the Everett team arrived at Northwestern before classes let out for the day, the administrators wanted to keep them someplace safe. They decided to lock the Everett players inside the school laundry room, a glorified cage made of chain-link fence. When the final class bell rang and the Northwestern students rushed past the players held captive in the cage, the white players' eyes grew large. They were terrified and looked to Johnson for reassurance.

"I told 'em all, 'Don't worry, everything's gonna be coooool,'" he says, laughing at the memory. During warm-ups the gym was already packed, with the students cheering wildly for each Northwestern dunk.

"All my teammates were watching them, wide-eyed again," Johnson says. "They were telling me, 'C'mon Earvin, start dunking!' I said no, not until the game starts. No point showing them your best stuff in warm-ups, and if I let the opponent change my approach to the game, they've already got me.

"Well, the game starts and we just blow 'em out. During the first time out, I said, 'See, I told you!' We were laughing then."

In the 1980 NBA finals, the Lakers returned to Philadelphia for game six, up 3–2, but had to leave Abdul-Jabbar at home to nurse his twisted ankle. Everyone assumed the Lakers would lose game six, then try to take the series with Abdul-Jabbar in game seven back in L.A.

Not Johnson. Just a twenty-year-old rookie, he committed a sacrilege by sitting in Abdul-Jabbar's seat on the team plane and copied Abdul-Jabbar's in-air routines. "Never fear," he said. "E. J. is here."

He took Abdul-Jabbar's spot at center for that game, too, and scored 42 points, going 14-for-14 from the line, with 15 rebounds, 7 assists, and 3 steals—a masterful performance.

Thus, when Johnson was suddenly thrust into the role of point-man for one of the world's most stigmatized epidemics, he had little trouble adjusting to his new responsibilities.

"I didn't panic," he says. "It's just another challenge. I'm a person who deals with it. 'Let's find a way to correct it.' I've always been like that."

After contracting a potentially lethal virus, Johnson has shown remarkable resilience, physically and mentally, and has readily accepted his role as spokesman for a maligned group of victims. He continued to work hard for other victims even after his health improved.

"He was the leader of the class, without a doubt," Greta Dart says. "All the other kids looked up to him. When we played kickball, he often picked the teams, but he was not someone who always had to have all the best players. He would take the poorer players and try to beat everyone."

Mrs. Dart's observation has been echoed by every coach Johnson has had: he had the uncommon ability to make those around him better. That quality, more than any other, has been his greatest asset since 1991, too.

"I get a lot of people calling with HIV, AIDS, or even other diseases," he says. "It's not just HIV or AIDS, it's life's struggles. One mom called up last week after her son was in a car accident. He wasn't doing very well, didn't have much motivation to get better. I told him, 'Don't give up. Life is too wonderful.' Later on he told his mom, 'Magic is right,' and he's doing better.

"I'm fighting a battle for other people now, to fight discrimination against people with HIV and AIDS, to get funding for those who don't have the money to get the medicines I have. I don't like publicity for what I do. It's not whether they see you helping out, it's whether you get the job done or not."

While many of the obstacles the HIV virus presented Johnson he had already encountered in some form before, one aspect was thoroughly new: for the first time, Johnson would test the loyalty of his friends and family. They came through, because Johnson never forgot them when he was flying high.

Johnson's longtime girlfriend Cookie Kelly had endured his numerous affairs but remained back in Michigan. They finally decided to get married just a few months before he tested positive for the virus.

In explaining why he waited so long to marry her, Johnson says, "I was afraid being married would change my basketball, and that always came first. It takes a strong woman to handle that. She says, 'Boy, I know when to leave you alone!'

"My wife is the reason I'm still alive and still ticking. She stayed by my side. She supported me, and loved me unconditionally. She keeps me grounded. She's a great mom and a great wife, and this is the only thing she ever wanted. I was a fool not to marry her before."

When he got the bad news, "The only thing I was really concerned about was whether I could be with Cookie the rest of my life, and see my kids grow up.

"I haven't changed in all these years," he says. "I've always known who I am."

That's not Magic. That's Earvin Johnson.

MAN VS. MACHINE

July 20, 1997
The Detroit News

Sometime this summer, Detroit's 39-year old defenseman Slava Fetisov will have to decide whether to return to the Red Wings for one final season, play somewhere else, or retire. For many players, this would be the toughest decision of their lives.

For Slava Fetisov, it's almost trivial.

Just a few days past New Year's, 1989, Fetisov sat in a room at the Hilton Hotel in East Rutherford, New Jersey, right across the swamp from the Meadowlands Sports Complex, debating the decision of a lifetime.

The Red Army leader and his team were in the middle of the "Superseries," a two-week run of exhibition games against NHL teams. A few hours before that night's game against the New Jersey Devils, their general manager, Lou Lamoriello, tried to convince Fetisov to defect right then and there, to leave his title, his team, and his homeland behind forever. But if Fetisov agreed, there would be no going back.

While teammate Igor Larionov translated for Fetisov, who could not speak English then, Fetisov's options became clear: he could defect and enjoy previously unimaginable wealth, a beautiful suburban home, and almost limitless freedom. Or he could stay with the Red Army team and earn the same modest pay as the worst player on the team received, spend eleven months of the year in an army barracks, and live his life as a glorified prisoner.

"Lou said, 'Defecting is easiest way,'" Fetisov recalled earlier this week.

That might have been an easy decision for most of us to make, but not for Fetisov. With little hesitation, Fetisov selected a third option, more arduous than the second: go back to Russia, try to beat the system that ruled his life, risk losing what few luxuries he had, and endure endless indignities in the process—all with no guarantee of success.

"I have to go back and fight for my rights," he told Lamoriello. "I want to open doors for others, and not just hockey players. Musicians, ballet dancers, all people."

Lamoriello remembers the conversation well. "He declined and under-standably so, knowing the type of person he is. I didn't ask twice."

Just a few months later, that single decision by a single man would dra-matically change the way hockey was played around the globe; it would help bring down one of the world's most powerful governments; and it would change one man forever.

This is Slava's story.

We know Fetisov as a solid, steady defender on the Red Wings' blue line, and as the "Papa Bear" of the five-man Russian unit.

But before he ever played a game for the Red Wings, before he even took his first shift in the NHL in the fall of 1989, Fetisov had already lived a full hockey life. His thirteen-year career for the Red Army and the Soviet national squad—probably the best hockey team ever assembled—earned him thirteen Soviet league titles, seven World Cup championships, and three Olympic medals.

Fetisov's first hockey life was filled with unbridled adulation, spirit-crushing frustration, and scorching public humiliation—but because of his iron will, it ended in a resounding international triumph.

Fetisov was born on April 20, 1958, in Moscow, where his father worked in construction and his mother toiled in the *Pravda* building. Slava started playing hockey on ponds at age four, in the Soviet national hockey camp at age eight, on the national junior team at sixteen, and on the Red Army team in 1975 at eighteen.

It was a heady time for Fetisov. Three years before he joined the Red Army club, also called CSKA, the Soviets shocked the hockey world by taking a team of Canadian NHL all-stars to the last minute of their eight-game Summit Series, before losing the final game 6–5, and the series, 4–3–1.

But the incredible Summit Series guaranteed many more emotional contests between the East and West. The final battles of the Cold War would be staged on a hockey rink.

The Soviet Union was hockey crazy. It was Leonid Brezhnev's favorite sport, and the perfect showcase to display the Soviet values of communal responsibility and shared rewards. In the Soviet Union's last decade, no-body represented that stoic spirit better than Slava Fetisov, the most popu-lar player on the team, and the best defenseman in the world. In his prime, Fetisov could run the puck end-to-end like the Red Wings' Paul Coffey, come back to play rock-solid defense like Boston's Ray Borque, and control the play in the middle of the ice like only Slava Fetisov could.

Although Fetisov scored 466 points in just 410 Soviet league games—a record that no one has approached—Hall of Fame goaltender and current Toronto Maple Leafs president Ken Dryden admires Fetisov more for his textbook work in his own end.

"The way he played defense was like a bulldog," Dryden told me, "always on you, yapping at your heels, never letting you go, never growing tired of it, just doing it all game long. And he of course was a great star. I've always been a big fan of Fetisov's."

But with age came responsibility, on and off the ice. In 1982, Fetisov's teammates elected him captain of both the Red Army and Soviet national squads. Not long after, he married Ladlena Fetisova. These two seemingly unrelated events would one day create a conflict between the incredible demands of the Soviet hockey system, and Fetisov's desire to lead a normal home life, which came to a head in the late 1980s and changed the lives of thousands of people.

If you are one of the top twenty players in the Soviet Union, you will likely be recruited to play for the Red Army squad, a team that won the Soviet league title thirteen times in Fetisov's thirteen years; a team that, during one of those seasons, lost *one game*.

Because most Red Army players also play for the Soviet national team, you will be forced to live eleven months each year at Archangelskoye, just outside Moscow. It's a beautiful barracks in a beautiful setting, but a barracks just the same.

You and a roommate will live in a small room with two beds, a sink and a tiny closet, like a college dorm room.

"No," Fetisov says, with a slight grin. "I have been in college dorm room—they are much better."

You work out four times a day, every day, then try to kill the rest of the time reading, playing chess, or talking, talking, talking with the twenty teammates you know better than your own wife. One player's wife added up the number of nights during the year he spent at home: thirteen.

Everything you need you must get through your coach, Viktor Tikhonov. He controls your access to hard currency, visas, cars, apartments, even day care for your children—and he is not bashful about using this power to coerce your cooperation.

Every night you rush to get in line to use the single phone in the lobby. After you finish your two calls, you must return to the end of the line.

"Sometimes you get lucky and go first," Fetisov says.

You might think of escaping, but you better think twice: the place has a twelve-foot-high fence, and a single gate which soldiers patrol twenty-four hours a day. Fetisov says lots of guys have tried to escape, but they were always caught, then punished severely. When you travel abroad, you will receive your passport and visa from a KGB agent just a few feet in front of customs, then you will hand them back to another KGB agent on the other side. They are not for you to keep.

In the global marketplace, you are one of the sport's greatest commodities. You are an international superstar, but you are treated like a prisoner.

"No, worse than prisoners," Fetisov says, grinning again. "Sometimes prisoners get out."

Then Fetisov's expression turns serious. "This was total control. When you're eighteen, you're so ambitious, you don't care about much else, just hockey. You live in barracks all year, it's okay. But later, you see life is too short to be robot."

Viktor Tikhonov is a driven man. According to Ken Dryden's excellent book, *Home Game*, Tikhonov dropped out of school after the seventh grade to work and play hockey, but he was a mediocre defenseman whose career fizzled in the 1950s. He went to night school to get his high school diploma, then pressed on to finish college and the four years of training necessary just to coach Midget hockey in the Soviet Union.

He embarked on a single-minded climb up the coaching ranks, reaching the pinnacle in 1977, when he was named coach of the Red Army and national teams.

The arduous climb instilled determination—Tikhonov only sleeps four or five hours a night—but also bitterness and insecurity. Tikhonov seems to resent being at the mercy of players with more talent than he had, and he's paranoid about losing his hard-won power to those who enjoy more popularity and respect.

"Only his wife and his dog like him," Alexander Mogilny said. "And I don't understand how they do."

With the noted exception of the United States' incredible upset of the Soviet Union in the 1980 Olympics, Tikhonov's first decade on the job was extraordinarily successful, capped by a gold medal in the 1988 Calgary Olympics. With their hockey supremacy restored and Mikhail Gorbachev's glasnost ("a policy of openness") gaining currency, Communist officials began entertaining Fetisov's request to join the New Jersey Devils, who drafted him in 1983 on a whim. Whenever talks warmed up, however, they abruptly ended, only to pick up again later.

"They play with my head all the time," Fetisov says of this confusing time. "Always go back and forth. They said as soon as 1988 season over, I'd start in NHL next season."

Still, nothing happened. Finally, Fetisov's close teammate, Larionov, who was fed up with the labor camp conditions and false promises of freedom, published a bold article in the USSR's most popular magazine, *Ogonyok*, writing that Tikhonov "doesn't treat his players like men. I used to say to him, 'You can't treat people this way. It's almost as if we are slaves here.' He says to me, 'There were guys like you before who said that. There'll be guys like you after. You're not going to change anything.'"

Fetisov had other ideas. With Fetisov playing at the top of his game, the team continued its dominance by crushing all comers in their 1988 *Izvestia* tournament, handily winning the championship. At the time many believed that would mark a peaceful end to the growing tensions. Tikhonov would step down, and Fetisov would be free to leave, with both in good standing.

That's when the Russian national team went to the United States for the Super-Series, Fetisov met with Lamoriello, and rejected the idea of defecting. Fetisov returned to Moscow optimistic that things could still work out for him and his teammates.

In early January of 1989, on the same day Fetisov signed a contract with the Devils, he received the Order of Lenin, given for outstanding achievement in science, technology, literature, or the arts. Previous winners have included Yuri Gagarin, the first human in outer space, chess champion Anatoly Karpov, and Stalin himself, but only two hockey players: legendary goaltender Vladislav Tretiak, and longtime captain Boris Mikhailov.

After the elaborate ceremony at the Kremlin, several high-ranking military officials came up to Fetisov and said, "Slava, you've done a good job for us. Now it's time for you to go somewhere else."

But Tikhonov never stepped down, and wouldn't allow Fetisov to leave either, stripping him of his captaincy just for asking.

The stage was set for a high-stakes showdown. On one side was Tikhonov, the Communist press, and the Communist system itself. On the other side stood Slava Fetisov, the greatest player in Soviet history, but just a man, alone.

As difficult as Tikhonov could be, Fetisov believes he was just a symptom, not the disease. Even if Tikhonov were replaced, Fetisov says, the system would still keep running. "Everybody in American press try to present my problem as player against coach," Fetisov said. "Really, it was human being against system. But Viktor represent old system very well, I would say."

The battle would leave all sides bloodied, but only one man standing.

"You feel once in a lifetime you have to do something special," Fetisov says. "So you take a chance."

Slava Fetisov took many. On January 16, 1989, he walked into Coach Tikhonov's office and said, "I will not play for CSKA anymore."

Fetisov's life would change literally overnight.

The morning after his announcement, Fetisov's wife, Ladlena, picked up their phone to discover it was dead. Once word got out of Slava's meeting with Tikhonov, the young couple lost almost all their friends. Fetisov was banned from practicing anywhere, even at his old childhood rink.

The Fetisovs' private troubles turned public the next day, in the pages of *Sovietsky Sport*. Tikhonov suddenly decided to explain why he had stripped Fetisov of his captaincy a few months earlier. After a fall game in Kiev, Tikhonov claimed, Fetisov had gotten drunk, punched out a hotel worker—who was also a decorated World War II veteran—then showered soldiers who tried to calm him down with punches and profanity. These workers, Tikhonov said, also happened to be national heroes, having fulfilled risky assignments after the Chernobyl disaster.

According to Tikhonov, Fetisov subsequently offended nurses at an alcohol rehabilitation center, then bellowed, "I am the famous Fetisov. I have received many honors. The NHL paid a million dollars for me. What about you?" Tikhonov concluded, "The famous Fetisov decided long ago to sell his famous soul."

The real story is less dramatic. "The police took me and beat me up," Fetisov says, without emotion. "Yes. They beat me up pretty good, and then blame me for it."

The same government officials who disconnected the Fetisovs' phone reconnected it a few days later—not as a peace offering, but the better to harass them.

"They tried to scare Slava, his parents, my parents—always calling," says Ladlena. "Some scream, some act like friends. They tell me, 'Slava can end up in Siberia, then you won't have apartment, hot water, bathrooms inside.' And I say, 'Okay, no problem—we'll just buy warm clothes and go there.'" Ladlena still laughs at this.

"They probably didn't know Slava so well," she says. "If he believes in something, he doesn't even question his own well-being. He must do it. He's that way. Nothing will change him. And that's probably why I love this man so much."

Since Fetisov was off the team, he had to put on his major's uniform, report every morning to a military office, and answer phones.

"Major Fetisov listening. How can I help you?"

Ladlena gave out the number to their remaining friends, and urged them to call and pester her husband. After a few calls Slava figured out the game and phoned home.

"What are you doing?" he asked his wife.

"I'm just giving you hard time," she said, laughing.

"During this time," she recalls, "we tried to make something funny from this situation."

Their sense of humor came in handy when the betrayals mounted.

After Tikhonov declared Fetisov persona non grata, many of his teammates were not willing to shake his hand, or even be seen in the same room with their former captain.

Fetisov and Alexei Kasatonov had been inseparable for twelve years. They were paired together on defense, they roomed together on the road, and they lived together in the barracks. They saw each other far more often than they saw their wives or families.

"Kasatonov was my best friend," Fetisov says. But where Fetisov is a worldly Muscovite who's read more American literary classics than most Americans, Kasatonov is a provincial farmboy. Where Fetisov is clever and stubborn, Kasatonov is gullible and easily manipulated. Where Fetisov is courageous, Kasatonov is cowardly. So, when Fetisov decided to take on the system, Kasatonov wanted no part of it.

"They told him they would give him everything, if he say these things," Fetisov says. "All of a sudden, he gets scared of system and say things to protect himself. Alex would scream at me in meetings, saying Tikhonov was right. It hurt, yes. But better to lose this kind of friend early than late."

Not all the Fetisovs' friends turned on them. Gary Kasparov, the Soviet chess champion, is an old friend of Fetisov, a lifelong chess player. During Fetisov's loneliest winter, Kasparov called him to bolster his resolve.

"'Only you can break system,' he tell me. 'You're going to break this world. But you have to realize it's going to be tough.' Well, I knew it was going to be tough, but not *that* tough. It was very scary time."

Soon after Kasparov told the Fetisovs how important their struggle was to the entire country, a chance encounter in a marketplace convinced them of it. A middle-aged stranger came up to shake Slava's hand. "You are not only standing up for players," he said, "but for all Russians." He was crying as he said this.

Three months after Fetisov made his stand in Tikhonov's office some brave teammates, led by Larionov, went on national television to say that if Fetisov did not play in the World Cup that April in Stockholm, they would not play either.

Their bold play worked. Fetisov was invited back to the team without having to rescind his request to leave for the NHL. All his teammates voted to reinstate him as captain, except one: Kasatonov.

Inspired by Kasparov's support, Fetisov decided to play a clever chess game of his own. Despite President Gorbachev's professed desire to instill democracy, almost all the people in power were Communists, but now they had to make a show of democracy to appeal to international opinion.

Fetisov calculated that an internationally recognized figure like himself might be able to call their bluff.

Tikhonov claimed he had signed Fetisov's release papers, but Dmitri Yazov, the minister of defense who would lead the coup attempt against Gorbachev two years later, would not sign them. Fine, Fetisov said, I'll go ask him myself. To do so, Fetisov had to meet Yazov in his elaborate, intimidating office, where he was surrounded by five generals at the table.

Yazov started stomping around the table, yelling at Fetisov.

"Why are you screaming at me?" Fetisov asked. "I only want to get out of the army. It's my right."

That made Yazov shout still louder to scare Fetisov. When that failed, Yazov changed tactics. "You can be a general of sport," he offered Fetisov, sweetly. "We'll give you a nice apartment, a dacha in the countryside."

"No thank you," Fetisov said. "You can give it to someone else."

Then Yazov turned angry again: "We'll give you ten days to accept, or send you and your family to Siberia."

This was not an idle threat, as millions of other Soviet leaders had suffered that fate over the decades. But the move only bolstered Fetisov's resolve.

"I know I could not back down now, or it's over for all players, all people," Fetisov recalls thinking. "No one would try such a thing again."

Fetisov could not know if he'd come out of this battle of wills safely, but he knew he couldn't go back the way he came.

"I tell him, 'In ten days all I want to hear from you is that you will release me from army.'"

Fetisov guessed right: they couldn't banish such a public figure with the world watching. Yazov did not send him to Siberia, but he did not release him from the army, either.

So, Fetisov then shifted strategies. "I tried to fight legally, openly, but it was not easy. It's a really tough system."

Since he couldn't get out of the army, Fetisov went to court to see whether a Soviet soldier could sign a contract with another party—in this case, the New Jersey Devils.

The Russian constitution is a private document, not hung in homes or taught in schools. Thus, it was widely believed that it was unconstitutional for an army soldier to sign a contract, but only a few knew for sure until Fetisov's unprecedented court case proved that it wasn't.

Once the Russian officials lost the case, they decided to turn lemons into lemonade by trumpeting Fetisov's success as proof that democracy was working in the Soviet Union. True or not, the additional publicity it created forced them to carry out Fetisov's wishes.

After an eighteen-month struggle, on August 13, 1989—a date Fetisov can recite as readily as his daughter's birthday—Slava and his wife waited in Moscow's international airport to board a 1:00 p.m. flight to New York. Problem was, they lacked passports, which they needed to get their visas, which were required to purchase their tickets.

Just a couple hours before takeoff, a government representative finally showed up with their passports, and furtively slipped them to the young couple.

"Nobody wanted to be responsible for this," Slava says, grinning once more. "Tough for them to decide who would be the giver."

The Fetisovs then had to rush across town to the U.S. Embassy, where their visas were waiting for them, then zip back to the airport, where they had paid someone to wait in the ticket line for them in their absence. They hugged their friends and family, all in tears, then boarded the plane going to America.

The Fetisovs were seated in first class, but stewed while they waited for the plane to pull out of the gate.

"Until Aeroflot plane took off," Fetisov says, "I didn't believe it would happen."

Though Fetisov had won a historic battle, his war wasn't over. When he arrived in the U.S., he recalls, "I was empty physically and mentally, and I got only two weeks to get ready."

Everything was new, from the language to the NHL's style of play, and none of it came easily for Fetisov. Making matters worse, thanks to the lingering hostility over the Cold War, Fetisov says, "People in my own dressing room hate me."

Current Red Wing Doug Brown was just four years out of Boston College when Fetisov joined the Devils, Brown's first NHL team. "Some of the boys weren't too excited to have him on the team," Brown confirms. "'You're taking our jobs,' 'Let the Commies stay over there,' all that stuff. But we became best friends almost immediately, and roomed together for four or five years. He's the godfather of one of my sons."

When the others got to know Slava personally, they came around, too. Unlike most Americans, Fetisov does not give off sparks when you first meet him, but if you get to know him, he radiates a quiet, lasting warmth like slow-burning coals. Fetisov is a man of great pride, but little ego—a rare combination that helped him adjust to his new role.

"The thing I found almost as amazing as Slava's stature before he left Russia," Dryden says, "is that he left at a time when his best days were past him. He didn't have that kind of standing [here]. He had to start over and earn it, and earn it when he was less able to earn it. Almost everyone I know in that situation has failed. They all seemed to pack it up and disappear from the scene.

"Well, Fetisov didn't leave the scene, he hung in there. Instead of being the head guy and the focal point, he had to become a support player, and I just really admire him for that. He gained that wonderful recognition that a support player can be an important player too—and that's a very difficult thing for a superstar to realize."

Having adjusted to the culture, Fetisov still had to master a fundamentally different style of play.

"If I was gonna dump it in for [Sergei] Makarov or Larionov, once, all right," Fetisov says of the Russian style. "Two times, they get pissed off. Third time, they say, '*you* go in and get it.' But in NHL, I get so much heat for holding the puck. The forwards would skate away from me, and I still have puck. I look like idiot!" Fetisov says, laughing again at his own expense.

Fetisov's new opponents were even less concerned with making him feel welcome than his teammates were.

"When you play in NHL for thirteen years, like Stevie [Yzerman], you don't have to prove anything," Fetisov says. "But I was new. All this close-checking from behind, you feel this atmosphere around you. Only my wife support me at this point—again."

Brown attests that Fetisov didn't get much help from the refs, either, who "constantly turned a blind eye."

Brown remembers Toronto's Wendell Clark taking runs at Fetisov during their first meeting, challenging him to a fight—something few European players are trained to do—and beating him up. The next time the two teams met, Fetisov lined up Clark for a thundering hip check, one that left Clark flat on his back long enough to reflect on what had just happened.

"I don't recall Clark taking too many runs at Slava after that," Brown says, with a chuckle.

"These [Russian] guys were tough," Dryden says. "They had to be tough to withstand Tikhonov, they had to be tough to become the best in their homeland, they had to be tough to ride out the fight to leave, and they had to be tough to make it here."

They were determined. The same season Fetisov joined the Devils, seven Russians signed with NHL teams. "The people in the Soviet Union are watching us, too," Larionov told *Sports Illustrated*. "We do not want to fail."

There were snags around every corner. Not willing to go through Fetisov's nightmare, the other Russian ex-patriots settled for fifty-fifty contracts, where they got half the money and the Russian Sports Federation got the other half, which they claimed would be spent on rinks and equipment—but the money ended up in various pockets along the way. But Fetisov had won the right to keep whatever money he earned.

People who file lawsuits and athletes who hold out for "renegotiated contracts" always say it's not the money, it's the principle. Almost as often, they're lying. Not Fetisov, who donated $100,000 of his own money directly to the youth organizations who needed the cash, and made certain it got there.

Only one other Russian player was allowed to keep his entire NHL salary: Alex Kasatonov, who joined the Devils midway through Fetisov's first season.

"Lou [Lamoriello] says, we need him," Fetisov recalls. "And I say, 'If it help the team, it's okay.' Never put own ego ahead of team. When Alex got here, I was still waiting for explanation, but it never happen. It was hurt, oh yeah. Tough to make good friends, tough to lose."

"Slava never allowed that to affect his play on the ice," Lamoriello says. "His professionalism never left him."

Nonetheless, when the Devils told Fetisov they were trading him to the Red Wings—right before the Devils won the Stanley Cup in 1995—"He was flying around the house, packing," his wife recalls. "And when Detroit traded for Igor [Larionov], Slava was so happy."

Instead of having to adjust to the NHL style, the Red Wings' five-man Russian unit could now make the NHL adjust to them, just like the old days.

Herb Brooks coached the University of Minnesota, the 1980 U.S. Olympic team, a pro team in Europe, and four NHL teams. He understands the Russian style as well as anyone. "This is not to take anything away from the tremendous hockey players in Detroit," he told me, "and that's important to say, but [the Russians] showed everybody what puck possession and regrouping means, how to play east-west hockey [instead of just up and down], and how to play without the puck. They've created another level of entertainment in the NHL."

With the Russian Five flying, Fetisov's final goal of winning the Stanley Cup seemed within reach last year, until the Colorado Avalanche stunned the Red Wings in the conference finals.

"So many ironies," Fetisov says. "We fight against the most powerful system in the world and Igor and I never cry. Then we get together again [in Detroit], and Igor is crying when we lose to Colorado. We get on the bus, and I said, 'Igor, our dream is gonna die.'"

But their dream did not die. After the Red Wings swept the Philadelphia Flyers this spring to win Detroit's first Stanley Cup since 1955, captain Steve Yzerman raised the Cup over his head, then handed it first to Fetisov and Larionov, something Yzerman had decided he would do a few days before.

"Those guys have been through so much," he said. "They deserved it."

Instead of taking jobs from Canadians, as originally feared, the influx of Russians, Swedes, and Americans has allowed the NHL to expand from a twenty-one-team circuit when the Russians first arrived to a thirty-team league by 2000, boosting the game's popularity to new heights.

Fetisov can readily tick off the nationalities of the Red Wings. "All Canadians except five Russians, three Swedes, one Yankee," he says, remembering Doug Brown. "So much trouble in the world, this has to be good. We are great example. That's why we're here, to help change people's minds."

The once despised Russian players are now treasured by fans and teammates alike.

"It doesn't take long," Fetisov jokes. "Only eight years."

Tikhonov is now a director of Russian hockey, and Kasatonov is his lackey, while Fetisov has become a beloved figure on two continents.

"Slava's so highly respected, both in sport and out of sport," Herb Brooks says. "I always tell him, 'You're going to be the president of Russia one day.'"

Nothing made Detroiters' affection for the Russians more obvious than their response to the recent limousine accident that injured Fetisov and left Vladimir Konstantinov and masseur Sergei Mnatsakanov in a coma. Fans held all-night vigils at the site of the accident and flooded the hospital with letters and packages, including dozens of teddy bears for Fetisov.

"We are quiet people, we don't socialize a lot," Ladlena says, "but after accident our neighbors started knocking on the door to go to the store, take care of our daughter, anything to help."

A few weeks ago, when the Fetisovs packed their car to go back to their home in New Jersey for the summer, Slava turned to his wife and asked, "Why are we going back? We have such incredible people here! So warm, so great." The Fetisovs are now considering building a permanent home in Detroit.

When asked if he could have imagined the American fans' incredible affection for him in the fall of 1989, Fetisov says flatly, "No . . . no." But then his face breaks into the craggy, warm smile his teammates know so well, the one that makes him look as if he's holding a happy secret. Just as surely as he believed Americans could never accept him eight years ago, he is just as certain now that they have not only accepted him, but embraced him.

For Fetisov, it's all been worth it.

"For some people, life is easy, but for me more difficult. My life was this way. But if I try another way, maybe I wouldn't be here now.

"If you have a chance to do something special, and not to help yourself but to help others, you have to do it or always you will regret. I realized I had a chance to help.

"This was my time."

JIM ABBOTT'S BIGGEST CHALLENGE

April 2009
Michigan Today

Jim Abbott is a rarity.

Of the four-and-a-half thousand players who've pitched in the major leagues this century, Abbott's 79 wins puts him in the highest 15 percent, at number 676. When the California Angels brought him straight to Anaheim in 1989, he became just the fifteenth player since 1965 to skip the minor leagues.

"Everyone talks about how many trials I've faced," Abbott says, "but there really haven't been that many. Baseball was never hard. You just go out and throw it."

Jim Abbott was always bigger, stronger, and more coordinated than the other kids, so he found it easy to excel in baseball, despite being born with no fingers on his right hand.

Earning respect was often harder.

When Abbott was still in grade school, one opposing coach ordered his batter to bunt, forcing Abbott to field the ball. Abbott pitched with his glove resting on his right hand. After he released the ball, he slipped his left hand into the glove, fielded the ball, then performed a nifty maneuver where he'd stick the glove under his right arm, let the ball fall into his left hand, and throw it to first base. One down.

"I don't ever remember it being something I had to master," he says. "It was just something I did."

He made the play as smoothly as a magician pulling a nickel out of your ear.

Thinking it was a fluke, the coach ordered the next batter to bunt—and the next. Finally, after six batters had bunted, and Abbott threw all six out, the coach called off the experiment. The only embarrassed person in the park was the coach.

When Jim Abbott was a junior at Flint Central, his Connie Mack base-ball coach, Ted Mahan, took him to Ann Arbor to show him the campus.

Mahan had been a catcher on Michigan's baseball team, and he hoped to get his star pitcher interested in his alma mater.

He showed Abbott the campus, the ballpark, even the football stadium—but the full tour wasn't necessary, because Mahan also took Abbott to Pizza Bob's, right on State Street.

"I had a torpedo sandwich and a chocolate chip mint shake," Abbott told me, more than a decade later. "That's all it took. I was sold."

But Michigan wasn't yet sold on him. Although Abbott had excelled at Flint Central, there was no ignoring the fact that Abbott had only one full hand, which could be a liability at the next level.

"In recruiting, I didn't do any favors," said Bud Middaugh, Abbott's coach at Michigan. "We were too competitive for that. I just hoped he'd be a competent college pitcher. He turned out far better than I imagined."

But after Abbott arrived as a freshman in 1985, Middaugh's caution seemed justified. Abbott was homesick, worn out, and overwhelmed. After a number of fruitless appearances on the mound, Abbott came on in relief against North Carolina, a perennial powerhouse.

Tie game, two outs, man on third. After Abbott threw just one pitch, and his catcher tossed the ball back to him, the Tar Heels' third-base coach started yelling at his runner to steal home, thinking Abbott couldn't possibly get the ball out of his glove and back to the plate fast enough. To the coach's surprise, Abbott made the transaction with time to spare, leaving the catcher an easy tag to get out of the inning. When the Wolverines scored in their next at bat, Abbott got his first college win—for throwing one pitch.

Abbott closed out his college career in 1988 with a 26–8 mark, a 3.03 ERA, and an average of seven strikeouts per game. He finished fourth on Michigan's all-time win list, and first in voting for the team's MVP, the Big Ten player of the year, Big Ten male athlete of the year, the nation's best amateur baseball player, and the Sullivan Award for being the nation's top amateur athlete, beating out such Olympic stars as basketball star David Robinson, volleyball legend Karch Kiraly, and Olympic gold medalist Janet Evans.

In short, Abbott took home virtually every piece of hardware a college baseball player possibly could.

The summer after Abbott's junior year, 1987, he joined the U.S. National Team, which flew to Havana to face the Cuban national squad.

"They had one of the best baseball teams in the world," Abbott recalls, "and we were just a bunch of college kids.

"It's hard to describe just how passionate they are about their baseball—

and how seriously they took that series. We played in the biggest stadium in the country, and they packed it for all the games, 50,000. And you hear them all night."

To loosen up his team of amateur players before facing the all-powerful Cubanos, manager Ron Fraser told his team, "Hey, they're not *that* good. They'd probably only finish third in the American League East."

"He was joking, but our mouths dropped open," Abbott recalls. "Hey, thanks, Coach! Big help!"

After the U.S. lost the first two games, as expected, Fraser gave Abbott the third start—and the Americans won, 8–3.

"For an American team to beat them on their own soil," Abbott says, "for the first time in twenty-five years—they didn't take it too well. They were smacking our bus the whole way back to the hotel, and kept us up all night. But we loved it."

A month later, the U.S. athletes at the 1987 Pan Am Games selected Abbott to carry the American flag into the stadium. The event wasn't just for fun, though. The U.S. team had to finish first or second just to qualify for the Olympics.

"We felt an incredible amount of pressure to succeed."

They barely qualified, finishing second to earn a spot in the 1988 Seoul Olympics. Close victories over South Korea and Canada, followed by a blowout over Australia, advanced the U.S. team to the finals against heavily favored Japan. There Abbott threw a complete game for a 5–3 victory and an unexpected gold medal.

What Abbott remembers most was not the game, but the celebration.

"Being on the bottom of that pile after we got the final out, everyone was just screaming and yelling—nothing intelligible for minutes. That wasn't an all-star squad, that was a *team*. We're still close to this day."

The California Angels drafted Abbott in the first round. Although he pitched well in his first spring training in 1989, and the Angels had an opening in their rotation, everyone expected Abbott to spend his first professional season in the minors—including Abbott.

"I'll never forget when Marcel Waxman, our pitching coach, walked in to tell me I was going to be in Anaheim with the big club."

Some critics accused the Angels of pulling a publicity stunt, but Abbott showed he belonged his first two years, compiling a 22–26 record. Abbott removed any doubt his third season, 1991, with a 2.89 ERA, an 18–11 record, and a remarkable third-place finish in the Cy Young voting.

Before that breakthrough year, the photos used for Abbott's baseball cards hid his hands behind his back or in his glove. It was only after Abbott established himself as a bona fide major league pitcher that the card companies showed him running the bases or pitching with his glove resting on his right hand.

"I'm glad for that, I'm proud of that," he says. "I want to be remembered not for having to overcome anything, but for making the most of what God gave me. If there wasn't some ability, and with that, some accountability, I'd probably just be remembered solely as the guy who pitched in the majors with no right hand."

Abbott enjoyed a solid ten-year run in the majors, highlighted by his no-hitter for the Yankees in 1993, but he still says winning the Olympic gold medal for his country marked his high point in baseball. It's a testament to a great career when you consider pitching a no-hitter at Yankee Stadium mere icing.

Abbott's low point is just as easy to pinpoint: 1996. After he had lost 15 of his 16 decisions for the Angels that year, they sent him to the minor leagues for the first time in his career.

"People are always saying, 'Well, you've overcome adversity before,'" he told me at the time. "Yeah, there have been other times, but this is harder, the toughest patch of my life. I realize a major leaguer struggling with his form is not exactly heart breaking, but baseball had been my crutch, my entry into acceptance."

Abbott's confidence in his pitching was virtually unshaken for more than 20 years, going back to his first year of Little League. To rekindle it, the Angels sent him to the AAA Vancouver Canadians in the Pacific Coast League. Thus, at age 28, after 227 major league starts, Abbott found himself warming up in the visiting bullpen in Tucson, Arizona, trying to regain his form.

He didn't get into that game, but after it ended, I watched him run a dozen sprints on the warning track, then lay down to do set after set of sit-ups. When he finished, the maintenance crew had disappeared. Abbott was the only person left on the field.

But not the only person in the stadium.

When Abbott finally finished his work, he signed autographs for the two-dozen kids standing patiently behind the chain-link fence. Wherever Abbott goes, kids with various disabilities find him. He is their one big league hero.

One of the youngsters, J.D. Cole, had a face Norman Rockwell painted a hundred times, and two fingers on his right hand. He was six years old, born two years after Abbott pitched his first game in the majors.

J.D.'s mother smiled bravely when she told the famous pitcher what an inspiration he'd been for her son, but before she completes her sentence, her eyes betrayed her, glistening with tears.

Abbott asked J.D., "What position do you play?"

"All of them!" J.D. said.

"And there's nothing you can't do, right?"

"Right!" J.D. said.

"Well, you keep it up," Abbott said, and passed J.D.'s baseball card back to him. The two said good-bye, then shared a left-handed hand-shake.

While Abbott turned his attention to the other kids, J.D. examined his card. Many autographs these days are nothing but a letter followed by a long line, but Abbott's was carefully rendered. The card was from Abbott's third season. It showed him bunting, his right hand on the handle, his left on the barrel. On the flip side, Abbott was leading off first base, both hands resting on his thighs.

J.D. showed me the card. He told me he had a dog named Chip, who just chews up everything, and a cousin named Eric, who used to bite him. J.D. likes street hockey, but he *loves* baseball. He plays it all the time. According to his dad, J.D. was playing about two years ahead of most of his peers. "I can throw the ball real far," J.D. said, "and sometimes I hit home runs."

When J.D. walked away from Abbott, he magically reverted back to the shy kid he was seconds before talking to his number one hero. Under his baseball cap J.D.'s eyes were once again half-closed, but they were gazing down at his card. His glowing smile gave away his secret: something inside him had changed. Things were possible. He knew it now.

The next afternoon, Jim Abbott was sitting in a plastic chair by the hotel's outdoor pool.

"Throughout all this," he said of his trying season, "the biggest lesson is, baseball's not everything. It's not who you are. When such a big part of your foundation is taken away, you find where the support is, where the real bricks are."

When he went to the minors, Abbott's bricks already included his wife of five years, with whom he hoped to raise a family, enough money for life, and the knowledge that, even if his comeback failed, his career had been an undeniable success, by any standard.

Abbott returned to the Major Leagues with the Milwaukee Brewers, where he went 5–0 in 1998, before retiring after the next season.

"But I'm thankful for the experience," he said of his stint in the minors. "When that success was taken away, I found I had way too much invested in being a pitcher. It was sort of a reckoning, that I'd better start seeing myself as more than that. Ultimately it was a good thing."

"I've been lucky—but I felt that way long before I made it to the major leagues. I never really battled against what I *didn't* have. I always tried to make the most of what I *did* have. I don't think I was ever in a position where someone should have felt sorry for me."

Today Abbott lives in Southern California, with his wife, Dana, and two daughters, the oldest of who now plays volleyball for Michigan. He travels extensively as a public speaker, which gives him a charge similar to the rush he got pitching.

"You can only prepare so much," he says. "And then you get the nervous energy you need to think on your feet. Whatever comes your way, you know you're going to have to go with it. I enjoy it."

Abbott keeps close tabs on his alma mater, especially during football and baseball seasons. In a career filled with honors, he received one of his most important on April 18, 2009, when the University of Michigan retired Abbott's jersey, only the fifth Michigan has retired, and the first Wolverine to receive this honor based solely on his play and not his off-field contributions.

"I don't think there are too many people out here who don't know I went to Michigan," he says. "I have a lot of pride in that. So I'm having a hard time getting my head around the idea of having my number retired on the outfield wall, the same place I was shagging balls as a freshman, not believing I was there.

"It's a long way from that Pizza Bob's torpedo sandwich and the chocolate chip milkshake—but I guess it all comes full circle."

DENARD'S DAY

October 14, 2011
The Wall Street Journal

Denard Robinson's Wednesday started at 6:30 a.m., when his alarm clock sounded in his off-campus condo bedroom.

He hit the snooze once, then twice, before getting out of bed to put on a pair of jeans, a red polo shirt, a pair of black Adidas training shoes, and his varsity jacket. Then he hopped into his roommate Devin Gardner's family pickup truck, a beat-up 2002 Dodge Dakota with a metal tool box behind the cab.

He rolled into Schembechler Hall, Michigan's football building, at 7 a.m. When he stumbled through the locker room door, he was met by a picture of the Paul Bunyan Trophy, which stays in the custody of the winner of the annual Michigan–Michigan State game. The picture said, "Home at Michigan State University since 2008." The Wolverines would try to get Paul back that Saturday.

Robinson looked half-awake when he walked into the training room for treatment on his left knee, which was swollen so badly you couldn't delineate the kneecap. After an hour of receiving treatments that looked like voodoo to a layman, Robinson went to a side room to do some physical therapy.

The worst part, said the Deerfield Beach, FL, native, was the cold tub, which is kept at 50 degrees. He slowly forced himself down in the water, grimacing the whole way. "'Y'all got it made,'" he said, mimicking the usual charge of his non-athlete classmates. "That's what everyone thinks. They don't see this!"

After undergoing a dozen various treatments, by 9:40 a.m. Robinson hopped back in Gardner's parents' pickup truck and raced back to their apartment to grab his roommate for their 10:00 class, "Crime, Race and the Law." Their first-floor apartment was modest, but bright, clean, and neat. "That's because we're never here!" Gardner said.

The two dashed to the Dennison Building and snuck into the classroom three minutes after the 10:10 start time—which they knew would get back to head coach Rich Rodriguez. Robinson found an empty seat against the right wall of the packed classroom. Gardner sat in the middle among the other students, or "normies," as the players called them.

Professor Scott Ellsworth, a middle-aged white man, started by discussing a documentary called "Murder on a Sunday Morning," which explored a case of mistaken identity in Jacksonville, Florida. It resulted in 15-year-old Brenton Butler, who was walking by to apply for a job at Blockbuster that morning, going to jail.

"Was Brenton Butler guilty of anything?" Ellsworth asked. Most of the white kids said no, but most of the African-Americans disagreed. Wrong place, wrong time, they said.

Gardner raised his hand more than any other student during the 80-minute class. Robinson was usually content to take notes in his spiral notebook. He wrote in careful penmanship that leaned left—a sign of an introvert. By the end of the class, he had written a page and a half, a little more than the suburban girl sitting next to him. Ellsworth told them to read Kafka's *The Trial*, and let them go.

While Robinson packed his things, a coed slipped him a small, handwritten note, which he tucked away.

He walked with Gardner and receiver Kelvin Grady across campus for lunch. He peaked at the note: "For your eyes only," it said in purple ink. "You seem like a really nice guy and I think it'd be cool to hang out with you. And no, I'm not a creepy stalker! Text me some time."

Robinson grinned and shook his head. Grady demanded to see it, then started laughing immediately. "Ahhhhh! Same note I got!" he said,

Robinson wanted to go to Wendy's in the Michigan Union basement, like usual, but Grady argued for Noodles & Co., a long block down State Street.

"Come on, man," Grady said, "I'm trying to expand your horizons!"

"I like Wendy's, man."

"But it's rivalry week!"

"Exactly why," Robinson countered, "I don't want to change my routine."

Robinson got his favorite, a Wendy's spicy chicken no. 6 combo meal, then sat down with his friends and teammates. The woman at the next table, reading an anthropology textbook, asked, "How's your knee?"

"What? My knee's fine. Where'd you get that?"

"They said on TV."

"Damn, already?"

After lunch, Robinson walked past a retail tent selling yellow T-shirts with "SHOE" at the top, "LACE" at the bottom, and an untied cleat in the middle, providing both Robinson's nickname and its source.

"Think they'd give me one?" Robinson said, walking by unnoticed.

"Only if you want an NCAA violation," I replied, recalling a similar conversation Chris Webber once had with Mitch Albom.

"That's crazy," he said, smiling. I didn't have the heart to tell him a replica of the number 16 jersey he wore on Saturdays was going for $70 down the block. Walking back across the street to Gardner's truck, a stranger coming toward us struck the Heisman pose, with no words spoken.

Robinson smiled and shook his head. "That's crazy, too!"

Next up, a one-hour meeting with a professor to discuss a paper.

"I like writing papers," he told me. "I don't like tests."

By 2 p.m., Robinson was back in the cold tub. While up to his chest in frigid water, with his elbows on the deck, he borrowed a cell phone to handle a national press conference with ESPN and others on the line. Robinson then rushed off to a quarterbacks' meeting at 2:30.

Practice started at 3:30. Members of Michigan's football royalty lined the field to watch, including former athletic directors and star players.

Like most teams today, Michigan hits only on Tuesdays, and even then, it's just glorified pushing and shoving. But on this Wednesday, you could hear the pads smack, each hit packing more punch than usual.

When practice ended, Robinson led the quarterbacks in their ritual chest bump, then showered and headed to the training room for yet more treatment. It was 6:49, and Robinson had already been on the go for 12 hours.

A trainer gave Robinson different knee pads to try on. Next, more ultrasound. All told, over the course of three sessions lasting three and a half hours, Robinson underwent more than two dozen treatments for his knee including the cold tub, a pool workout, the stationary bike, a dead lift, micro-electrodes, ultrasounds and low-level laser therapy.

At 7:30, Robinson sat down with a few teammates in the commons for dinner and conversation. In less than an hour, Robinson ate two biscuits, 16 chicken wings, two Gatorades, two caramel cheesecakes, and a big scoop of rice. All told, he consumed well over 4,000 calories that day—which paled in comparison to the linemen's max of 14,000 calories a day.

Afterward, in the team meeting room, Robinson and teammates Vincent Smith, Junior Hemingway, and Darryl Stonum hunkered down to watch film of the previous year's loss to Michigan State on the big screen.

The players were struck by how poorly they had played in the 26–20 overtime loss.

"Man, we played so bad in this game," Stonum said, "and we still almost won it."

"I can't wait for game time," Hemingway said. "I wish it was tomorrow."

"Any requests?" Stonum asked, going through their film catalogue.

"Third and longs," Robinson said.

While Stonum fished around for the file on the computer, the players talked about how long their day had already been.

"Classmates say, 'You look tired,'" Hemingway said. "Yes, I just finished lifting for 90 minutes, before you woke up."

"Or they say, 'You walk slow,'" Robinson said. "Yes, I do. It's because I'm dead."

After working like crazy during conditioning and practice, when the players leave the football building they walk slower than their grandparents, barely lifting their feet.

At 10:34 p.m., they finally walked out of Schembechler Hall for the last time that day—only to be met by middle-aged autograph seekers who would post their new prizes on eBay 30 minutes later. Robinson would be in bed by 11, then do it all again the next day—plus a workout and study table.

I had only followed him that day—and I was exhausted.

Leaders

Leadership is important in every field, of course, but it's much easier to study in sports. We get to hear their philosophies, watch their players develop, and chart the results.

From the time I started playing sports, I've always been drawn to great coaches, so it's probably not surprising that I've written more about coaches than athletes. Fortunately, in Michigan we have had no shortage of great leaders to write about, especially in the college ranks, where I believe coaches can make a bigger impact than in the pros.

On the surface, the people in this section might look very different. Bo Schembechler was a screamer on the sidelines, while Red Berenson rarely changed his expression on the bench. But whether you're looking at Tom Izzo or Carol Hutchins, when you boil it all down, they all seem to have the same basic philosophy: they care deeply about their players as people, yet they insist on pushing them to be their best.

That has never gone out of style—but it's a lot harder than it looks.

BO'S BACK WHERE HE BELONGS

I first met Bo Schembechler in 1975, when I was a ten-year-old kid asking for his autograph at a Michigan hockey game—so nervous I could not think of my own name. I met him again in August of 1996, when I was writing a section on Fielding Yost for a book on Michigan football. We got along, and he agreed to let me tag along for a week in October of 1996—a very generous offer, to say the least. By mid-week, I already knew I had a great story, and called my editor at the Detroit News from a pay phone (that'll date you) in Grand Rapids, urging him to spare all the space he could. He did, giving me 2½ pages, and the story earned national awards. When I met Bo in his office four days later, he told me, "Well, Bacon, you didn't screw it up—and frankly I'm surprised." In the next breath he asked if I wanted his papers—16 big boxes' worth, with everything from correspondence to transcripts to game plans. I soon realized he had given me the raw materials for the book we would write together ten years later, my first bestseller. But it started with this story.

November 3, 1996
The Detroit News

The last time Bo Schembechler's name was at the top of the sports page, he was at the bottom of his life. Tom Monaghan had just fired him as president of the Detroit Tigers, and Bo's wife Millie was dying of adrenal cancer. According to Lynn Koch, Schembechler's secretary of twenty-seven years, "Bo was just devastated."

Four years later, the Millie Schembechler Foundation has raised over a third of the $3 million necessary to establish an adrenal cancer research center at the University of Michigan Hospital. Bo is married to the former Cathy Aikens, who's got him eating right, exercising regularly, and dressing like a Ralph Lauren model. He's incredibly busy raising money for the Foundation, helping his former players any way he can, giving speeches around the country, and simply enjoying the fruits of his labor.

In short: Bo is back.

In early 1990 Schembechler retired as Michigan's all-time winningest football coach, with a record of 194–48–5. At the same time, he stepped down as U-M's athletic director and became president of the Tigers. Two years later the Tigers' organization had unraveled, with Schembechler serving as the fall guy for the decision to fire Ernie Harwell and the lightning rod for those protesting a new stadium.

In February of 1992, fed up with Monaghan and the Tigers, Bo and Millie flew to Hawaii for a three-week vacation with Jim Brandstatter and his wife, Robbie Timmons.

"At that point," recalls Brandstatter, "Bo was just beginning to say, 'To heck with this mess,' and smell the roses with Millie. One week later Millie gets sick."

The timing was cruel, but the disease was merciless. Adrenal glands are almost insignificant, roughly the same size, shape, and weight of almonds. If the doctors discover adrenal cancer soon enough, it's relatively easy to remove the glands altogether. But if they don't, the cancer spreads like a brush fire to the liver and lungs. That's why medical texts describe the disease with terms like "grave" and "rapidly fatal," saying, "Only rare patients survive more than a few years."

"Bo's the kind of guy who wants to fix everything," secretary Lynn Koch says, "and the cancer was like beating his head against a wall." Schembechler has always relied on effort and integrity to solve problems, but those weren't enough to battle two tiny, cancerous glands. "He was at the hospital all the time. He was just a broken man."

Monaghan fired Schembechler on the same day Bo and Millie celebrated their twenty-fourth wedding anniversary. Millie Schembechler died a few days later, on August 19, 1992.

"After Millie died," Bo admits, "I didn't do anything."

Schembechler had lost his characteristic spark, he wasn't active, and he looked gray and flabby. If mourning is measured not by days but by depth, the nine months following Millie's death were an eternity.

Concerned about Bo's condition, some friends invited him down to their home in Florida, then took him out to a party where everyone knew him. Everyone, that is, except Cathy Aikens. She had been widowed five years earlier herself, but was still financially secure and eye-catching. She had plenty of suitors, but no one who captured her imagination.

"I guess I had just about given up on finding someone," she says. "It's tough when you're older and alone."

Bo noticed Cathy across the room and asked someone about her, but before he could meet her he headed back to his friends' house to watch the Michigan basketball team play in the NCAA tournament.

Bo's eager friends called him at halftime. "We heard you were asking about Cathy," they said, and tried to arrange a meeting. Problem was, Schembechler was going to the Bahamas for a fishing trip the next day. "Okay," they said, "we're going to pick you up at eight for breakfast, and she's going to be there."

"I didn't know anything about this dating business," Schembechler confesses. "I actually showed up for that breakfast in my fishing gear."

"He looked awful that morning," Cathy says, demonstrating her ability to give Bo a good ribbing—a hallmark of all his close friends.

Cathy is more interested in literature than linebackers, so when Schembechler told Cathy he was a football coach, she asked, "Is that all you've done?"

Bo laughed and said, "Lemme tell you something: *that* was a *full-time job!*"

The two hit it off that morning, but afterward Schembechler stalled. Three weeks later, when Schembechler's plane stopped in Minneapolis for a two-hour lay-over, he told himself, "If you've got a gut in your body, you'd call her."

He did. They met again two weeks later at her Florida home. They were supposed to go out to dinner, but instead sat on her couch and talked—and talked and talked—until it was midnight. At that late hour, Bo challenged her. "I came down here to see the ocean, and it's right out that door. If you've got a gut in your body, you'll put your swimsuit on and we'll go swimming in that ocean.

"Well, she did it! I was splashing around in the water. I felt like a kid again!"

Schembechler slept on that couch that first night—and the four nights that followed.

"We talked about everything," Bo recalls. "We have a lot of the same interests, we think alike. She's well-read, she knows a lot about a lot of things. And she's even more conservative than I am!

"Now, I may not know much about dating, but I do know recruiting. I know if you're in that house for five days, something good is happening."

Cathy felt the same way. "Bo's the first man I've completely trusted—ever."

Bo's friends are unanimous: Cathy was the right person at the right time to get Bo back to being Bo. Even President Ford, a former U-M football player, weighed in with his approval. "It seems Bo's got a little extra pep in his step since he met her," he told me.

After more than two decades of Oprah-esque weight fluctuations, Bo says his diet now consists of "skim milk, no sugar, no butter, no fun." Combined with his regular workouts, Bo is now "197 pounds of blue twisted steel," as he says.

"He looks twenty years younger," says John Wangler, one of Bo's favorite quarterbacks, who still talks to his old coach every few weeks. "It's a godsend that those two met. Bo would be miserable by himself. It's great to see him get a chance to finally sit back and enjoy the fruits of his labor. You can just see the light in his eyes."

Contrary to his "football-mad" reputation, Schembechler is interested in virtually everything, from the Ann Arbor bus system to teacher training to racehorse breeding to politics. He's a voracious reader, with a weakness for Tom Clancy books, and also loves music, from Cole Porter to Tina Turner (no kidding). Wherever Bo goes, whatever he's doing, it's a safe bet he's humming some song or other. It resonates in his chest, and occasionally bubbles up to form a verse, which he delivers in a deep baritone, with extra vibrato. "With YOU, I've gone from RAGS to RICHES, I feel like a MILLion-AIRE," then returns to humming while he files some papers.

For all the recent changes, friends will tell you the biggest change since he met Cathy is not his renewed health or spunk, but his attire. "He's dressing a lot sharper since he met Cathy," Wangler says. "He finally got out of all that damn seventies polyester and into the natural fibers, and I'm really impressed."

"If I go into the office," Bo told one audience last week, "I promise you it's going to be an interesting day."

When Bo's in town, he'll drive to Schembechler Hall about 10:00 a.m., park in "Reserved Space 01," and trundle down the second-floor hallway to his office. Schembechler might have been a great coach, but he'd make a terrible spy; he has a complete inability to whisper, sneak up on anyone, or speak anyone's name in lower case letters. "Hey, *Mary!*" he bellows at one end of the hallway, "Howya doin'? Hey, *Big Jon Falk!* What's the good word!"

Schembechler walks into his modest, comfortable office, but before he can even get his black Polo jacket off, the phone starts ringing.

He leans forward, snaps up the handpiece and shouts, "Hel-*lo!* This is *he!* Heyyyyy! How the hell are ya?!" and leans back contentedly in his chair, wearing his famous teeth-clenched grin. Chances are good he's talking to one of his 640 former Michigan players, like Rob Lytle, Tony Gant, or Brad Cochran, all of whom called last week. Or he might be interrupted by visits from Jamie Morris, Rick Leach, or Carlitos Bostic, who stopped by.

Whether they were all-Americans or walk-ons, Schembechler invariably remembers their names, their positions, their hometowns, and what they were up to the last time they talked. Follow him for a few days and you'll hear a dozen people marvel at his ability to remember his former players. Not surprisingly, virtually all of his former players keep in touch.

When his phone conversation ends, no matter what kind of mood he's in, he slams the handpiece down on the receiver like he's spiking a football—*bang!*—every time. Of the dozens of phones in Schembechler Hall, only Bo uses the ancient, chunky model, and it's a good thing: those fancy, sleek devices wouldn't last any longer in Bo's hands than his old headsets.

When Schembechler's not answering calls, he's answering mail—stacks of it. He opens about twenty pieces a day, mostly requests for autographs. These come from charities like the Rock and Jock Celebrity Auction ("I suspect I'm among the rocks," he jokes), or from idolizing fans. They usually neglect to include a photo or a return envelope, which he finds frustrating, but they always include a gushing letter, which he finds embarrassing.

"'Dear Coach,'" he pretends to read, "'You are the greatest person who ever lived in the history of the game.' Man, some of these letters are too much." He also gets letters from old friends ribbing him for some ad they recently saw him on, former players asking for recommendations or inviting them to their wedding, and from lawyers. "I always open the ones from law offices," he cracks.

Second only to the requests for his autograph are the requests for Schembechler's time. When he checks his calendar, he sees a grid filled with about twenty-five hours of commitments each week—interviews, speeches, appearances, recruiting help, foundation work, you name it— and every one of them is highlighted in fluorescent yellow.

"That's so I don't forget 'em!" Schembechler explains.

But Coach, they're *all* highlighted.

"Hey! If I told 'em I'm going to be there, I've gotta be there!"

The phone rings again. It's Ryan White, a writer for U-M's student newspaper. "So, you wanna be a sportswriter?" Bo says, a mischievous grin on his face. "Yeah? Now Ryan: didn't your parents have higher aspirations for you than that?"

He laughs, finishes the interview, and slams the phone down—*bang!*— and it rings again.

"Hel-*lo*! This is *he*! What? Let me get this straight: They want *me* to do a speech for the University of Wisconsin Alumni Club of Milwaukee? Who the hell's idea was that?" After declining, he hangs up—*bang!*—and chuckles. "I can't believe some of these requests."

Bizarre or not, Schembechler answers them all, which is why he rarely leaves the office before 5:30.

Schembechler is mystified by the public's demand for him. "Hey, I'm not Jonas Salk," he says. "Football coaching should not have so much status attached to it."

Schembechler doesn't get it. People are not attracted to him because he was a successful football coach, but because he's *Bo*.

Here's proof: a couple years ago Schembechler received a letter from a university professor in Poland, who read one of Bo's books to improve his teaching. The professor didn't care about Schembechler's Big Ten titles (nor, mercifully, his anemic Rose Bowl record), but about his passion, his humor, and his values.

Winston Churchill once said of Franklin Roosevelt, "Meeting him was like opening your first bottle of champagne." Meeting Schembechler is like busting open a whole crate of the stuff. As much as possible, Schembechler tries to splash himself around so everyone gets a sip. Some men build a fortune over their careers, and spend their retirement giving it away. Schembechler spent his career building a philosophy, which he has been sharing with thousands since he retired.

Despite getting a D in his college speech class at Miami of Ohio ("I was so petrified I skipped class when it was my turn"), Schembechler can now command up to $10,000 for a speech. However, his fee is considerably less for former players, colleagues, and almost anyone who works for the U-M hospital or cancer research: nothing.

One such request came from Craig Mutch, an attorney who played linebacker for Schembechler twenty-three years ago before his knee gave out. When he asked his former coach to give three different speeches in Grand Rapids last week, Bo readily agreed.

"I gotta admit, I like this kid an awful lot," Schembechler explains on the drive to Grand Rapids. But when he sees Mutch, he doesn't tell him that. Instead, he growls, "You're late!"

"No, I'm not!" Mutch says. "I've been here for twenty minutes!" But he can't help checking his watch to reassure himself—three times.

"Okay, you're safe," Bo says. He smacks Mutch in the chest. "God, you look skinny. I hope you're not going around telling people you played linebacker for Michigan!"

After catching up over some iced tea, Mutch escorts Schembechler to

Grand Rapids Christian High School, where his son plays tight end. A few adults walk over to expound on Bo's legacy. Bo listens politely, but lets it all blow past him without comment.

"I hate that stuff," he tells me later. "It's embarrassing."

Bo is much more comfortable joshing with the kids. To one player he says, "Your dad's a judge? Well I guess *you* ain't getting away with much!" and pokes him in the chest.

In front of Craig Mutch's son, Bo asks the head coach, "Tell me about Chris Mutch: is he worth a damn? Because his dad sure wasn't."

When Bo addresses the Eagle players, he says, "Let's listen up here, men. My name's Schembechler. How many of you remember who I am?" They all raise their hands, which surprises the famous coach. He talks for about fifteen minutes about teamwork, honesty, fundamental values; how integrity, above all else, is what they should be getting out of football.

Then he gets to the business at hand. "Gentlemen, your record is not good. One and five is nothing to brag about. My understanding is you've been close in a lot of games, but haven't quite pulled it off. The difference between winning and losing is a little more hard work—then you start winning those games. There is no greater feeling in all the world than to go back to that locker room with your teammates after a victory. You'll know then that the extra effort is worth it.

"I hope you win those last three games—and I'll be checking on you!"

His message apparently sunk in. Two days later the Christian Eagles crushed their opponent, 46–6.

After Schembechler's talk to the team, Mutch whisks Schembechler to a reception for the boosters, where Bo spends an hour kibitzing with the guests before speaking.

Hobie Loranger, thirty-five, is one of the sixty people who spent $100 to attend this fundraiser for the Grand Rapids Christian football team. Loranger sports a maize-and-blue Nike shirt, a ready smile, and a stainless-steel wheelchair he's been using since a car accident paralyzed his legs when he was fifteen. He tried to attend Michigan, but found getting around the expansive campus too difficult. But, thanks to Michigan Stadium's user-friendly ramps and platforms, Hobie's been going to Michigan's football games for more than two decades. Three years ago he met his wife, Tammy, in a Grand Rapids bookstore; today he's about to meet the man he calls a "god."

As soon as he sees Hobie, Bo says, "Hey there!" He shakes Hobie's hand, and asks his name. "Hey, Hobie!" Bo points to the Michigan helmet in Hobie's lap. "Betcha want me to sign that? Well then that's what we'll do." Bo also signs Hobie's videotape, *The Schembechler Years*, then tells him, "You gotta watch this once a year!"

"That's all I wanted for Christmas this year," Hobie happily confesses.

"Aw, c'mon, Hob! You gotta want more than that!" Bo cracks, and they both laugh. Bo asks Hobie where he works, how he likes it, and what he thought of the Northwestern game. In mere seconds Schembechler has transformed their relationship from one of a god and his disciple to just a couple guys talking Michigan football.

Bo is pleasantly surprised to see two of Mutch's former Michigan team-mates, Jim Hackett and Gerry Szara, at the reception. They should know by now that they will be fair game.

"Everyone asks what I'm doing these days," Bo says to open his informal talk to the boosters, "and it seems that I'm as busy as you people with jobs!

"Since I retired it's very difficult for me to say no to one of my players, especially a guy like Craig. Everyone says Michigan players are just getting ready for the pros, but look at these three guys," he gestures behind himself to his former players. "These guys weren't in it for a pro contract—and it's a damn good thing! The objective is to have a meaningful experience, to learn how to play together, to fight together, as a team—and that's all good. So I think you're doing the right thing supporting your football program. I really think I missed something by not coaching high school kids—because they'll listen to you!"

After telling a half-dozen stories, Schembechler says for the third time, "Okay, this is going to be my last story!" and the crowd laughs again.

"This past weekend I went down to Ohio State for the thirty-fifth reunion of the 1961 Buckeye team, which Woody coached and I assisted. The organizers said, 'We've invited you every five years and you've never come because there's always some Michigan game that weekend. Well, we checked your schedule this time, and Michigan ain't playing. You're coming down for the Wisconsin game!'

"So I'm in the stands sitting next to Ann Hayes [Woody's widow]. She's eighty-three, and she's still coaching up a storm—'Bo, they should've done that, and Bo, they should've done this.' The reunion guys tell me, 'Bo, we're going to introduce you at halftime.'

"I said, 'I don't think you guys understand.'" He waits for the laughter to subside. "'Like hell you are! They're going to boo me out of there!'"

"'Oh, no they're not,' they tell me. 'They really want to see you!'

"So they announce my name—and sure enough, the crowd boos me! At the reception afterword I said, 'I *told* you guys they'd boo me!'

"And they said, 'No, no, Bo—that was the *Wisconsin* fans!'"

When the laughter finally dies down, Bo asks, "Okay, any questions?"

"Hey Bo, are you still in the pizza business?"

Bo claps his hands and says, "That ends this little speech!" The crowd erupts. He chuckles and waves goodbye, then heads out the door for his next speech.

On the drive to the Calvin College auditorium, Bo says, "Now, think about that Hackett for a minute. He didn't play much, but he worked hard, and I loved that kid. Now he's the CEO of Steelcase, the largest manufacturer of office equipment in the world, and every one of his fourteen hundred employees—from the janitors to the vice presidents—can call him up and get an appointment.

"Wouldn't you be proud if you had three great kids like those guys? Jesus! Wonderful!"

After being introduced at the Calvin College auditorium, Schembechler gives them the ten commandments of teamwork, Bo style. Although the speech is tailor-made for a corporate meeting, its universal themes of self-lessness, commitment, loyalty, and goal-setting are eagerly absorbed by the diverse group of five hundred people who paid five dollars each to attend.

Unlike a lot of corporate speeches, there's nothing calculated or cynical about Schembechler's message. Everything Schembechler says he believes in passionately, and has experienced firsthand. The speech is a classic—a local radio host will play it on his show the next morning—but Bo's delivery is just as fascinating.

Everything Bo's college speech teacher tried in vain to teach him, he does naturally now. He builds resonance by repeating phrases. He gradually raises his voice to a crescendo, then suddenly brings it down to a hush. He walks casually around the stage, then plants his feet firmly on the edge of the broad stage to make his point. He rattles off a litany of evidence, then stops cold for the conclusion. If you remember the opening scene of *Patton*, in which George C. Scott delivers his famous speech in front of a huge American flag, you're halfway there.

"You must have a job description for *every single player*," he says, punctuating the sentence with his finger. "If I'm talking to Anthony Carter, your job is to catch a lot of passes and score a bunch of touchdowns. If I'm talking to Craig Mutch . . ." Bo gestures toward Mutch sitting down on the stage, shrugs his shoulders, and puts his palms up, then lets the laughter roll over the two of them.

"Hey, look at Jim Hackett, CEO of Steelcase. Look at Gerry Szara, director of human resources at Steelcase. Look at Mutch—he's a lawyer, and I apologize for that."

By nine-thirty, Schembechler has talked for ninety minutes, without a single lapse in energy or focus. Schembechler never goes longer than ten minutes without pulling your heartstrings or tapping your funny bone. The audience has tracked his entire speech. His masterful performance makes you wonder: what are the guys who got As in that college speech class doing now?

"Have I talked long enough?" he asks, looking at his watch. "My god! I've talked over an hour! And you should *never* do that—especially when you're not getting paid!"

After another rousing close, Schembechler receives his third standing ovation of the evening.

When he stops at a restaurant on the way home, he doesn't talk of the audience response, his busy day, or the money raised for Mutch's group. He talks about Hobie Loranger, the thirty-five-year-old car accident survivor in the wheelchair. Bo is still impressed by Loranger's pluck and good humor.

"Ol' Hob," Bo says, shaking his head, grinning. (The two would stay in touch the rest of Bo's life.)

When it's time to recharge his batteries, Schembechler returns to his humble office in Ann Arbor. He's not there to bask in his accomplishments, but in the camaraderie of old friends who know they can find him there.

"My memories are not in a plaque or a trophy or a ring," he says, explaining why none of those things are displayed in his house, in his office, or on his hands. "Mine are running into someone I coached or worked with. That's the best way to have memories."

This is not to say Bo's reminiscing would be appropriate on a Hallmark card. Most of Bo's friends can take it and dish it out with equal aplomb. Shrinking violets don't last long around these offices.

When retired assistant coach Tirrell Burton walks into his office, Bo takes him on immediately.

"Burton, if you had a *backbone* in your body—which you don't!—if you weren't gutless, yellow, and just plain *scared*, Burton—you'd be *man* enough to do battle with Bo Schembechler on the golf course!"

"Just so long as I give you fourteen strokes, right?"

"Yeah, that too," Bo says.

Schembechler sees veteran U-M equipment manager Jon Falk walk past his open door, and yells, "Hey, *Falk!*"

Falk comes in, and within seconds they start swapping stories.

"Best story about Falk," Bo says. "A couple days after I left for the Tigers, I came down here to work out, and my name had already been removed from my locker! I said, 'Jon, what the hell is this?' And he just shrugs and gives me a line from *The Natural*: 'They come and they go, Hobbs, they come and they go.'"

They come and they go, but Bo came back.

Everyone knows where to find him, just like the old days.

"I think that's the real reason he came back here," Lynn Koch confides. The secretaries say you can't count how many of his old players return to see him.

And if Schembechler feels like taking a break from all the calls and the letters, he'll yell, "'Hey, Koch! C'mon in here!' And we'll just talk," Koch says. "He's the kind of person—and there aren't many—that you could just sit down and listen to for hours."

Even fewer people are honest—truly honest, all the time, to everyone, regardless of the cost. Henry David Thoreau once wrote that he'd happily walk several miles through the woods just to meet such a man.

If there's one thing every player and colleague of Bo's agrees on, it's this: "You may not always like it, but with Bo, you always know where you stand." Honesty has become so rare in a society that prefers image over substance, glad-handing over conviction, that Bo's bedrock values seem almost extreme to us now.

What's more surprising is how likable, how compassionate, how humble he is when you meet him in person. As they say, some men are like mountains: the closer you get to them, the greater they are. Schembechler impresses people not by playing the star, but simply by being one of the guys.

Bear Bryant used to lord over his visitors by sitting behind a six-by-eight-foot desk, and looking down on them sitting in a soft couch, two feet lower.

Schembechler takes the opposite approach. When he was still coaching, Bo used to help out the Special Olympics in town by playing basketball with mentally handicapped kids. He loved it because they had no idea who he was, and didn't care.

"I was just some old guy who came down to play basketball with them."

And that's how Schembechler sees himself now: Just some guy who coached football.

We know better.

TOM IZZO: IRON MOUNTAIN MAN

A few months after my first interview with Bo Schembechler, I met Tom Izzo in his office. We were scheduled to talk for 30 minutes, but three hours later, we were still talking. People forget that he was still not very popular in the midst of his second season as MSU's head coach, which would end with the Spartans finishing in the bottom half of the league again, leaving plenty of people doubting he could do the job. But after meeting him, I had no doubt. He was confident, direct, and down-to-earth, with a captivating energy. This first interview led to many others over the past two decades, and I've enjoyed every one of them.

As we're going to press, we still don't know the outcome of the various investigations at Michigan State, nor how they might impact Tom Izzo. But I stand by my impressions of the man at the time I wrote this, 21 years ago.

January 12, 1997
The Detroit News

After a twelve-year apprenticeship, the crown prince finally became king—but Tom Izzo's long, rigorous climb to become Michigan State's head basketball coach reads more like *Coal Miner's Daughter* than a basketball biography.

Izzo's arrival to the coaching big time is one of the unlikelier stories you'll find in college basketball. It's a story of long odds and hard knocks, offset by incredible tenacity and loyal support.

The key to Tom Izzo, forty-five, lies 585 miles all the way back to Iron Mountain, Michigan, a town of about fifteen thousand people built on the old iron mines in the Upper Peninsula. Izzo's great-grandfather worked in those mines, and was killed in one. His grandfather was a shoe cobbler, and his dad did everything from installing carpets to fixing awnings—and he's still doing it.

When his father was about the age Tom is now, he went back to high school, not night school, to get his diploma. He graduated, then ran for president of the Iron Mountain School Board—and won.

"I've been lucky," Izzo says of his blue-collar background. "My parents gave their kids discipline. People work hard up there, they're straight with you. You've been brought up that way, and that's the only way you know. It's in your blood."

Izzo has also received constant support from his best friend, Iron Mountain native Steve Mariucci, now the 49ers' head football coach.

"I was at the Catholic grade school and he was at the public school," Mariucci remembers, "and he was the star down there, and I hated his guts."

They got over it when they became high school classmates. "The day we became teammates in high school," Izzo recalls, "was the day we became best friends."

Izzo drew on that friendship after each setback—and there were many. In 1972, when the two were high school juniors, their team made it to the Upper Peninsula basketball finals. With seconds to go and Iron Mountain trailing by one point, Izzo was fouled at the buzzer, putting him on the line for a one-and-one free throw attempt.

The five-eight point guard had already scored sixteen of his team's fifty points—but he missed the first foul shot, sending his team down to defeat and young Tom Izzo down to the hardwood, crying.

"Oh geez, I had to pick him off the ground," Mariucci recalls.

When Izzo failed to receive any scholarship offers, the school's assistant principal put a call in to the late Glen Brown, the Northern Michigan basketball coach, and said, "This kid's lower than a snake's belly. Can you give him a shot?"

Izzo and Mariucci both walked on at NMU, Izzo in basketball and Mariucci in football, and given their prospects, both probably should have walked off.

"It was a rough, rough year," Mariucci says of their first season on campus. "But misery loves company. We kind of fed off each other. It was almost a contest to see who could work harder. We ran and lifted every day when the other guys were out partying—this was the seventies, remember—and you'd have to say, 'What's wrong with these guys?' We once took a maximum oxygen intake test, and the only other athletes on campus who could compete with us were the cross-country skiers."

Still, Izzo languished on the freshman team. Northern had a combined twenty-five players on the varsity and freshman teams, but when injuries and eligibility problems set in, the numbers dwindled.

"We had only thirteen guys left on the varsity and five guys on the freshmen team," Izzo remembers. "We always traveled with fourteen, so I figured, heck, I *gotta* make it by default. I came up to locker room, saw the list on the wall, and everyone's name was on it but mine!

"When we had twenty-five guys on the roster and I wasn't traveling, I could pretend I was better than five or six guys. But when it was down to nobody left and I still wasn't traveling, I couldn't pretend anymore."

He couldn't quit, either. Through his tenacity and Mariucci's support, Izzo climbed from the twenty-fifth man on a twenty-five-man team to team captain, MVP, and Third Team Division II All-American by his senior year.

"I think I can always get up one more time than I'm knocked down."

Fortunately for Izzo, his coaching career progressed faster—at first. After graduating from NMU in 1977, he became the head coach of Ishpeming High School, got an overachieving team into the regional finals, then returned to Northern as an assistant the next season. Four years of good work there put him on the coaching map, and some money in his bank account.

He needed that money when he accepted the post of MSU's part-time assistant in 1983, which paid $7,000 a year.

"He was broke!" recalls his former boss, Jud Heathcote.

Izzo became Heathcote's full-time assistant in 1986, when Izzo was thirty-one. He quickly made a name for himself as a top recruiter. In a field rampant with fast-talking, sleazy coaches providing illegal incentives and false promises, Izzo tried a completely different approach: He decided to tell kids the truth, promise them only an opportunity to succeed, and offer them nothing but a college scholarship.

It was just crazy enough to work.

Former Spartan great Mike Peplowski recalls his first contact with Izzo in 1986, when Izzo was in his first year as a full-time assistant and Peplowski was just a freshman at De LaSalle.

"Where everyone was going for the hard sell," Peplowski remembers, "sending me all kinds of junk mail, Coach Izzo called me up one afternoon, and said, 'Listen, I've just been put in charge of recruiting here, and I want to know how you want me to handle it.'

"I said, 'Don't call me at home, I'll call you. Send me letters and I'll read 'em, but not the junk mail, and send everything to the high school.' He said if I ever want to come up and visit, give him a call. I was also looking at Indiana and Purdue, but Michigan State won out because, right off the bat, he respected my wishes."

"I'm just a regular guy," Izzo explains. "When I'm recruiting, I figure people want to be treated honestly, with respect, same as me. I try to be as positive as I can be, but I don't sugarcoat anything. A lot of guys tell 'em what they want to hear, but I'm not going to do that."

That approach works just as well now that Izzo's the head coach. His first two recruiting classes were both ranked in the top twenty-five. A white guy coming into the inner city being honest and caring about a player's future is not something such kids see very often. Izzo's biggest catch so far, Mateen Cleaves, came to MSU because of Izzo.

"He just came to me from his heart," Cleaves says. "He didn't tell me what I wanted to hear. He was honest with me—and *that* was very unusual. Man, some of these coaches will tell you they're gonna name a TV show after you, whatever you want to hear, just to get you to sign."

The 1992 *Sports Illustrated* college basketball preview issue called Izzo "One of the top evaluators of high school talent." He was gaining a big reputation for his recruiting skills, strong integrity, and energetic work in practice. But Heathcote was not just the head coach, he was a legend. Izzo would have to wait his turn.

"The younger (assistant) coaches nowadays don't realize you have to be aggressive, sure, but also patient," Izzo says.

He was. And it might have been his best move.

"I probably coached two years longer than I intended," Heathcote says today. "But I worked hard to help get Tom the head coaching job. I'm convinced if I had quit when I originally intended, Tom would not have gotten the job because he lacked head coaching experience. But he's clearly the right guy for the job."

Early in Izzo's first season as head coach, 1995–96, it might not have seemed so. The Spartans won only three of their first seven games, their worst start in sixteen years. Izzo didn't panic, finishing his first year with a respectable 16–16 record, 9–9 in the Big Ten.

"Tom was in a learning process," Heathcote said. "He had to go from making suggestions to making decisions, but he's kind of like a sponge, always learning. If Tom has a fault, it's that he almost works himself into exhaustion. But I wouldn't say Tom is old shoe. I'd say Tom's a modern workaholic."

Izzo clearly respects and appreciates Heathcote, but he recognizes his style can't be the same as his mentor's.

"The difference between Jud's generation and mine is that my era has to explain things more," he says. "If there's one thing I want to do a little differently, it's in practice. If I want to yell and scream, I will, but kids today don't react well to criticism in front of others."

Peplowski, who had Heathcote for a head coach and Izzo for an assistant, said, "Jud was the biggest jerk I knew in my entire life—there's no other way to put it. What's more important than all of that is that he was that way for a reason. That's why I became the player I did. Izzo could get on you too, but he had the ability to smooth things over."

A couple years ago a few players missed class, so Izzo sat them out of the next game, and left the players to explain the situation to the press.

"You want to build a program that will last," Izzo told me. "The program is bigger than the players, it's bigger than the coaches. I almost *want* those guys to be a little embarrassed. They'll learn."

In these situations Izzo recalls the advice he received from Buck Nystrom, the retired NMU football coach, when Izzo became MSU's head coach. "He called me and said, 'Izzo! Remember this: *all* kids *want* to be disciplined—doesn't matter where they're from or who their parents are.' I believe that. Discipline is a form of love."

If that's so, Izzo's players receive a lot of love.

"He expects a lot from us, and we know that," Cleaves says. "All he asks of all of us is that we work. But if you work hard for him, he's 110-percent behind you."

Despite the blue-collar ethic, Izzo is still considered a player's coach. He has also somehow managed to get at least ten players in each game. The uncommonly generous approach creates more headaches for Izzo, but it motivates those players on the court and on the bench.

"We know we're going to get in," Cleaves says, "and the guys who're in know they're not gonna stay in for the whole game—so everybody works harder."

"I work for you, you work for me," Izzo says. "It's a simple marriage."

If you want to see Izzo work, really work, you need only watch him during a game. Even sitting by himself on the sidelines before tip-off, Izzo looks like a man sitting in a rocket ship about to blast off to the moon. Relaxed, he is not—but neither is he nervous. Just intense.

Very, very intense.

During a game Izzo's face is as taut as a trampoline. Pizza Hut could give out free pizzas each time Izzo smiled and not hand out a single one. When his players complete a beautiful, textbook pass play ending in a ferocious dunk, Izzo simply drops his head and walks away from the play—as close as he comes to a celebration.

Whatever the fans are doing, it's a safe bet Izzo is doing the opposite. If they cheer, he looks down; if they moan about a turnover, he frantically points out what needs to happen next; if they yell at the ref, he yells at his player. The crazier things are, the calmer he is—and the calmer things are, the more frantic he becomes.

"I try to act on what's needed," he says. "If people are celebrating, they don't need me to celebrate. If the guys are quiet, they need me to get 'em going."

Unlike most of his peers, however, Izzo rarely gets frustrated or nasty. He's just trying to squeeze every drop of effort out of his team.

"He'll yell, but he won't get in your face," one referee said. "We told 'em last year, 'Tom, you got to slow it down, you're gonna have a heart attack.' But he can't stop. That's just how he is. He wants it so bad."

"This school and this administration are so good, I just gotta believe we can win it here," Izzo says. "There are so many positives, that if I can't get it done, they *should* fire me. You gotta get breaks, and I got one, and I'm gonna run with the SOB as far as I can."

Those who know how far Izzo has already run to become Michigan State's head coach would never bet against him running all the way to a national title.

CAROL HUTCHINS:
THE BIGGEST WINNER ON CAMPUS

June 1, 2012
Michigan Today

This spring, the University of Michigan women's softball team won its fifteenth Big Ten title, and fifth in a row. It went to the NCAA tournament for the eighteenth straight season, and won its fourteenth NCAA regional crown, before losing on Friday in the super-regional to third-ranked Alabama.

In other words, just another typical season for Michigan softball—a team led by Carol Hutchins, one of Michigan's best coaches, of any sport, in any era. Winning titles is what they do—and this was not even one of Hutchins' best teams.

That's how well this machine runs—and make no mistake, it *is* a machine. Hutchins' teams have won more Big Ten titles than the rest of the conference *combined*. But it's a machine she put together, part by part, one that took years of tinkering just to win its first race.

That Hutchins even got the chance was a bit of a miracle. She grew up in Lansing, the fifth of six kids. Her mom didn't see the point in her playing sports, let alone competing. But Hutchins refused to quit.

She attended Lansing Everett High School, where she shared the court with a young man named Earvin Johnson, better known as Magic. Even in high school the differences between men's and women's sports were glaring. Magic's team got nice home and away uniforms and practiced after school. Hutchins's team wore reversible "pinnies," and practiced late at night.

When both Magic and Hutchins enrolled at Michigan State, the contrast became even greater. The men's basketball team traveled by private plane, and stayed two to a room in nice hotels. The women drove rented vans, and slept four to a room at the cheapest places they could find.

But none of this dampened Hutchins's love for sports. She switched from basketball to softball, and from the Spartans to the Wolverines. When she interviewed at Michigan for a position split between assistant softball coach and administrative assistant, former athletic director Don Canham asked her one question: "Can you type?"

Hutchins thought about it for a moment, then replied with complete conviction, "Yes. Yes I can." Except, of course, she couldn't. If she had told the truth, however, Michigan would have missed out on its all-time winningest coach in any sport.

Fresh off her master's degree, Hutchins received a whopping $3,000 her first year, which had her mom shaking her head all over again. Two years later, Hutchins became Michigan's head softball coach. In 1992, her eighth season, her team won its first Big Ten regular season title—and her teams have won fourteen times since, falling short only six times.

But the national crown proved far more elusive, with Hutchins' teams getting eliminated in their first eight Women's College World Series appearances. Finally, in 2005, her team became the first softball squad east of Oklahoma and north of Cal-Berkeley to win an NCAA title—about as stunning as a hockey team from Alabama beating all the Northern teams for the national title.

How does she do it? First, her players love her, and so do her assistants. The seniors cry at their banquet, realizing a great phase of their lives has just ended. Her assistants never leave, despite getting good offers to go elsewhere.

When you're on her team, you get to see her goofy side—"and no one else gets to see that," recent graduate Kristin Larsen says.

During a road trip, Larsen managed to get Hutch and the team hooked on *The Office*. When they got back to Michigan, they set up a camera in the clubhouse for "confessionals," and the players would actually tape these during games—including a ten-run inning to cap a come-from-behind victory during the 2008 NCAA regionals. A few days later, Hutch herself showed up for practice dressed as Dwight—and the players howled.

When you get to third base, Hutch—as even her players call her—gives you peanut M&Ms out of her back pocket. Hit a homer, and she tosses a few in the air for you to catch as you round third.

This is not to say Hutch is always warm and fuzzy. Her high standards on and off the field are non-negotiable, and while she's not a big yeller, her glare is something all her players work to avoid. But ultimately, her secret is developing young women who can motivate themselves to excel.

Former athletic director Bill Martin said, "If every coach at Michigan was stamped out of the same mold as Hutch, you wouldn't need an athletic director. Her kids thrive in the classroom, and she's a great colleague and mentor to other coaches. She was an absolute pleasure to work with—except after a loss."

For ten years, Martin's office was right next to hers. He quickly learned, on a Monday after Hutchins' team lost even one of the four games that weekend, "Don't come in. She is a big grump!"

Well, as Woody Hayes often said: Show me a good loser, and I'll show you a busboy. Hutch's mom should be glad to know: her daughter is no busboy.

HARBAUGH COMES HOME

August 13, 2015
The Wall Street Journal

It's seems like eons ago now, but in the summer of 2014, Michigan football coach Brady Hoke appeared poised for a solid season. With eight or nine wins, Hoke's job would be safe, athletic director Dave Brandon would give him a contract extension, and the Brandon-Hoke Era would continue for many years.

On the West Coast, everyone expected Jim Harbaugh's 49ers to make their fourth straight trip to the playoffs and perhaps their fourth straight NFC title game.

So, in the summer of 2014, the idea that Harbaugh would return to Michigan any time soon seemed ridiculous. Even if Michigan's head coaching position somehow magically opened, the experts said Harbaugh would stay in the NFL. But that last theory took a hit on a summer weekend in Northern Michigan.

In mid-July, when Jim and Sarah Harbaugh traveled to Northern Michigan for a wedding, they flew in a day early to spend the evening with Todd Anson, a San Diego attorney, his wife, Terri, and a dozen or so of Anson's friends, including yours truly. I had gotten to know Todd while researching my previous two books.

At about six p.m., the entire party boarded the S.S. *Boike*, a pontoon boat with ample bench seating and a couple of coolers. The boat's owner, Bill Boike, just happened to have a recording of "The Victors" handy, and couldn't resist blaring it through the speakers.

The passengers hadn't gotten too far into Michigan's fight song when Boike's boat encountered another boat with a few Spartans on it, and their green flag flying high. It turned out they just happened to have their own fight song ready to blast, while the two boats raced down the lake—for reasons I still can't understand, but whatever. When Harbaugh stood up to lead his boat singing "The Victors," the S.S. *Boike* won the battle of the bands.

Defeated, the Spartans turned their boat around, while a young lady stood up and proudly mooned us as they took off.

When Harbaugh sat down, he was thrilled. "This stuff just doesn't happen in the NFL!" I realized you probably don't have boats with 49ers flags and Raiders flags racing each other in San Francisco Bay, with their fight songs blaring. They don't even have fight songs.

Harbaugh turned to his wife and said, "You've got to learn this song!"

"Jim was *sooo* happy," Sarah told me later. "It was easy to see he still felt very much connected, and excited!"

Even the notoriously unpredictable Michigan weather, which turned chilly and gray that evening, couldn't dampen Harbaugh's enthusiasm. When he told Sarah he loved this type of weather, and hated the way the sun always beat down on you in California—things you don't hear too many people say—she just smiled and nodded.

After the other guests had left, Todd, Jim, and I stayed up until 2 a.m., catching up and talking about mutual friends, Ann Arbor, and Michigan football. In the middle of our conversation, Harbaugh said, "I think it's great to grow up in a college town, don't you?"

Yes, yes it is, I thought. Why do you ask, man with three young children?

"He's said that many times to me," Sarah later told me. "'Wouldn't it be great to raise our kids in a college town?' Palo Alto is great, but it's not really a college town like Ann Arbor. That's always been in the back of his mind."

There were still a dozen of obstacles between Harbaugh and the Michigan coaching job. Only a lunatic would have made that bet in July of 2014.

But that night, two bits of conventional wisdom—that the Harbaughs were unwilling to leave California and the NFL, and they had no interest in Michigan—were revealed as illusions. They did not exist.

It turned out the exact opposite was true. Harbaugh had never lost his feeling for Michigan, and his desire to coach there was as strong as ever.

That's what Michigan's interim athletic director, Jim Hackett, was betting on. When he fired Brady Hoke after he finished the 2014 season 5–7, the national press kept saying Michigan had no chance at Harbaugh, the wheels were coming off Hackett's head coaching search, and Michigan didn't have a clue. Hackett showed considerable restraint and confidence in ignoring all of it, and keeping his eye on the prize.

Over the next four weeks, Hackett and Harbaugh had long talks on Saturday nights, and occasionally other times, developing a good rapport. (To avoid anything leaking to the media, Hackett always referred to Harbaugh internally as "Unicorn," another indication of where Hackett placed Jim on their list: the one-of-a-kind dream candidate.)

"The interesting thing is," Hackett told me, "we never talked specifically about Jim being head coach. We talked about what Michigan needed. After a few weeks of this, we're going back and forth and getting really excited about the possibilities, and Jim says, 'We're getting excited about this, aren't we?'

"Yes, we are," Hackett said.

"You didn't offer me the job, did you?" Harbaugh asked.

"No, I haven't."

"I didn't accept, did I?"

"No, you didn't."

It wasn't an agreement, by design, Hackett says, "But that gave me the confidence, no matter what pressure the media was putting on me, I could stick to my guns."

At one point in their conversations, "I shared with him my time line," Hackett says. "'Here's my walk away date: Saturday, December 27, 2014.'"

Day by day, it became clearer to Hackett that Harbaugh was sincerely interested in leading Michigan's program, and Harbaugh certainly didn't have to wonder if Hackett, or just about anyone else who mattered, wanted him to do so.

But by Saturday, December 27, 2014, the day before Harbaugh's last game as the coach of the 49ers—who were not going to make the playoffs for the first time since Harbaugh took over in 2011—Hackett still didn't have a contract, or any ironclad assurance from Harbaugh that he'd be signing one. That date also happened to be Hackett's self-declared "walkaway day," when he promised himself he'd stop pursuing Harbaugh and move on to his next candidate.

"I figured the minute Jim's season was done," Hackett told me, "he'd be open season for the NFL teams, and he'd get flooded with offers that night. So I wanted to make Saturday my day."

Hackett dialed up Harbaugh for their weekly phone call. It was no longer about relationship building. Hackett needed an answer—a firm one.

"I need to trust you Jim, and I need to know if you're going to come back to Michigan."

"I need to finish my commitment here," Harbaugh said, "so I can't sign anything until we finish the season here. You understand that, yes?"

"Yes, I do," Hackett said.

"So I can't sign yet," Harbaugh repeated. But then he said the words

Hackett—and three million Michigan fans—longed to hear: "But I want to come."

Hackett needed a clear answer. Then, he recalls, "There followed a long pause. Long pause. Long pause. Finally, Jim says, 'Yes.'"

"That's enough for me," Hackett said.

Looking back on it, Hackett says, "I don't know in business if I would have done that, just accepted a verbal commitment. If I have the commitment with no contract, I'd be facing a lot of heat from the Regents and others—but I would explain: 'Look, this is Michigan, and two guys who played for Bo. If we get to the point where we both get excited, and this is for God and country, I have to trust that.'

"But with this system—Michigan football—I knew I could, because it was a system we'd both been raised in. We know what it means. We know how we're to conduct ourselves. I had faith that he learned what I learned—that your word has to be good. There is a currency we could call on as Michigan Men."

Proving the early rumors false, Sarah was on board, with both feet. When Todd Anson's army of friends, former teammates, and childhood idols started calling Jim, and even saying on TV how much they wanted him back in Ann Arbor, "That's when I said, 'Wow, they really want you!'" Sarah recalls telling her husband. "'Very few people can do that in a lifetime, be that person that everyone wants. You gotta go!'

"A lot of people say, 'You made it to the top, you've got to stay at the top,'" she told me. "Not that he's taking a step down by coming to Michigan, but he's pursuing something that he always he felt was his destiny.

"It happened so fast, I was in shock. But not for one minute did I not see the good in coming to Ann Arbor. We were in a great place, but I'm coming back home in a sense. I'm Midwestern, and I always will be.

"Say you have this guy pursuing you and he's in love with you, but he hasn't come out and said it yet, he's just admiring you from afar. But you're dating this big macho guy who gets all the ladies, but he doesn't treat you right. And you finally come out and say it, and decide to give the other guy a chance, this nice guy just waiting, and that's when you realize it's a match made in heaven.

"And you ask yourself, 'Why didn't I go out with this person ten years ago?' Well, maybe it wasn't the right time yet.

"Michigan was that guy, who loved you the whole time. So you finally say yes, and you can't believe you didn't say yes years ago.

"It was such a fragile process for everyone. If it had not been handled just that way—if you had someone who was pushing you, not letting you make the decision, not giving you your space—I don't think it would have happened.

"Feeling the love. That's what it came down to."

On Monday, December 29, 2014, just minutes before Harbaugh got on the plane that would take him, Sarah, and three of their kids from California to Michigan, he signed the long contract.

The same reporters who said Harbaugh would never return to Michigan were now convinced Hackett must have offered Harbaugh a record contract. Harbaugh repeatedly told his friends, however, that "It's not about the money."

It turns out he meant it: Harbaugh's Michigan contract is roughly the same as his deal with the 49ers—about $5 million a year, plus incentives, including a $2 million signing bonus. It didn't exactly qualify as a vow of poverty, but it was undoubtedly less than several NFL teams would have been eager to pay. Harbaugh didn't even try to find out, immediately letting the NFL teams know he had committed to Michigan, ending the dance before it started.

The morning of Harbaugh's introductory press conference, Hackett told me, "Jim *insisted* that he not be the highest paid coach in college football, or even the Big Ten. I think that tells you something about his values."

When I asked Harbaugh about this, he said, "Let's not make this sound more noble than it is. I'm not on the same dance floor as Mother Teresa. I like a buck as much as the next guy. I wouldn't kill for it, I wouldn't marry for it, I wouldn't cheat for it, I wouldn't steal for it. But I'm open to *earning* it.

"But," he added, "I would say that I didn't pick Michigan because I thought they were going to pay me the most. We didn't wait around for teams to start some bidding war, or even make offers."

The decision was simpler than that, he said.

"Earlier that week, I was talking to my dad on the phone, and I finally cut to the chase. 'Well, whatya think, Dad?'"

"Well, Jim," his dad said, "you make great decisions; you always have. I'm not going to tell you what to do. Follow your heart."

"And that," Jim Harbaugh said, "is what I did."

Some jobs are for God and country.

This was one of them.

Michigan had its man.

RED BERENSON DID IT ALL, WITH HONOR

April 13, 2017
The PostGame

This week, Michigan hockey coach Gordon "Red" Berenson announced he was retiring after thirty-three years behind the bench. He leaves behind the greatest legacy in Michigan hockey's long and enviable history, but it all hinged on a couple lucky moments.

Berenson loved the game from the start. When he was a six-year-old kid in Regina, Saskatchewan, for Christmas his parents gave him new skates, new gloves, and new shin pads. He was so excited, he called his best friend on the party line—at 6:00 a.m.

When his friend's mom answered, she asked, "Do you know what time it is?"

Berenson replied, "Yes—but this is important!"

Hockey has always been important to Berenson. And if you grew up in Regina, Saskatchewan, it probably would be to you, too. Regina, the provincial capital, is a tight circle of a city with no sprawl to speak of, which 180,000 farmers, politicians, and businessmen call home. For more than a century, Regina's main businesses have been grain and government, neither of which are terribly thrilling to watch grow.

But if you're a hockey fan—or better yet, a hockey player—Regina's the place to be. The list of Saskatchewan natives who've played in the NHL runs twelve pages long, a remarkable feat for the only province west of the Maritimes that's never had an NHL franchise. The list includes Sid Abel, Ace Bailey, Johnny Bower, Glenn Hall, Eddie Shore, Bryan Trottier, Theo Fleury, and a guy from a tiny town called Floral—a town so small it's not even listed on the atlas index—named Gordie Howe.

Berenson and his friends would skate outdoors on Regina's natural rinks and ponds all day, and go home for dinner with their skates on so they could rush back out to play some more as soon as they were excused from the table. When the snow drifted up to the top of the boards they shoveled it off, and when the forty-mile-per-hour winds rushed across the plains from Alaska, they leaned into it and kept skating.

"Some days," Berenson recalls, "skating into that wind felt like you were going uphill."

When Berenson was still in high school, the Montreal Canadiens' general manager, Frank Selke, for whom the NHL named an award for the league's best defensive forward, invited him to turn pro as soon as he graduated. But the staunchly independent Berenson decided to conduct a thorough investigation of U.S. colleges first. In the spring of twelfth grade, he and his hockey buddies trotted down to the only library in town to find out which college had the best combination of academics and hockey. Berenson knew the college for him when he saw it.

"It was pretty clear Michigan stood at the top," he says. "After I came down on a visit, I came back and told the other guys, 'This is where we're going.'" And just like that, a pipeline of fourteen blue-chip hockey players was formed between Regina and Ann Arbor.

When Berenson told Frank Selke, the Montreal GM who had drafted Berenson, about his decision, Selke warned him, "If you go to an American college, you'll never become a pro."

Fully aware he might be sacrificing the dream of every Canadian boy to play in the NHL—and for the Montreal Canadiens, no less—Berenson didn't flinch. After sitting out the two semesters the NCAA required then, and playing one semester for the Canadian national team, Berenson suited up for his first college game on February 5, 1960, against Minnesota.

"Ninety seconds into his first game he takes it all the way down the ice and scores," his former coach Al Renfrew recalled. Minnesota head coach John Mariucci yelled to Renfrew, "'Man, at this rate we're going to lose, 60–0!'"

Almost. Berenson assisted on another goal five minutes later and scored a third later in the game. They had just seen the future of Michigan hockey, and it looked bright indeed.

Berenson scored forty-three goals his senior year, in just twenty-eight games. Although they usually play ten more games now, Berenson still holds the school record. He was simply the best player Michigan has ever produced.

Berenson's senior year ended when Clarkson upset Michigan in the 1962 NCAA semifinals. Minutes after Michigan won the consolation game the next night, Berenson got a ride to play 24 hours later for the Montreal Canadiens. When Berenson took the ice, he became the first college player to go straight to the NHL—and proved Frank Selke wrong. Berenson also became the first NHL player to wear a helmet who hadn't already suffered a head injury.

Three years later, in the 1965 Stanley Cup playoffs, Berenson's Canadiens played the Chicago Black Hawks for the Stanley Cup. One day Berenson was holding Bobby Hull's line in check in the seventh game to win the grail, and the next he was sitting in a Michigan business school classroom taking his first class for his M.B.A. (There is drama in Berenson's final games.)

Although Berenson's B-school classmates didn't know who he was, Berenson remembers "very clearly what a good feeling it was to be there. I was preparing for life after hockey."

"I always thought about what I'd do when it was over, but for one reason or another, it hasn't ended," he says. "I was lucky. With [NHL] expansion and the World Hockey Association [expanding opportunities for players], I played until I was thirty-eight."

Along the way, he was named to six all-star teams, played in the famous 1972 Summit Series between Team Canada and the Soviets, served as an assistant captain in Detroit and the captain in St. Louis, and once scored six goals in a single game, still a post–World War II NHL record.

Berenson hung up his skates in 1978, and was named the St. Louis Blues' head coach midway through the next season. In 1980–81, his first full season as the Blues' head coach, he was named Coach of the Year. The next season he was fired, which shows you what the NHL is all about.

University of Michigan athletic director Don Canham had tried to recruit Berenson to take over his alma mater's team twice before, but both times Berenson was under contract to NHL teams. When the Berensons brought their oldest son, Gordie Jr., to Ann Arbor in the spring of 1984 on a campus visit, word got to Canham that the Red Baron was back on campus, and hurriedly invited him down to his office to offer him the head coaching job once more.

The third time proved to be the charm. Berenson took it.

"Red was brought in to save the program," said former PR man Jim Schneider. "If he didn't, it was gone."

That might be an overstatement, but not by much. The once-proud Michigan program found itself on the bottom of a new league, the CCHA. The situation was undeniably dire.

"I never saw myself as a college coach—but then I never saw myself as a coach," Berenson says. But there he was, the fourth Michigan captain to be named head coach, standing up at his first press conference to tell people how he intended to restore the emaciated program to its former robust health.

"My first goal is to change the image of the program," he said. "I have a good feel for Michigan, the tradition, the excellence, and what I call a 'Michigan kid.'"

He rebuilt it, but he did it the right way, which takes longer. He honored the scholarships of the players he'd inherited. He followed the NCAA's countless rules—even the absurd ones—and he graduated his players.

Six years later, Michigan returned to the NCAA tournament—and kept it up for twenty-two straight years, an NCAA record. Under Berenson, Michigan won twenty CCHA league titles, went to eleven Frozen Fours, and won the NCAA title in 1996 and 1998. Perhaps most impressive: Four players from those national title teams would graduate from Michigan's medical school.

That is how you do it.

And that's why Berenson's players will tell you Berenson was invariably more proud of what they did off the ice than on it. Perhaps that explains why his players maintained a 90 percent graduation rate until they started jumping early to the NHL—making Berenson a victim of his own success.

Berenson knew what Michigan stood for, and he was able to identify which recruits understood that by turning the tables on them. Instead of telling them all the great things Michigan was going to do for them, he looked them straight in the eye and asked, "Now, what are you going to do for Michigan?"

Fifty-two years after Berenson started preparing for life after hockey, he will actually start his life after hockey, at age seventy-seven.

Nobody needs to ask what Berenson did for Michigan. The answer is simple: He did everything he could.

Legends

One of the most satisfying aspects of sports writing is researching legends who have been reduced to two-dimensional characters, and restoring them to their full selves. Looking past the clichés, the famous figures described here all proved to be more compelling than the cardboard cutouts handed down over the decades. Their flaws made them more interesting to me—and in most cases, more admirable, because they allow us to see how they overcame their very human weaknesses to achieve a manner of greatness.

Of all the stories in this collection, these are some of the most emotional for me. If I occasionally laughed out loud (at my own expense) writing the first-person stories, I just as often pulled a tear composing these pieces. That may seem corny, but when you feel like you're really getting to know your subjects—living or dead—they pull you in. Hopefully, you'll see what I mean.

HALIFAX, EXTRAORDINARY HEROISM,
AND HOCKEY

December 21, 2017
Time Magazine

Joseph Ernest Barss is one of the most important people in the history of Michigan athletics, and by extension, college hockey. But you wouldn't have guessed that from his background—and certainly not from his family's.

Like 60,000 other British colonists, Barss's great-great-grandfather, Joseph Barss Sr., left New England for Nova Scotia before the American Revolutionary War. His son, Joseph Barss Jr., served as a privateer in the War of 1812, when he captured, sank, or burned more than sixty American ships, making him the most wanted man on the East Coast.

His great-grandson, Joseph Ernest Barss, was born in India in 1892, the son of Baptist missionaries. He grew up in Wolfville, Nova Scotia, just a few miles from Windsor, Nova Scotia, the birthplace of hockey. He attended the hometown Acadia University, which his grandfather helped found, where he starred in football, hockey, baseball, and boxing.

"He was sort of a stocky fella, big thighs, who carried himself very straight," recalled his son, Dr. Joseph Andrew Barss, in a 1999 interview. "A tough guy. His ankles were so strong, he didn't have to lace up his skates."

After graduating cum laude in 1912 at age nineteen, Barss moved to Montreal, where he rose to become a district manager for Imperial Oil, earning $1,500 a year—big money for a twenty-two-year-old at the time. Barss seemed to have a steady supply of friends and romantic interests.

Life was good for Barss in just about every way we typically measure for a young man: career, finances, and fun. He did not want for ambition, talent, or charisma.

But Barss's letters give the unmistakable sense that his current lifestyle, appealing as it was, did not leave him fulfilled. He came from a line of people who had something else in spades: a profound sense of purpose. His ancestors attacked enemy ships on the high seas, built fortunes in business, started universities, and went on missionary trips to India. And that essential piece was something the good life Ernest Barss was living in Montreal did not provide.

That changed one Saturday in 1915, during the second year of the Great War, when one of his rowing club friends read out loud that the Germans had gassed a famed Canadian unit, the Princess Patricia's Canadian Light Infantry (PPCLI), killing 461 of the 1,068 men in the unit, including friends of theirs from Montreal. The four men were "filled with indignation," Barss wrote, and decided to enlist right then and there.

In his early letters back to his parents, Barss was bursting with enthusiasm for the cause, and the role he was training to play: machine gunner. The reason the PPCLI was in such need of reinforcements, he explained, was because "there are only 53 left out of 1,500. So we have some reputation to keep up. Of course, as you have probably noted, I am full of this thing. So are the other fellows."

Barss's bravery and equanimity would soon be tested when the prospect of being killed in the trenches shifted from a far-off hypothetical to a cold reality he would face every day. But no one could claim his new life lacked purpose.

As the killing continued all around him, however, with no progress for either side, his letters revealed growing doubt, fear, and disillusionment. A little more than a year after he volunteered, after seeing countless comrades go down and surviving a few close calls himself, Barss wrote to his parents on May 31, 1916, from Belgium, just a mile from the worst fighting the world had ever seen. He told them his unit was going "into the line" that night for eight days, which he hoped would be their last trip.

"I think we are all heartily sick of the whole show," he wrote. But, he added, after this they needn't worry about what's next, because "it can't be any worse."

But it was. On June 2, 1916, a German shell landed near Barss and sent him flying, knocking him unconscious for hours, and seriously injuring his back and left leg. He spent six months in a body cast in England, then transferred to Halifax in early 1917, where the doctors reported Barss had suffered complete paralysis "of left foot and up the leg to three inches above the ankle joint."

Almost a year after Barss had been evacuated from the battlefields, he still could not extend or flex his left foot or toes, and could walk only with "a marked foot drop," hardly the stuff of a hockey hero. A question on the form asked the attending physician, "To what extent will injury prevent his earning a full livelihood in the general labor market?" The doctor answered, "30%." On another form, under "Probable Duration of Incapacity," a doctor wrote, "Indefinite."

Barss's shell shock hadn't abated either, including "insomnia, nervousness . . . some tremor of his hands." Today doctors would likely conclude Barss suffered from post-traumatic stress disorder, or PTSD. After being released, he returned to his parents' home in Wolfville to continue his self-directed rehabilitation program, which entailed walking all over town with a cane, trying to sell Victory Loans and prove the doctors wrong.

He was also trying to figure out what to do with his life. He knew he didn't want to run the family grocery store, work for a corporation in Montreal, or return to the trenches. But he didn't know what he wanted to do—or what he still *could* do.

On the morning of Thursday, December 6, 1917, a French munitions ship called *Mont-Blanc* was very eager to get inside the safety of Halifax Harbor as soon as the underwater metal gates, designed to keep German U-boats out, were opened—and with good reason. Five days earlier the longshoremen in Brooklyn, New York, had finished loading her down with an unprecedented quantity of high explosives, including TNT: a staggering six million pounds, or thirteen times the weight of the Statue of Liberty, which would be used to fill shells to drop on the Germans.

While *Mont-Blanc* was anxious to get inside Halifax Harbor, the Norwegian ship *Imo* was just as eager to get out and go in the opposite direction to New York. There it would load relief supplies intended to alleviate the desperate situation of the civilians in German-occupied Belgium. At Halifax Harbor's narrowest stretch, *Imo*'s impatient captain, who had no idea what *Mont-Blanc* was carrying, passed several ships on the left, against nautical convention. This set up a game of chicken with *Mont-Blanc*, which bailed first, pivoting to the left at the last second—just as *Imo*'s captain lost his nerve and veered the same direction.

At 8:46 a.m., *Imo* struck *Mont-Blanc*'s bow, knocking over barrels of airplane fuel. Fire swept across the decks, sending *Mont-Blanc*'s crew scurrying to the lifeboats, while Halifax longshoremen, office workers, and schoolchildren watched the ghost ship slip perfectly into Pier 6 at the base of the city.

At 9:04:35 a.m., *Mont-Blanc* erupted, leveling 2.5 square miles of Halifax, rendering twenty-five thousand people homeless, wounding nine thousand, and killing two thousand more—all in one-fifteenth of a second, less time than it takes to blink. It was the largest manmade detonation prior to the A-bomb. In 1942, J. Robert Oppenheimer set up a conference at California-Berkeley to study Halifax, accurately concluding that the atomic bomb would be only five times more powerful.

About an hour after the explosion, which blew out windows fifty miles away, Barss received a call from a mentor, Dr. Elliott, who had gotten word by telegram that a crisis had occurred in Halifax. "Of course, we thought it greatly exaggerated," Barss wrote to his uncle, Andrew Townson, "but when about half an hour later an urgent call came for doctors and nurses we began to think there must be something in it."

There was something to it.

Dr. Elliott was essentially recruiting Barss to return to a war zone—not to fight this time, but to help. Despite Barss's infirmity and shell-shock symptoms, all of which could be aggravated by this demanding mission, once again he didn't hesitate to answer the call.

If Barss's outlook had changed dramatically during his first trip to the trenches, slowly turning his optimistic bravado into fatalistic defeatism, this second call would transform his life once again.

When he got off the train, he wrote, "No reports could exaggerate the terrible damage and loss of life. We couldn't get within three miles of the city, for the whole space in between was a blazing mass of ruins. I saw some terrible scenes of desolation and ruin at the front, but never, even in that old hard-hammered city of Ypres, did I ever see anything so absolutely complete. In that entire area of over three-square miles in the immediate vicinity of the explosion there was not one stick or stone standing on another. Every house and building had just crumpled up and the whole was a raging mass of flames.

"Practically the whole waterfront was wrecked. All the large new steel and concrete piers just completed recently were wrecked beyond repair. People were killed everywhere, all over the city, and there was hardly a whole ceiling or pane of glass in the city or within a radius of five miles."

Although Barss had no medical training beyond the basic first aid all soldiers received, the city was grateful for anyone who could still walk, see, and lend a hand, so he was permitted to perform tasks normally reserved for medical professionals.

"The wounds were terrible," he wrote. "There was every kind I ever saw at the front, but a great majority had head wounds. Hundreds of people lost their eyes. In one of the operating rooms where they took only eye cases, the surgeon took out one hundred eyes the first day, and then handed the patients over to the next man to operate.

"The stench of blood was almost overpowering. Several of the trained nurses keeled over at the sights. As for me, I had seen so much of that kind of thing that it didn't bother me at all. I was assigned a trained nurse and a V.A.D. [Voluntary Aid Department nurse] to help me, and my how we worked; I dressed every kind of wound, set several fractures, and did a number of [surgeries] as well."

When Barss was relieved at four the next morning, Friday, December 7, he had completed a nonstop fourteen-hour shift. He got a few hours of sleep somewhere, then came back at 8:30 Friday morning for more—and did it all again Saturday. If he ever wondered whether medicine might be his calling, it would be hard to concoct a more intense introductory course to find out.

That Saturday afternoon the beleaguered town received relief from an unexpected source: Boston, which had fought against "British North America" in 1776 and 1812, and whose government's Speaker of the House advocated the annexation of Canada from the floor of the U.S. Congress in 1911—and received hearty cheers for it, just six years before the explosion.

Yet it was Boston, not Montreal or Toronto, which sent two trains and two ships loaded with one hundred doctors, three hundred nurses, and a million dollars' worth of supplies (about $20 million today)—all without being asked. Some of those medical professionals relieved the exhausted Barss after three very long days in the operating room with almost no sleep. The Americans' unexpected act of chivalry was enough to transform 141 years of animosity and aggression into a century of peace. Boston's overwhelming generosity even converted the great-grandson of Canada's greatest privateer.

"You know we have always been a trifle contemptuous of the U.S. on account of their prolonged delay in entering the war," Barss wrote his uncle. "But never again! They can have anything I've got. And I don't think I feel any differently from anyone down here either."

The explosion and its aftermath did something else, too: it changed Barss's outlook. On the long train ride home it came to him: having taken part in both fighting and healing, Barss wanted to spend the rest of his life practicing the latter. When he told his uncle Andrew Townson of his new-found desire, he gave Ernest $100 to enroll at the University of Michigan in 1919, back when that was enough to get started. How Ernest Barss picked Michigan, however, remains a mystery.

"Darned if I know why he went to the University of Michigan," his son, Dr. Joseph Andrew Barss, told me, "but it's always been a first-class school."

In Ann Arbor, Barss started becoming a new man, with a new mission, and a new name: Joe, because that's what his professors read off roll call. He found time to sing in the First Congregational Church under the leadership of Lloyd C. Douglas, who would go on to write *The Robe*, which sold two million copies and became a movie starring Richard Burton.

In the fall of 1920, he went on a blind double date that "neither of us wanted to go on," recalled Helen Kolb, a Michigan undergraduate from Battle Creek. "But we had a wonderful time. I never thought anything serious would come of this date, as Joe had so far to go to become a doctor."

When Barss and a classmate, Bob Breakey, picked up their dates the next day to go to a football game, Barss brought Helen two big mums and a box of Whitman's chocolates. The man seemed to have a plan, and "worked very hard to be invited to my home for Christmas," she recalled. Shortly after the holidays, Barss asked Helen to marry him, then did something even more surprising: he became a naturalized American citizen. If anything demonstrated the distance the two nations had traveled since the Halifax explosion, it was the simple, small decision of Joseph Ernest Barss, descendent of a notorious Canadian privateer, to become an American, something he could not have conceived when he joined the British forces in 1915, grumbling about the Americans sitting out the war.

The couple wed in 1922 and had a son, Joseph Andrew, in 1923, and a daughter, Elizabeth, in 1927.

Even while Barss was busy starting a family and finishing his medical education in peaceful Ann Arbor, he was still occasionally haunted by the Great War. Like most veterans who'd seen combat, Barss was a stoic man who rarely talked of the epic battles in which he had fought. But early in their marriage, Helen was startled to discover that this otherwise self-possessed person would get choked up whenever he heard bagpipes, as it was bagpipers who led his unit into the trenches and it was bagpipers who led them back out, with the soldiers carrying the writhing victims of shells, gas, and bayonets behind them. Helen also noticed whenever he heard a whistle or a loud bang he would drop to the ground, a survival instinct he had learned in the awful days when enemy shells were dropping all around him.

Through the steady support of his family, his friends, and his own strong spirit, Barss was gradually able to let his memories of war recede, and the simple pleasures of civilian life take their place.

Barss knew he would lose his hard-earned progress re-learning to walk if he quit pushing himself, so he made it a point to go down to Michigan's rudimentary rink, a building with only three sides, and cajole himself to get around the rink until tears streamed down his face.

According to the box scores of Michigan's "informal team," Barss officiated many of the club's hockey games in 1922. Perhaps it was his desire to return to a normal lifestyle and have some fun again that motivated him to find time in his already overburdened schedule for such a trivial pursuit. It's easy to imagine the lightheartedness Barss must have felt as he became reacquainted with the happiness a hockey game could bring. And having gotten a taste, he wanted more.

To get more, however, Michigan needed a varsity hockey program—something the club players had asked for and been denied three times over the previous decade. When the Great War broke out, Michigan sponsored only five varsity teams: baseball, football, track, tennis, and basketball.

To change that, Barss paid a visit to Michigan's legendary football coach and athletic director, Fielding Yost, to ask if he could start a varsity hockey team. Yost, a native of West Virginia, didn't know much about hockey, but he knew a good coach when he saw one. Yost agreed, on one condition: Barss had to become the program's first coach.

Barss agreed, which meant he had to "rush home from classes, eat dinner, have a taxi waiting, go to the rink and coach, return by a little after nine and study for the next day's classes until midnight," Helen recalled. Because the rink lacked artificial ice, or a fourth wall, they were at the mercy of the weather. "The tin roof [on the rink] caused him some trouble because we had to live by the weather report and temperature."

Barss attached a thermometer outside their bedroom window, which Helen Barss checked every morning. If it was too warm to skate on the Coliseum's outdoor rink, she simply rolled over and let her young husband steal a golden hour of sleep until he had to go to class. But if it was cold enough for the team to practice, Helen would stir her bone-tired husband out of bed to get him to the rink on time. After everything he'd seen in France and Halifax, however, Barss was not likely to complain about a little fatigue.

Before he stepped down in 1927 he had built the Michigan hockey team into one of the most popular attractions on campus, with a 26–21–4 record (.553) and two league titles. The program was strong enough to inspire Yost to buy the rink, enclose it, and install all-important artificial ice. These crucial elements helped Michigan hockey survive both the Great Depression and World War II—one of only two programs west of the Alleghenies to do so. Michigan has since won an NCAA record nine national titles.

Dr. Barss became chief of surgery at the Hines Veterans Hospital in Chicago before setting up a private practice in Oak Park, Illinois, Ernest Hemingway's hometown.

"He sure gave me a good upbringing, in terms of character and honesty," Barss's son said. "He was absolutely true-blue. He was very aware of what was right and what was wrong. My dad was a helluva guy."

In 1966, at age seventy-four, Dr. Barss took his wife, Helen, his son, and his grandson Joe back to Nova Scotia. In Wolfville, he showed them where he had learned to skate, where he had gone to college, and where he sold victory bonds. In Halifax, he showed them where he had recuperated, where *Mont-Blanc* had blown up, and where he'd helped victims at Camp Hill Hospital start their own recoveries.

But he didn't tell them how he had left Acadia University a confident young man with no sense of purpose, returned from the Great War a broken man searching for one, and went to Halifax for three long days, where he found his life's mission—and pursued it at the University of Michigan.

THE TRUE STORY OF "THE GIPPER"

I stumbled on this story by pure dumb luck. A friend put me in touch with the woman who happened to have George Gipp's love letters to her great-aunt, and they were surprisingly emotional and well-written from a man who had a reputation as a drinker, gambler, and womanizer. But I could not convince the Detroit News sports editor to assign the piece.

In late January of 1997, there was no reason to run a college football story, except for one reason: my boss was on vacation. I worked my tail off for five solid days with little sleep, while the graphics department put together a great package spanning two-and-a-half pages. Late on Friday night, with everything completed and the staff gone, I sat there contemplating what the consequences could be, with my finger twitching over the "SEND" button. I knew it could cost me my job, but after going back and forth, I decided, "No guts, no glory," and punched the "SEND" button. It was off, and my fate was flying with it.

The story ran on a Sunday. That Monday, I awaited the inevitable reaction. But just as the section editor was marching in, the publisher beckoned him into his office to say the story was one of the best things they'd run in a while, and it went on to win national recognition. By the time the editor walked out of the publisher's office, he didn't have anything to say to me.

No guts, no glory. Glad I hit "SEND."

January 5, 1997
The Detroit News

Probably no athletes in any sport feel the richness of their past, or its weight, more acutely than Notre Dame's football players.

The man most responsible for building that tradition is Notre Dame's winningest coach, Knute Rockne. And the player most responsible for making Rockne famous was George Gipp, more commonly known as "The Gipper."

Gipp died in 1920, just twenty-four days after his last game. Thanks in part to the famous phrase "Win one for the Gipper," and a 1940 movie starring Ronald Reagan, George Gipp is one of the best-known athletes of this century—and one of the most misunderstood.

George Gipp was more human than the sanitized, one-dimensional character Reagan played, and deeper than the hard-living antihero revisionists have created since. Gipp's brief life was filled with devilish habits and angelic gestures, athletic heroism and crushing heartbreak. His death was preceded by a private act of honor, and followed by a national outpouring of grief.

This is the real story of George Gipp.

First, the facts: George Gipp was born on February 18, 1895, in Laurium, Michigan, located on the Keweenaw Peninsula, just one mile from Calumet and thirteen from Houghton. He enrolled at Notre Dame in 1916, earned four varsity letters in football, and died on December 14, 1920.

The 1940 movie *Knute Rockne: All-American* solidified Gipp's reputation as an outstanding natural athlete, and a clean-living character.

They got it half right: George Gipp was truly a phenomenal athlete. He was built like the powerful, versatile athlete he was, standing six feet tall and weighing 180 pounds, very big for the time. He could run the 100-yard dash in 10.1 seconds, throw the old oblong football 50 yards with accuracy, and drop-kick it 60 yards through the goal posts. He was also an excellent basketball and hockey player, and even won a gold watch for ballroom dancing. His best sport, however, was baseball.

"My buddies and I used to look through the knotholes in the fence of the ballpark to watch Gipp play for the Calumet Aristocrats," recalls William John Foster, eighty-eight, a Calumet historian. "He was terrific! He could move, I'll tell ya. We idolized him."

Lillian Gipp Pritty, eighty, is the daughter of Gipp's oldest brother, Alexander. "I remember my dad telling me there wasn't anything Uncle George couldn't do, and do better, than the other guy," she says. "Uncle George could throw a ball from his knees at home plate with just his wrist all the way to second base, and the second baseman would say, 'Hey, Gipp not so hard!'"

In a town filled with numerous athletes who played for college and professional teams, Gipp was the best in every sport—despite his efforts.

"He was quite a lazy guy," says Manila Gipp, ninety-four, who married Gipp's cousin. "My husband had to get him out of bed to play baseball games."

George Gipp was the seventh of eight children born to Isabella and Matthew Gipp, a Baptist preacher—something you'd never guess from George's lifestyle.

Gipp was considered very bright, but his high school grades were so bad he never earned a diploma or even a varsity letter. When he wasn't sleeping or playing ball, Gipp liked to smoke, drink, play cards, and shoot pool.

"George lived a very high life," says Ruth Maynard, eighty-eight, who still lives on Gipp's old street in Laurium. "He didn't take care of himself."

The revisionists who've written about Gipp's freewheeling lifestyle as a Notre Dame student generally assume he fell into those habits when he was blinded by the "big-city lights" of South Bend, Indiana—yet another myth. When Gipp left Houghton County for South Bend in 1916, he left a booming area of almost ninety thousand people for a far quieter hamlet of fifty-three thousand.

The source of Houghton County's wealth could be found deep in the ground. The first mining boom in the United States wasn't the California gold rush of 1849 but the Michigan copper rush of 1844. From the Civil War to the turn of the century, Michigan produced 70 percent of the nation's copper, with Calumet producing more than half the state's total. If you bought a single share of Calumet mining stock when it opened for business in 1866 for a dollar, you could sit back and collect the 700 percent annual dividend, or sell it for a thousand dollars fifty years later. The place where Gipp grew up was like the Wild West, plus culture.

With the Copper Rush on, Houghton County's population exploded from nine thousand in 1860 to almost ninety thousand by 1910. The county had ten trains a day going to and from cities like Milwaukee, Chicago, and Detroit. They had street cars running every fifteen minutes, twenty papers in four languages, seven theaters, and two gorgeous opera houses.

The vibrant area attracted such luminaries as John Phillip Sousa and actress Sarah Bernhardt. Civic leaders could also boast thirty churches, thirty schools, and sixty bars—ratios that suited Gipp's lifestyle.

In the midst of this unprecedented prosperity, the miners went on strike in 1913, which marked the beginning of the end. The strike lasted nine months, and culminated in disaster.

On Christmas Eve, 1913, the strikers packed a local hall for a holiday party. The revelry was interrupted when somebody yelled "Fire!" The alarm was false, but the resulting panic was real.

"Hundreds of people ran to escape," local historian William John Foster says, "but there were only two doors and they opened inward. The folks at the front were getting crushed and couldn't get the doors open. That's when the people started to pile up and suffocate. Fifty-three children, eleven women, and nine men died—seventy-three total. They had to use the Calumet town hall as a morgue.

"The union blamed the company for yelling 'Fire!' and vice versa, but to this day no one knows for sure," Foster says. Either way, the area's decline hurt everyone. Houghton County's population averaged a population drop of ten thousand every decade until it leveled off at about thirty-three thousand in 1970—a third of what it used to be.

"I saw it go up," Foster says, "and I saw it go down."

The Keweenaw Peninsula's surprising boom and tragic bust closely paralleled the life of its most famous son, George Gipp.

After Gipp dropped out of Calumet High School in 1913, just a few months before the holiday disaster, he worked construction in the winter, drove a taxi in the summer, and played semipro baseball—in addition to keeping up his nocturnal rounds of the saloons and pool halls.

When three of his Calumet friends left for Notre Dame, he was persuaded to join them. So, in 1916, Gipp accepted admission to Notre Dame—to play baseball.

Gipp's collegiate baseball career lasted all of one game. According to James A. Cox's 1985 article in the *Smithsonian*, when Gipp's manager gave him the bunt signal, Gipp disregarded it, electing to blast a towering home run instead. Back in the dugout the irritated manager asked Gipp why he'd ignored the signs.

"Because," he said, "it's too hot to be running around the bases after a bunt."

His teammates chuckled, until they realized their new teammate wasn't joking. He quit the baseball team next day.

Rockne discovered Gipp when Gipp and a friend, wearing street clothes, were punting a football back and forth to each other. Gipp's kicks were so prodigious, Rockne invited him out for the freshman team.

Smart move. In Gipp's first away game, against Western State Normal of Michigan (now Western Michigan University), the teams were deadlocked at seven late in the contest. When the Irish stalled on their own forty-eight, the quarterback ordered Gipp to punt. Gipp characteristically disregarded this order, too, and drop-kicked a sixty-two-yard rocket for the win—setting an NCAA record that stood for decades.

In 1917, at age twenty-two, George Gipp made Notre Dame's varsity football team—the first varsity letter he earned in any sport, for any school.

The skills Gipp mastered on Calumet's fields helped him conquer Notre Dame during the day, and the skills he learned in Calumet's pool halls helped him conquer South Bend at night.

For most of his five years at Notre Dame, Gipp eschewed the dorms for city hotels. He rarely showed up for practice before Thursday, and ignored curfews to give him more time to break other rules for smoking, drinking, and gambling.

One headline of the day described Gipp as "Notre Dame's Cool Gambler." The author probably didn't realize how accurate that was. A 1992 article in *Sports Illustrated* quotes the late Hunk Anderson, who grew up with Gipp on the Keweenaw Peninsula, played at Notre Dame with him, then went on to star for the Chicago Bears and coach for Notre Dame, Michigan, and the Detroit Lions.

"Every once in a while some of the hotshot pool players from Chicago would come to South Bend looking for action," he recalled, "and George would play them at $100 a game or more at Hullie and Mike's pool room. They were crackerjack players who made their living shooting pool, but George would take them almost every time."

When you consider that $100 in 1916 was equivalent to $1,460 today, it's obvious Gipp didn't lack for nerves. In a sardonic boast, Gipp said, "I'm the finest freelance gambler ever to attend Notre Dame."

Joking or not, he had a case. Fred Larson, another Calumet friend who played for Notre Dame, recalled Gipp's brief time in the dorms. "I once asked him how he was doing at poker, and he told me he had made at least $5,000 ($73,000 in 1997 dollars) the previous year and, from the looks of things, would top that amount that year."

It was common in Gipp's day for opposing football teams to eat together the night before their game and place friendly wagers with each other. Gipp took it to a new level, frequently betting hundreds with bookies and bar patrons on Notre Dame games. Before TV, Gipp took advantage of the fact that fans often couldn't recognize him. He made large bets that "that Gipp fellow" could outscore the opposition single-handedly. Gipp would then go out and do just that the next day, then return to the bars that night to collect.

Despite his obvious flaws, Gipp was remarkably well liked by his teammates, friends, and coaches—if not his professors. Gipp ignored team rules not out of contempt but indifference. He made no attempt to hide his weaknesses. He had no artifice, refusing to live a hypocritical double life, and never sought publicity for his athletic exploits. Gipp rarely read his own clippings, often avoided interviews, and frequently pulled himself in blowouts so he could stand on the bench to cheer on the second-stringers.

Gipp freely displayed his worst traits, openly pursuing his night life, while keeping the "better angels" of his character private, away from the press—the antithesis of many modern athletes.

"He let the wrong side show," says his niece, Lillian Gipp Pritty.

According to his roommate, Arthur "Dutch" Bergman, "Nobody around South Bend could beat him at pool, billiards, poker, or bridge. He was the terror of the parlors. I've seen him win five hundred dollars in a crap game and then spend his winnings buying meals for destitute families." When steak cost twenty-five cents a pound, five hundred dollars could buy a lot of steak dinners. "No wonder he was idolized by the South Bend townies."

He was also idolized by his teammates. During Gipp's time there were no athletic scholarships, and the total cost for one semester at Notre Dame ran about five hundred dollars. Gipp occasionally covered the amount for his friends to see them through another term.

For all Gipp's street smarts, he had one notable blind spot: he failed to distinguish between games of skill, like pool, poker, and football games, and games of chance, like dice. With his inflated sense of invincibility—or perhaps a secret bent for self-destruction—Gipp gambled as boldly on things he could control as he did on those he could not.

It would prove to be his fatal flaw.

Gipp's off-field pursuits didn't seem to affect his performance on the field. His rushing totals grew steadily each of his first three years on the varsity, from 244 yards in 1917 (with a 3.8 yard-per-carry average), to 541 yards his second season (5.5 average), to 729 yards in his junior year, with an impressive 6.8 average.

Those figures don't include his passing yardage, which increased from 40 yards to 293 to 727 over the same three years, nor his punting, which totaled 2,593 yards. He remains the game's greatest triple-threat player.

By the end of his junior season, Gipp had begun to attract national attention. His team fared even better, going 9–0 to steal the title "Champions of the West" from Michigan.

Rockne knew that his team's chances of repeating the next season depended largely on Gipp. What came hard to others came easily to Gipp: athletics, gambling, and casual charm. But conversely, what came easily to the average man was hard for Gipp: getting up, going to class, staying out of bars, and living clean. Gipp seemed as content to squander his opportunities as exploit them.

By his junior year, Gipp's aversion to rules included not just Rockne's, but also the school's and the NCAA's. His lack of classwork finally got him booted from Notre Dame, prompting him to return to semipro baseball leagues for cash (the same sin that cost Jim Thorpe his Olympic medals), and play football with some Irish teammates for money one day in Rockford, Illinois. Fortunately for him, the NCAA never found out.

When revisionists consider Gipp's "dropout" mentality, they often portray Gipp as a happy-go-lucky party boy with little depth, like Babe Ruth. While it's tempting to wink at his disregard for the rules, his flurry of off-field distractions seemed to cover a broken spirit. Look a little closer at George Gipp, and you can't help but think there was something essential missing in him, some lack of zest for life, some part of him that could not be happy.

"He was a strange person, fun-loving in a way, yet withdrawn," said the late Fred Larson, who met Gipp in Calumet, and played with him at Notre Dame. "George had no real close friends—Hunk [Anderson] and I were as close as any. He was friendly enough, but I always got the feeling he didn't want to get too close to anyone, even those of us who had known him for years. He was a very complex person."

Tolstoy wrote that all happy families are the same, while unhappy families are all unhappy in their own way. The Gipp family seemed to be in the second category. Gipp's father, Matthew Sr., was a strict German preacher who gave off little warmth. His wife, Isabella, was remembered by one granddaughter as being very "domineering" with her children.

Dorothy Frueh, seventy, another Gipp niece, grew up in Isabella Gipp's home. "Whenever I came in to ask my mom to go swimming or get a bike, I always heard Grandma Gipp telling her from the other room, 'Don't let her do it, Mary, she might get hurt!'" she recalls with a vivacious laugh. "That was my everlasting image of Grandma Gipp—laying down the law."

Frueh recalls, however, that her mother, Mary Gipp Martin—Gipp's sister—"never seemed a real happy woman, and Uncle Matthew never seemed happy."

Perhaps that explains why Gipp never seemed truly happy, either. His apathy almost cost him the one thing that genuinely inspired him: a woman named Iris Jeanne Trippeer.

"The girls around South Bend would have given anything to meet and go out with him," Larson once said, "but George stayed aloof, more interested in his poker, pool, and football."

That was only partly true. Gipp's late teammate Paul Castnor once recalled that Gipp enjoyed the company of a few bar girls, particularly a woman named Mattie Blake. But nothing awoke Gipp from his complacency until 1919, when he met Iris Trippeer at a school dance.

Trippeer, a twenty-year-old who worked as a secretary for the Indiana governor, was visiting a friend at St. Mary's College, Notre Dame's sister school, after a football game. Iris's niece, Gloria Trippeer Lyons, sixty, recalls her aunt as a "pretty nice-looking lady, in an upper-class, classically elite manner. That's how she carried herself: a lady through and through."

A bar girl she was not.

"Aunt Iris was very smart but soft-spoken, never a splashy person," Lyons adds. "She was kind of sensitive, which is probably one reason George and Iris thought so much of each other, because they were both quiet, sincere."

Gipp was smitten.

Iris's parents, however, were not taken by him. "I think they both disapproved," Lyons says. "Most people in those days thought athletes were kind of wild and ne'er-do-wells."

Not without reason. In 1919 there was no NFL, so there was no money to be made playing the sport. Even professional golfers were decades away from being allowed in the clubhouses of the courses where they competed, professional baseball players worked in the winters, and the Black Sox scandal was just coming to light. The idea of marrying an athlete, even one as notable as Gipp, was not something an upright father wished for his daughter.

That might explain why Iris's parents had her ten-year-old brother, Glenn, "tag along to keep an eye," Lyons says of her father. Gipp could have resented the lad's presence, but instead treated him like a welcome friend. "Dad liked Gipp very well, thought he was a very kind man. Dad said Gipp was always, *always* very generous with him."

Iris's niece says the young lovers had intended to get married, but "my aunt was given pause because he was not sure what he was going to do with himself after university. She wanted him to become a regular person and get a regular job and be a regular Joe—and he was not the kind of person for that."

The conflict between their growing love and disparate aspirations tore them apart after Notre Dame expelled Gipp for poor grades in the spring of his junior year, 1920. To make a few bucks, he sold his services to a number of baseball teams before settling in Flint, where he worked in the Buick factory by day and played for their team at night.

His letters to Iris that summer chart his struggles to "go straight," and show two sides of himself rarely seen elsewhere: commitment and passion.

On August 21, 1920, Gipp wrote to Iris at her parents' house in Indianapolis.

"Finally able to wield the pen once more. Have been considerably under the weather since Tuesday. Never had an experience quite like this before. Didn't miss a day at the factory tho but oh I wanted to."

Two days later Gipp sent another letter, in which he mentions the "little war" between them—no doubt over Gipp's lack of direction.

"Dear,

"Cold and windy, seemed as the summer had fled overnight . . . Iris honey I'm mighty lonesome tonight. Just think of you all the time dear and oh I've been waiting and waiting for some little word. Don't you believe dear that I'm being good? I want your life to be always happy but if you refuse to believe in me I don't see how it can be. I'll do anything to assure your happiness honey but dear don't please don't treat me as though I was an object of contempt. That isn't fair because I've been true to just you for a long time honey and oh don't let our little war overbalance the love that is yours ever yours.

"Always, George."

On August 27, Gipp seemed to claim he'd find honest work. He poured his heart out to her again, and sent it special delivery.

"Dear,

"Came home at four today expecting to play but it started to rain so once more a postponement. Iris dear you know what thoughts the rain drops accentuate? The sunny happy days we had together and Iris of music. Some day we'll have them all again forever tho this time not just a few sweet hours. But those little hours dear changed my whole life. I've conquered every little doubt honey because of you so there will be only one little year honey and then honey oh you'll never doubt any more.

"Yours always, George."

After Gipp returned to Notre Dame that fall, he wrote Iris again.

"Dear Iris,

"Well I don't want you to be sick anymore so remember what my manager always shouted to me when the count was two and nothing. Hang in little champion and someday the happiness that is due you shall come.

"I know it will Iris because you deserve it. The average has to be even some day so think of all the happy days that must come to balance the dark ones . . . Good-bye dear and keep the proud little chin up as the champion should.

"Always yours, George."

Whether the incorrigible Gipp could have kept his promise to straighten up, we'll never know. One thing is for sure: Gipp biographer Jim Beach's claim that Gipp couldn't possibly have uttered the famous "Gipper" speech to Rockne because "such a romantic notion would have been completely out of character for a pool player and gambler like Gipp," mistakes the man considerably.

Thanks to Gipp's expulsion, Rockne had no small task getting him back on campus for the 1920 season—especially with the University of Michigan and the University of Detroit now competing for his services. An early myth held that Gipp passed a stiff oral exam to get reinstated, but the reality is less glamorous: alumni and students simply pressured the administrators until they buckled.

It should be said, though, that Gipp was no dumb jock, writing a thesis on the plight of the Jewish people, and why they were so often forced to migrate.

But when his efforts to impress Iris apparently fell short, he slipped from being merely apathetic to downright self-destructive. His senior year he moved into the Oliver Hotel for good, and redoubled his debauchery.

Everyone marvels at Green Bay Packer Max McGee's hungover heroics in Super Bowl I, but Gipp pulled the same trick almost every game—playing both directions, no less. With Gipp leading the way, the Irish won their first four games by a combined score of 125–10.

Their fifth game, on Saturday, October 30, 1920, pitted the Irish against a formidable Army team at West Point. Crucially, they played in front of the Eastern press, the first chance many in the New York media had to see the famed Gipp. At halftime, with the Irish down 17–14, Rockne gave a typically rousing speech which sent the players screaming onto the field—except Gipp, who leaned against a door jam, looking bored.

Seeing him there, Rockne said, "I don't suppose you have the slightest interest in this game."

"You're wrong there, Rock," Gipp replied. "I've got 400 bucks on this game, and I don't intend to blow it."

He didn't. Using his running, passing, and punt returning to great effect, Gipp racked up a total of 323 yards—more than all the Army players combined—to secure a 27–17 Notre Dame victory. This game, more than any other, established Gipp's legend.

Under the headline, "Gipp Plays Brilliantly," the *New York Times* said, "A lithe-limbed Hoosier football player named George Gipp galloped wild through the Army on the plains here this afternoon, giving a performance which was more like an antelope's than a human being's."

A week later, on November 6, 1920, the morning of the Purdue game, South Bend scribe Walter O'Keefe saw Gipp stumble out of the Oliver Hotel's elevator unshaven, unshowered, and clearly in a bad state from a night of smoking, drinking, and gambling. A few hours later Gipp ran for 129 yards, passed for 128, punted for 339, and returned a Purdue punt for 35. He capped the day by running 80 yards for a touchdown to seal a 28–0 Irish victory and a 6–0 record, leaving Notre Dame just three wins from a perfect season.

Several accounts claim that a week later, on the morning of the Indiana game, Iris broke up with Gipp for good. Early in that contest Gipp severely injured his shoulder, probably dislocating it. With his team down 10–0, Gipp sat on the bench with a blanket around him, but couldn't stand to watch an Irish drive falter at Indiana's two-yard line. He threw off his blanket and ran onto the field against Rockne's protests. On the second play, Gipp took the ball on a tough run right up the middle for a touchdown.

A few minutes later, when the Irish stalled on the Indiana fifteen-yard line, Gipp came off the bench for a dropkick. The Hoosiers rushed, Gipp faked, and then floated a pass to a teammate who took it to the one-yard line. On the next play Indiana keyed on Gipp, who smashed into the line to sell the fake convincingly, while quarterback Joe Brandy walked untouched into the far corner of the end zone for the game's last points. Notre Dame 13, Indiana 10.

By this time Gipp's normally pale complexion was sickly, he ached all over, and he had a bad cough. Whether this was a continuation of the bug he caught that summer, we don't know. But we do know that, instead of returning to South Bend with the team, Gipp traveled to Chicago to give a lesson on dropkicking to a former teammate's prep school team, where the cold winds off Lake Michigan compounded Gipp's respiratory problems. Only a man with little regard for his own well-being would have made the trip.

Gipp spent the following week in his bed at the Oliver Hotel, but roused himself to play at Northwestern that Saturday, November 20. Gipp's late teammate Paul Castnor said that, heading into that game, Gipp had fallen behind to his bookies. They made him a simple offer: if he stayed out of the Northwestern game, they'd wipe his debts clean. Since Rockne wanted Gipp to sit out anyway to recuperate in time for their season finale against Michigan Agricultural College (now Michigan State University), it seemed like an easy solution.

Gipp dressed for the game but stayed on the bench covered in a wool blanket, shivering with fever, while the Irish built a 20–7 lead. His teammates didn't need Gipp to make a rescue mission this time—but perhaps Gipp's conscience did.

In the fourth quarter George Gipp once again discarded his wool blanket, and ignored his failing health and gambling debts to complete five of six passes for two touchdowns late in the game, to give Notre Dame a 33–7 victory, and an 8-0 record.

In an era when people frequently died from strep throat and pneumonia, Gipp probably knew that by entering the game he was tempting death. We can only speculate about that, but this we know for certain: his 55-yard touchdown pass that Saturday was George Gipp's last play.

Three days after the Northwestern game, the Notre Dame administration, alumni, and fans organized a team banquet on Tuesday, November 23, 1920, at the Oliver Hotel, Gipp's unofficial home. The Irish were one win away from their second consecutive undefeated season, and with it, their second Champions of the West crown.

During the meal Gipp started coughing, and could not stop. After the banquet, he entered St. Joseph's hospital, where he stayed during Notre Dame's last game, a 25–0 Thanksgiving Day trouncing of Michigan Agricultural College.

A few days later, Gipp's doctors determined he had contracted pneumonia and strep throat. Today penicillin will cure both in a week—but the miracle drug was still years from common use. With nothing to stop the bugs, over the next two weeks, Gipp suffered infection, fever, and delirium.

Rockne telegrammed Iris Trippeer. "George some improved. Still critical. Wishes to see you today."

Trippeer answered Gipp's plea. On December 7, she telegrammed her parents. "Improved somewhat. Urged me to remain a while."

Even without their daughter's updates, Trippeer's parents could easily follow Gipp's struggle in any local or national paper. Headlines read:

"George Gipp Fighting Brave Battle."

"Gipp Gains in Battle for His Life."

And finally, "Little Hope for Gipp."

Even as Gipp's body was failing him, the accolades rolled in. While in the hospital he became the first Notre Dame player to be named to the All-American team. Walter Camp tapped him as the year's outstanding back. When Rockne told Gipp the Chicago Cubs had offered him a baseball contract, Gipp opened his eyes and said, "Well, that's jake, Rock."

As Gipp fought to survive, the editors of a daily paper in Calumet provided hourly updates by printing Gipp's status on a large card and placing it in their front window.

At about seven o'clock on the evening of December 14, 1920, the editor solemnly placed a card in the window that announced to Gipp's friends and relatives that George Gipp had lost his struggle. He was gone.

Of all the athletes who have died young, Gipp's legacy looms the largest. The most obvious reason is the famous passage attributed to him by Knute Rockne. Eight years after Gipp's death, Rockne brought Gipp's tale to light when Notre Dame faced a far superior Army team before a standing-room-only crowd in Yankee Stadium.

"Boys, I want to tell you a story," Rockne said. "I never thought I'd have to tell it, but the time has come."

Rockne then proceeded to pass on what Gipp had told him from his deathbed.

"I've got to go, Rock," Gipp said. "It's all right. I'm not afraid.

"Sometime, Rock, when the team's up against it, when things are wrong and the breaks are beating the boys—tell them to go in there with all they've got and win just one for the Gipper. I don't know where I'll be then, Rock. But I'll know about it, and I'll be happy."

Rockne's boys ran out to post a tremendous upset, 12–6.

Despite the doubters, Rockne insisted the story was true to the day he himself died tragically, when his plane went down in 1931. You can decide for yourself what to believe, but contrary to revisionist wisdom, from his letters to Iris alone, there is little question George Gipp had it in him.

What is sometimes lost in the debate over the "Gipper" speech is how good an athlete George Gipp really was.

Late in his life Fred Larson said, "He was the greatest I ever saw, and I played against Jim Thorpe."

Notre Dame has produced more Heisman Trophy winners and All-Americans than any other school, but none of them could break their first All-American's career record of 2,341 yards until 1978, more than a half century after Gipp set it.

A little-known fact, perhaps, but it's far better known than Gipp's greatest attributes, including his generosity, his humility, his devotion, and his ultimate act of integrity.

Perhaps the greatest testament to Gipp came from Iris Trippeer. Before she died in 1975, Iris showed her granddaughter Victoria Phair her collection of mementos from George Gipp, including his national championship bracelet, and asked her to protect them.

When Iris gave them to Phair, Iris admitted, "George Gipp was the only man I ever loved."

No myth can top that.

THE BIG HOUSE AFTER HOURS

In the fall of 1995, Jim Russ, a former editor of mine at the Ann Arbor News, called from his new post at the Detroit News, and asked me to interview for the position of sports feature writer. This often led to columnist, as it has for Bob Wojnowski and others. For a guy who had never held a full-time position at a newspaper of any size, this was a great opportunity. The interviews went well, but being a largely unknown quantity, they wanted to give me a try-out.

After I turned in my first piece—on Traverse City adding a second high school, and what that does to the town—I pitched the News on a story about the Big House after hours. Because I lived two blocks away from the stadium at the time, I ran the steps on a regular basis, and was struck by how busy the Big House actually was between games. The editors gave me the green light, I wrote the story (and revised it many times, with the help of smart friends), turned it in, and they liked it enough to stop the try-out then and there. I had the job— probably the biggest break of my career.

Sadly, Michigan's policy of letting visitors inside during the week ended when athletic director Bill Martin stepped down in 2010.

October 22, 1995
The Detroit News

The Michigan football game's over, the crowd files out, and now the storied stadium settles in to hibernate until the next game.

Right?

Wrong.

Dead wrong.

When the masses leave, the real work—and the real fun—begin.

For starters, the day after a game a 500-person cleanup crew will come in to transform 300 overstuffed 55-gallon trash cans into 72 cubic feet of compressed trash—two long dumpsterfuls. On Monday the builders will resume their 10-year renovation project, completing about $2.5 million of repairs a year. While all this is going on, thousands of tourists drop by from every state in the union—yes, even Alaska—just to see the Big House. And at night a couple might attempt to join the Fifty-Yard-Line Club, which is like the Mile-High Club, without the altitude.

As almost everyone knows, Michigan Stadium is the largest college-owned stadium in the country. With a capacity of 102,501 the building could play host to the entire population of Ann Arbor until just a few years ago. They've sold out every game—125 straight—since November 8, 1975.

With those kind of numbers, no one questions why Michigan has such an incredible facility for only six events a year (eight if you count graduation and the spring scrimmage). But why did the University build such a monstrosity way back in 1927 when the population of the students and city combined barely topped 35,000?

Two words: Fielding Yost.

The legendary football coach and athletic director actually wanted to build a 140,000-seat stadium, but settled for 85,000 with room to expand. As quixotic as it probably seemed at the time, the oversized stadium started paying off in only its third week.

According to author Al Slote, after the dedication game—a 21–0 victory over Ohio State—senior captain Bennie Oosterbaan and Yost walked home together, talking. "Mr. Yost was feeling pretty good," the late Oosterbaan remembered. "We'd won, and the stadium was completely filled. He lighted up his cigar and turned to me and said, 'Bennie, do you know what the best thing about that new stadium is? Eighty-five thousand people paid five dollars apiece for their seats—and Bennie, they had to *leave the seats there*.'"

Now it's left to other generations to keep Yost's stadium clean.

"People who walk in here for a game don't have *any* idea what goes into it—and that's the way it should be!" says stadium supervisor Leon Tweedy, fifty-four, now in his twenty-third year at the Big House. "They shouldn't have anything to worry about."

Tweedy, a native of Kentucky, still speaks with an accent as warm and rich as the six-gallon vat of homemade chili he makes for his coworkers and friends every home game. They start eating it at 6:30 a.m. in Tweedy's office, which is wedged under the seats of section 41—so obscure it took athletic director Joe Roberson a few years to find it.

Leon Tweedy is as lean and precise as a mechanical pencil but as sturdy and comfortable as a good pair of work boots. Good qualities for a man who must show his staff how to do everything from picking up mountains of trash to replacing concrete supports without letting the stands cave in—which is sort of like removing a table cloth without disturbing the china.

"After a while," stadium worker Pete Brow jokes, "you see the games in terms of the trash they create."

"Something is being done at the stadium every day," Tweedy says. "*Every* day. New seating, concrete restoration, painting this place from one end to the other. It takes a lot of money to keep this ol' gal up. Everything is really jumping around here . . .'cept my salary."

Because Tweedy almost always leaves the gates open during weekdays, they get a steady stream of visitors, both invited and uninvited.

"We *like* to have people come in, see the field, and take their pictures," Tweedy insists. "We have hardly any trouble."

While it's true that most Big Ten schools are casual about locking up their stadiums during the week, none seem quite as officially determined to accommodate the public as U-M. Tweedy and his staff host over two hundred tours each year, including schools, senior citizen groups, prospective students, and Japanese businessmen—all for free.

Most just stand and gawk. "Very rarely do they really walk around," says Bob Patrick, who's the director of the U-M Public Safety Department, which patrols the stadium. They don't run between the pews or carve their initials in them. "You do not see that type of vandalism. They treat it like a historical landmark."

Of course, some want to do more than watch. Tweedy says such folks almost always do one of four things: run through the tunnel, make the famous Desmond Howard catch in the northeast corner ("I've seen that catch over a thousand times," Tweedy says), do Howard's Heisman pose in the endzone, and see how far out they can kick a field goal. In addition to the Desmond wannabes, the stadium also attracts a handful of runners each day, who test themselves against the world's biggest StairMaster—4,476 steps in all.

As Tweedy talked, the stadium received John and Ruth Heyer, both retired, who traveled from California to see Amish farms in Ohio, the Indianapolis Motor Speedway, and, of course, the Big House. Julie Granito, a junior at Michigan, drove her old Connecticut high school friend straight from the airport to the stadium before dropping off her luggage.

They were joined by a group of third-graders from Dearborn, almost all of them from Yemen, Iraq, or Lebanon. The kids formed two neat lines at the mouth of section 11, clutching the railing and oohing to themselves as if preparing to go on their first roller coaster. Once they were sitting safely down by the south goalposts, their fear was transformed into a happy log-jam of questions.

"Are you the boss of this?" one student asked tour guide Trenna Garner.

"No, President Duderstadt is," she explained.

"He made this all by himself?"

"What's that for?" asked another student, pointing to the press box.

"That's where they have the speakers," a classmate said, "to tell people who's winning."

As much as Tweedy enjoys the wide spectrum of visitors, even his southern hospitality has its limits. Officials at both schools will tell you the Michigan-MSU game is usually the busiest week for trouble.

"Funny part is," Officer Patrick says, "it doesn't matter where that game is being played. Both schools have to watch it."

Good news: vandalism is very rare these days at Michigan, MSU, or any other Big Ten field. Most intruders are lovers, not fighters—which brings us to the Fifty-Yard-Line Club. To join, a couple must sneak into the stadium and reunite at midfield—if you get my drift—a practice that probably started at Penn State.

"On the old term system, school didn't let out until late May," one Penn State alumnus told me. "With the warm weather students would migrate to Beaver Stadium, sometimes a dozen couples at a time. Some nights you had to settle for the thirty-yard line."

"Jed Thompson" (not his real name) is a Michigan alum and campus restaurant manager who recently joined Michigan's Fifty-Yard-Line Club. "I'd been thinking about it for years," Thompson told me.

When he and his girlfriend decided to go for it, they discovered it wasn't as easy as they expected. Lest you think it might be cool to join the Club, be forewarned: to get into the stadium at night requires climbing over a perilous ten-foot-high chain-link fence with a couple feet of barbed wire at the top. One coed recently got her hair got caught in the barbed wire, and another guy broke his leg climbing over it—and wasn't found until security made its rounds. And if all that doesn't scare you off, Jed Thompson's partner in crime discovered how difficult it is to get the yard-line paint off her back. She went home that night with a white stripe on her spine just like the female lead in a Pepé Le Pew cartoon.

"I was on the fifty twice," Thompson says, "and there won't be a thrice."

It seems Officer Patrick's men caught Jed Thompson and his friend during their escape.

"We do prosecute," Officer Patrick says. "We have to be completely consistent—no exceptions. We can't discriminate between students and nonstudents or anything else."

Jed Thompson was quickly sentenced to seventy-two hours of community service. He's working it off at the Wildflower Bakery, a local nonprofit outfit which usually has a few court-ordered helpers on its staff.

"We hear a lot of good stories," Wildflower's Dave Morris says of their temporary workers. "But Jed's was one of the best."

"I asked Thompson what he did," says fellow baker Dan Calderone, "and he said, 'I got busted on the fifty-yard line.' I asked, 'What game?' and he said, 'It wasn't football.'" Calderone and Morris laughed all over again.

Jed Thompson, meanwhile, is busy learning the art of the sesame seed bun. "Turns out there's a top and a bottom to the balls of dough that become the buns," Jed says. "Get it upside down and you get a rose effect. You don't want that. Hey, I can't turn out an inferior product."

Jed Thompson's going to have ample opportunity to perfect his technique, since he has sixty hours left on his sentence. But even Jed Thompson's disavowal of the Fifty-Yard-Line Club hasn't dampened his affection for the stadium that inspired it.

"Now, whenever I'm watching a Michigan game on TV and they're on the fifty, I have to chuckle to myself—and it doesn't matter if Michigan's looking at fourth and ten. You can never watch a game there the same way.

"When you're in the Big House by yourself, it's incredibly quiet in there. And all you see are the silver stands around you, and the sky above.

"There's nothing else like it."

BRANCH RICKEY AND JACKIE ROBINSON

April 19, 1997
The Detroit News

More than any other figure in American history, Jackie Robinson stood alone.

Abraham Lincoln had an army.

Martin Luther King Jr. had a movement.

All Jackie Robinson had was a baseball bat. But in his hands, it was enough.

Robinson used that bat to gain entry into one of our nation's most stubbornly segregated institutions. Once inside, Robinson started dismantling the system with his skill, his discipline, his pride, and especially his courage.

If Robinson didn't have an army, or a movement, he did have Brooklyn Dodgers general manager Branch Rickey—and that made all the difference.

"Rickey needed Jack as much as Jack needed Rickey," said Rachel Robinson, Jack's wife.

Like Robinson, Rickey was a very complex man. If you didn't look closely at Rickey you would never predict that he would be the one to pursue the "Great Experiment" any more than you'd predict Robinson would be the best candidate to carry it out. Like Robinson, there was much more to Branch Rickey than met the eye.

Politically, Rickey was ultra-conservative. Topping his list of social evils were Franklin Roosevelt, Communism, and welfare. But he believed in fairness above all, often taking on cases for African American defendants on a pro bono basis when he was convinced they had been wrongly accused. This predisposition had been developed in Rickey as much by his legal education as his religious background.

On December 20, 1881, Wesley Branch Rickey was born in Lucasville, Ohio, and soon after surrendered to the four passions of his life: religion, education, business, and baseball. Rickey enrolled at Ohio Wesleyan in 1901, where he played catcher and coached baseball before embarking on brief stints with the Cincinnati Reds, the St. Louis Browns, and the New York Highlanders, now called the Yankees.

His refusal to play on the Sabbath—and his .239 batting average—were enough to convince him to enroll at the University of Michigan law school while coaching the school's baseball team, performing both tasks with aplomb.

The legendary sportswriter Red Smith once wrote, "Rickey was a giant among pygmies. If his goal had been the United States Supreme Court instead of the Cincinnati Reds, he would have been a giant on the bench."

"If he ever played 'Jeopardy,'" Joe Garagiola said, "he would have swept the board."

Since Rickey could have applied his considerable talents to business, law, or the clergy, you wonder why he spent his life in baseball. Sometimes he did, too.

Rickey once remarked, "I completed a college degree in three years. I was in the top ten percent of my class in law school. I'm a Doctor of Jurisprudence. I am an honorary Doctor of Law. Now, tell me: Why did I just spent four mortal hours today conversing with a person named Dizzy Dean?"

He once asked himself, in a more thoughtful moment, "why a man trained for the law devotes his life to something so cosmically unimportant as a game."

Perhaps because Rickey recognized he could do more good for his country in baseball than he could in law, business, or even the church.

We can be certain of this: Rickey never treated baseball as just a game.

For all that he might have done, Rickey seemed born to be a baseball general manager. He practically invented spring training, Ladies' Day—to bring women into what was originally a male domain—and baseball's minor league system. Former Cardinal great Stan Musial said, "An all-star team of our top farm clubs probably could have finished third behind the Cardinals and Dodgers. This was Branch Rickey's masterpiece."

When Rickey moved to the Brooklyn Dodgers in 1942, his new players quickly learned that Rickey was as cheap as he was smart. Said Dodgers outfielder Gene Hermanski: "Mr. Rickey had a heart of gold—and he kept it."

When Rickey coached the University of Michigan baseball team, he recognized freshman George Sisler's talent immediately. After Sisler finished his Hall of Fame career, he accepted Rickey's offer to work for him as a scout. In that capacity, Sisler saw Michigan outfielder Don Lund play against Wisconsin, and was sufficiently impressed to sign him to a minor league contract. After Lund played the 1946 season for the Dodgers' top farm team in Montreal, where he teamed with Jackie Robinson, Rickey invited Lund to his office in Ebbets Field.

"After we talked about Michigan for an hour or so," Lund told me, "Mr. Rickey finally asked me what kind of contract I wanted, and I said I wanted a major league contract with a $7,500 bonus. He said, 'Sure, no problem'— and right there I knew I'd blown it," Lund recalled with a laugh. "Branch Rickey *never* would have said yes so fast unless he was getting the better deal."

Brooklyn second baseman Eddie Stankey recalled a similar negotiating session. "I got a million dollars' worth of free advice," he said, "and a very small raise."

Rickey might have been tight with a nickel, but he overflowed with courage—and he would need it.

It is tempting for us to look back on American history as a slow but steady climb for African Americans. It's tempting, but wrong.

"In fact," Pulitzer Prize–winning author George Will told me, "from 1865 to 1947, things got worse for blacks. Consider the rise of Jim Crow laws and the KKK at the turn of the century."

In the eighty years between the end of the Civil War and World War II, the biggest legal change in the status of blacks was entirely negative. In *Plessy v. Ferguson* (1896), the Supreme Court coined the phrase "separate but equal," legalizing segregation—a case Rickey would have studied thoroughly at the U-M Law School, a little more than a decade after the ruling came down, alongside a number of African-American and female students. The wrongheadedness of this ruling struck him immediately.

As World War II ended, Rickey believed it was high time to change this—and he believed the national pastime was the place to start.

"It took a big man to do what he did," Negro League legend Buck O'Neil told me. "A lot of guys were against it, see. It could have killed Rickey in baseball if this thing had blown up."

Said rival general manager Larry MacPhail: "When Rickey makes up his mind, he'll walk through a ten-foot brick wall."

The question was: who could do it?

Rickey was looking for the man best suited to survive this dangerous experiment. The man he found wasn't the best player available, and he certainly wasn't a pacifist.

In 1944, while a captain in the U.S. Army, Robinson refused to move to the back of the bus—eleven years before Rosa Parks—for which he was court-martialed.

This act of defiance didn't turn Rickey off, but impressed him. Rickey once said, "I don't like silent men when personal liberty is at stake."

Despite Robinson's temper and rough skills, Rickey figured that with Robinson's competitive fire, social awareness, and uncommon discipline, he was the right man for the job.

In August of 1945 Branch Rickey invited Robinson to his Ebbets Field office. After some small talk Rickey got to the business at hand: He wanted to bring Robinson up to the major leagues in a year or two, but he needed to know if Robinson could survive long enough to establish a foothold. Could he put up with southern hotel clerks, racist waiters, and cutthroat runners who would want to "haul off and sock you right in the cheek"?

"Mr. Rickey," Robinson asked, "are you looking for a Negro who is afraid to fight back?"

"I will never forget the way he exploded," Robinson wrote years later.

"Robinson, I'm looking for a ballplayer with guts enough *not* to fight back."

After thinking it over, Robinson answered Rickey quietly and deliberately. "Mr. Rickey," he finally said, "I've got two cheeks. If you want to take this gamble, I promise you there will be no incidents."

"You're asking the man for quite a bit," Buck O'Neil says today of the arrangement. "To be that strong you had to know exactly what it meant for a black man to play in the major leagues. Lucky for us, Jackie did."

In signing Robinson first, Rickey didn't make the obvious choice. He made the bold one—and the smart one.

Some critics accused Rickey of bringing Robinson up solely to win games and fill seats. No doubt the competitive and business advantages of breaking the color barrier appealed to Rickey, but Rickey's deeply held belief in social justice, especially in light of the incredible risk he was taking with his own career, suggest higher motives.

Filmmaker Ken Burns told me, "I feel in my gut that Rickey knew, beyond any business considerations, that [integrating baseball] was good for mankind."

About Robinson's debut, Rickey said, "It's not a move, it's a movement."

"The most important black person in American history is Martin Luther

King," said George Will. "A close second, I would argue, is Jackie Robinson. He came before King, and began the consciousness-raising of whites and blacks that resulted in King's career."

When Jackie Robinson broke the color barrier, virtually no institution in American life had been officially and completely integrated. Not the schools, not the government, not the military—and certainly not baseball, where resistance seemed greatest. Rickey's and Robinson's act not only preceded all the advances, it made them possible.

Ken Burns spent almost a decade researching his documentaries on the Civil War and baseball. "The first *real* progress in race relations after the Civil War, sorry to say, was Jackie Robinson," he told me. "Jackie Robinson was the man who continued the work Lincoln laid out."

Martin Luther King Jr. counted himself among Robinson's many admirers. "Jackie Robinson made it possible for me in the first place," he once said. "Without him, I would never have been able to do what I did."

The Robinsons often said the same thing about Branch Rickey himself.

"I owe him a debt of gratitude," Robinson said. "I will always speak out with the utmost praise for the man."

In 1965, Branch Rickey died at age 84. When a reporter called Robinson to pass on the sad news, Robinson fell silent, unable to speak. Finally, he turned to his wife Rachel and said, "Rae, take this call. Mr. Rickey has just died."

Later, Rachel said, "Rickey needed Jack as much as Jack needed Rickey."

Buck O'Neil agreed. "Don't ever forget," he told me. "When you say Jackie Robinson, to say Branch Rickey too—see, because you couldn't have one without the other."

HOW PRESIDENT HANNAH MADE MICHIGAN STATE

December 13, 2013
The Ann Arbor Chronicle

Since Mark Dantonio arrived in East Lansing in 2007, Michigan State has won three Big Ten Championships and five bowl games, the most by any coach in Spartan history. But what's more impressive: Michigan State no longer needs a ranked football team to be a world-class university.

Every university has got its giants, of course, but those schools born around the Civil War needed bigger men than most to carve these campuses out of forests, then build them to rival the world's greatest institutions—and to do it all in mere decades.

The list of icons includes the University of Chicago's William Rainey Harper and Amos Alonzo Stagg, who put their new school on the map; Michigan's James B. Angell and Fielding Yost, who built the foundation for what Michigan is today; Notre Dame's Knute Rockne, who made Notre Dame famous, and Father Ted Hesburgh, who made it great.

At Michigan State, that man is John A. Hannah.

Born in Grand Rapids in 1902, he was a proud graduate of Michigan Agricultural College in 1923, earning a degree in poultry science. He rose to become the school's vice president, whose job description included serving as the state's secretary of agriculture. He married the school president's daughter, then succeeded his new father-in-law as president in 1941.

Hannah's timing was unusually good, with the G.I. Bill opening the doors for 2.2 million returning veterans nationwide, and the auto industry's golden era, generating unprecedented wealth for the state's citizens, who dreamed bigger dreams for their children. Seemingly unrelated, the University of Chicago's football team dropped out of the Big Ten in 1939.

Hannah cleverly exploited all three opportunities. Back when state schools were actually funded by the state, Hannah knew he needed more help from Lansing, which had long favored the flagship university in Ann Arbor. So, while U-M president Harlan Hatcher rolled up to the capital in a chauffeured Lincoln Town Car, the unassuming Hannah hopped in his pickup truck for the trip up Michigan Avenue to the statehouse—and got more money each time he did it from his friends in the legislature.

When Hannah gathered enough funds for a new dorm, he built a beautiful brick building with green trim, filled it with former GIs, then took their tuition and built the next dorm—and kept doing it, for decades.

He also lobbied hard to take Chicago's place in the Big Ten. He had to, because Michigan coach and athletic director Fritz Crisler, a proud alumnus of the University of Chicago who had played for Stagg, didn't want to see the Spartans replace his Maroons.

In 1947, President Hannah fought back by hiring Clarence "Biggie" Munn, who had been Crisler's captain at Minnesota, and his assistant at Michigan. To gain stature, the next year Michigan State started an annual rivalry with Notre Dame, which was only too happy to help the upstart Spartans stick it to their mutual enemy, Michigan, which had effectively kept Notre Dame out of the Big Ten for years.

When the Spartans finished both the 1951 and 1952 seasons as undefeated national champions, nobody could deny they could play football in the Big Ten. The Spartans enjoyed their greatest success during Hannah's last two decades, claiming four more national titles and a 14–4–2 record against Michigan.

Hannah attended every Spartan football game, home and away, throughout his tenure. *Ripley's Believe It or Not* even published a piece on his streak. He recognized the central role the Spartans' success played in raising the profile of the former cow college, which in turn helped attract more state funding, more skilled students, and more first-rate professors to East Lansing—following a familiar formula used by Chicago, Notre Dame, and other major schools.

Hannah's strategy transformed the humble Michigan Agricultural College, with just six thousand students he had inherited, into the forty-thousand-student Michigan State University, a major research center good enough to be admitted to the prestigious Association of American Universities—and he did it all in about two decades, one of the most remarkable success stories in the history of higher education.

Perhaps most important, what President Hannah built has endured, surviving the state's turbulent economy, the Big Three automakers' troubles, and the Spartan football team's sporadic performance. In the forty-three years since Hannah retired, the Spartans have won five Big Ten titles and no national crowns—but the stature of the university he built has continued to grow.

In President Hannah's penultimate State of the University address, delivered on February 12, 1968, he stated: "The university is an integral part of a social system that has given more opportunity, more freedom and more hope to more people than any other system."

President Hannah greatly increased all three through improved state funding, the G.I. Bill—and Spartan football.

Michigan State University would not be what it is today without President Hannah or his beloved Spartans.

THE TIGERS' LOVE FOR LAKELAND

March 1997
The Detroit News

LAKELAND, FL — If you think the divorce rate among U.S. couples is high, check out the recent rash of break-ups between major league baseball teams and their spring training sites. In the past 40 years, all but four of Major League Baseball's 30 teams left their spring training towns at least once, and only half of them still train in Florida.

The divorced include the Cincinnati Reds, who were in Tampa for 41 years before moving to Plant City, Florida in 1988, Sarasota ten years later, then Goodyear, AZ, in 2009. The New York Yankees spent 33 years in Ft. Lauderdale before taking the Reds' place in Tampa in 1996. Even the St. Louis Cardinals' 51-year run in St. Petersburg came to an end when they moved to Jupiter, Florida.

In this permissive environment of town-swapping, the Tigers stand as a pillar of fidelity. Except for three years during World War II, when they trained in Evansville, IN, the Tigers have been coming down to Lakeland every year since 1934. That's a total of 84 seasons, by far the longest marriage in the majors.

But why Lakeland? Compared to tourist magnets like Tampa Bay, Sarasota, and Ft. Lauderdale, Lakeland is a relatively small, inland town with few tourist attractions—hardly the most glamorous date at the Spring Training prom.

But as many divorced couples know, looks don't last. Lakeland's attributes may not be immediately obvious, but they have proven more valuable in the long run. According to Tigers' former general manager Randy Smith, Lakeland has always given the Tigers "everything we've asked for," often anticipating the team's needs without being asked. The people of Lakeland have showered the organization with appreciation at every turn, including an annual barbeque they put on in the Tigers' honor. It's worth noting that a mere "barbeque" done Lakeland style feeds about 1,100 people and costs about $30,000.

The rock-solid bond between the Tigers and their winter hosts is a direct result of the close relationship between former Tigers' president Jim Campbell and Joker Marchant, who served officially as the director of Lakeland's park and recreation department for 35 years, and unofficially as the "Boss Hog" of this city, getting things done that no one else would dare.

They're both gone now, but the bond they created between the Tigers and this town is still thriving today.

Major league baseball teams started migrating to Florida during the Roaring Twenties, when a St. Petersburg businessman named Al Lang convinced some of the owners to bring their teams down to Florida for preseason practice. Some came down, but most bounced around for years, including the Tigers, who practiced in nine states and fourteen cities, including such far flung sites as Shreveport, San Antonio, and Sacramento.

Lakeland's early economy was built on railroad tracks, strawberry fields, and seedless grapefruit. When the Tigers arrived in 1934, Lakeland only had about 20,000 people, and not much to do. For decades, that's how things stayed.

Hall of Fame broadcaster Ernie Harwell has been visiting Lakeland since 1941. "When we first started coming here the county was dry, so you didn't have many good restaurants," he says. "The Elks Club was allowed to serve whiskey, and therefore was very popular. Nothing happened here but morning, noon, and night—and sometimes they skipped one of those."

From 1960 to 1980, Lakeland's population had stabilized around 40,000. During the state's second boom in the 1980s, Lakeland's population almost doubled to 78,000, bringing the economy along with it.

"Lakeland's a whole lot more than it was when I got here 25 years ago," says Dave Miller, the Tigers' minor league director. "There were only two or three places to go out then. But now you've got dozens of choices."

"Downtown was really dead five, ten years ago," said one waitress. "But now they've got bars and restaurants going, so it's fun to go downtown again."

Lakeland still may not be on the travel agents' short list of tourist destinations, but it's good enough for Lou Whitaker and Chet Lemon to make their permanent homes here—along with approximately 12,000 other former Michiganders.

As one transplant said, "Lakeland grows on you."

As for the Tigers, they were smitten with Lakeland from the start. The club's leaders never cared much about the number of restaurants or tourist attractions; they've only wanted what's best for their baseball team.

Lakeland sits a half-an-hour from the Gulf of Mexico and an hour from the Atlantic, but right in the middle of the baseball action. Tourists may love Ft. Lauderdale, but baseball players don't. It's the most unpopular bus ride of the spring season—one the Tigers aren't even making this year.

"Our location couldn't be better," Dave Miller says. "We're close to most of the other teams, and it might actually be to a ball club's advantage to be a little more removed from the ol' nightlife. Our guys are focused on baseball."

By far the most important consideration for a major league club, however, is the quality of the facilities. On that score, Lakeland has always ranked among the best in baseball—maybe the very best.

"We've got it all right here in Lakeland," Dave Miller says. "And all on one site. It's a real advantage."

The facilities are impressive, but Lakeland's support is more so. It's the Lakeland taxpayers, not the Tigers, who own the elaborate Tigertown facilities. Lakeland devotes $500,000 of their annual $7 million parks and recreation budget just to maintain the Tiger camp. The city puts 16 of their 186 parks workers on Tigertown detail during spring training, and keeps 8 of them there year-round.

That's why, when Dave Miller needs a couple bulletin boards hung on his office wall, it's two guys from the parks department who come in and do the work—usually the same day. It's also why, just seconds after a half-dozen Tigers finish a twenty-minute bunting drill, two other city workers make the base paths as smooth as felt on a pool table, as if no one had played there.

Because of the Lakeland staff's excellent work, the Tigers are one of the few major league teams that can afford to leave their entire grounds crew back home. As Tigertown crew chief Walter Clayton says, "We're on the ball."

For as much as the people of Lakeland give the Tigers, they get quite a bit in return. Their $500,000 annual investment is more than matched by an estimated $19 million the Tigers and their fans pump back into the local economy each year.

Nonetheless, the many jilted spring training cities must have figured out this simple equation, and yet they still lost their teams. Why has Lakeland been able to keep their team while the other towns failed?

"It's really pretty easy to explain," says Bill Tinsley, who worked for Joker Marchant for two decades before succeeding his former boss. "It's about two very stable organizations: the Tigers and the Lakeland Parks department. And it's about two unusual people: Jim Campbell and Joker Marchant."

Tiger fans will remember Jim Campbell, a reserved Northerner who was most comfortable in a coat and tie, but probably know Joker Marchant only for the stadium named in his honor. He was born Marcus Thigpen Marchant in tiny Phoenix City, Alabama, in 1908, and accepted a football scholarship to Lakeland's Florida Southern College, back when that school had a football team. He stayed on to become the director of parks and recreation for 31 years, including the years Jim Campbell worked for the Tigers.

Among Marchant's old friends, estimates of his height range from 5'-7" to 6'-0". When pressed, most conclude that he was probably a small guy who had an aura of bigness about him, especially since he wore a big white Stetson hat wherever he went. Marchant had a taut body, leathery skin, and a deep Southern drawl. He always drove a pick-up truck, never a sedan, and kept working until his body just couldn't do it anymore.

His only indulgence was leaving work every day at 5 p.m. to go home and watch re-runs of *Gunsmoke*. Then he'd hop back in his pick-up truck and work some more.

"Joker knew everybody and everybody knew him," Harwell says. "He didn't stand on ceremony. He got things done."

And he wasn't about to let petty little things like politicians, rules, or budgets get in his way.

"He always figured it was easier to ask for forgiveness than permission," Tinsley says. "If we needed something, he'd go out and buy it, then try to figure out how to pay for it.

"A few decades ago he installed our first playground equipment, despite not having any money in the budget for it. Then he went to the commission and said, 'We need to pay $2,500 for playground equipment. Now, we don't *have* to keep it—but I just drove by that playground on the way to this meeting and saw 50 kids playing on it, and I don't want to be the one to tell those kids we gotta send it back.'"

"Of course, they paid for it," Tinsley says, chuckling at the memory. "Joker was a tough guy to supervise, but a great guy to work for. He never asked us to do anything he wouldn't do himself, and he would never, *ever*, let you down. Joker Marchant's word was his bond, and Campbell was the same way. Joker had more pull than any elected official in town."

As a result, Marchant could open his department's books for the Tigers—a practice the city follows to this day—and not worry about his superiors' disapproval. This way Campbell could work directly with Marchant, instead of going through a bunch of political committees, and still be confident whatever they decided would be carried out.

"You want to know how they made Tigertown?" Tinsley asks. "Campbell and Joker walked out to the middle of a field, drove a stake in the ground and said, 'Here's Tigertown.' And that was that."

These two men, as different on the surface as they could be, shared a deep devotion to their work, a penchant for details, and the ability to size up someone's character in a five-minute meeting. Despite their differences, they both saw in the other a kindred spirit.

"We had a minor-league pitcher in the mid-80s," Dave Miller recalls, "and he came to spring training with a boa constrictor, a huge one. I went to Joker and said, 'What're we going to do with this?' He said, 'We have an extra room in the cafeteria, so let's put him in there.'

"Campbell hears about this, of course, and he's hotter'n a firecracker. He's givin' me the business up one side and down the other, every expletive in the book and he even threatens to fire me. Finally I said, sort of meekly, 'Joker said it was okay.'"

At that, Campbell stared at Miller, bulged his eyes, pursed his lips and simply walked away.

"*That's* how close those two were," Tinsley says. "But my best memory of those two guys is just them eating breakfast together every morning in the old cafeteria, pretty happy with the lives they had led. Here was a guy from big city Ohio and the other from small town Alabama, but they had bonded more closely than any two guys I'd seen."

Almost as close as the devoted couple they left behind: Lakeland and the Tigers.

THE VOICE OF THE TIGERS

May 5, 2010
The Detroit News

If you grew up in Michigan in the seventies, as I did, Bob Seger sang the soundtrack to your summers, and Ernie Harwell provided the voice over.

Who is Ernie Harwell? Well, if you were listening to a baseball game and the announcer somehow claimed to know that the fan who just caught the foul ball is from Calumet, Kalkaska, or Kalamazoo, it's a safe bet you were tuned in to Ernie Harwell.

Our family trips up north were always accompanied by Harwell's comfortable cadences filling the car. He didn't simply broadcast baseball games. He turned them into stories. In Harwell's world, a batter didn't merely strike out. He was "called out for excessive window shopping," or "caught standing there like the house by the side of the road."

Like millions of others, my love of baseball was fostered by Ernie Harwell. He covered more games than anyone in baseball history, including forty-one years' worth for the Tigers. When *Sports Illustrated* drew up its all-time baseball dream team, it tapped Harwell as the radio announcer. In 1981, he became the first active announcer to be inducted into the baseball Hall of Fame, and his voice has appeared in six films, including classics like *Cobb*, *Paper Lion*, and *One Flew Over the Cuckoo's Nest*.

"TV, and especially the instant replay, made the analyst the number one guy in the booth, not the play-by-play man," Harwell told me. "And if you try to tell a story on TV, the graphics will pop up in the middle of it. Baseball is still the perfect game for radio, because you can tune in and tune out throughout the game while you're doing something else."

Unlike most modern announcers who prattle on with mindless patter and meaningless factoids, Harwell preferred to treat his listeners to a few homespun stories and a healthy dose of "companionable silences," something Zen masters refer to as the delicious "space between the notes."

"I don't believe much in stats," Harwell explained. "I'd rather keep quiet than say a guy has hit safely in six of the last eight games, or is two-for-six lifetime against this particular pitcher. When you're quiet, you can let the listeners enjoy the sounds of the ballpark itself, which I think is better."

Just about everybody, it seems, agrees with his philosophy.

"There is a timelessness," Bob Costas writes, "to [Harwell's] approach."

Like most members of baseball's first generation of radio stars, Harwell was raised in the South, in a time and a place that valued relaxed conversation over the rush of commerce. Born in Washington, Georgia, in 1918, Harwell grew up delivering the daily paper for *Gone with the Wind* author Margaret Mitchell, reading the *Sporting News*, and listening to Atlanta Crackers minor league games on a crystal radio set. Harwell understood at an early age the special relationship between announcer and fan.

"My dad had multiple sclerosis," Harwell said. "He rarely left his wheelchair, and the highlight of his day was listening to the Atlanta Crackers games on the radio."

At age sixteen, Harwell pitched *The Sporting News* for the post of Atlanta correspondent—and he got it. At twenty-nine, he realized another dream when he became the Crackers' play-by-play man. Just two years later, in 1948, the listener-friendly Harwell caught the ear of the Brooklyn Dodgers, who were so impressed they offered to give the Crackers catcher Cliff Dapper in exchange for Harwell, making him the only broadcaster in baseball history ever traded for a player.

Harwell's timing was perfect. TV hadn't yet invaded radio's turf, and New York was about to become the capital of baseball, with the Brooklyn Dodgers, the Yankees, and the New York Giants dominating the sport throughout the fifties. New Yorkers could debate which team had the game's best centerfielder, the Dodgers' Duke Snider, the Giants' Willie Mays, or the Yankees' Mickey Mantle, and who had the best lead announcer, Brooklyn's Red Barber, the Giants' Russ Hodges, or the Yankees' Mel Allen—southerners all.

"New York was great for me," Harwell says. "The fans were supercritical of the players and the announcers, but with three teams in the city, they'd listen to all three broadcasts. It kept you honest."

The unusually competitive conditions soon thrust New York's announcers and managers into a game of musical chairs. Harwell moved across the river to the Giants' Polo Grounds to become Russ Hodges's sidekick, while a young man named Vin Scully replaced Harwell in the Dodgers booth.

During the Harwells' years in New York, his son Gray's teacher asked the students what their fathers did for a living.

Gray piped up. "My father doesn't work. He just goes to the ballpark."

"So many guys are just working for paychecks," Harwell said, "that I just appreciate the fact I've got a job I love."

When the American League created the Baltimore Orioles in 1954, Harwell left the Giants to become the new team's lead announcer. There he witnessed Brooks Robinson's debut—and a lot of bad baseball —before pulling up roots for the fourth and last time in 1960, moving his wife Lula and their four children to the Motor City.

"If life was too smooth," Harwell said, "it wouldn't be much fun."

In the four-plus decades that followed, Harwell became more closely linked with the Tigers than Harry Carey was with the Cubs. Along the way Harwell saw more than a few highlights, including the Tigers' World Series triumphs in 1968 and 1984.

"A magical year," Harwell recalled of the time the Tigers jumped out to 35–5 start and never looked back. "It all just came together."

He'd tell you Willie Mays was the best player he'd ever seen, that Jackie Robinson was the most courageous, and that a lovably quirky Tigers pitcher named Mark Fidrych, who used to get on his knees to groom the mound before each inning, "was probably the most charismatic guy we've ever had here in Detroit. A real breath of fresh air."

"We throw around words like 'legendary' and 'excellent' and 'exceptional,'" longtime *Detroit Free Press* baseball writer Gene Guidi told me, "but Ernie really is. He treats everyone the same. He makes new reporters feel like they've been in the business for fifty years, and *he's* the rookie."

In 1997, I was one of those rookie reporters, lucky enough to cover spring training for the *Detroit News*. My first day there, Ernie Harwell himself sidled up next to me on a bench. We sat there, watching baseball, and chatting like old friends—just the way everyone of us imagined we already were, listening to him on the radio all those years. He invited me for dinner that night with his wife Lulu. We enjoyed a long talk, he picked up the tab, and we stayed in touch from that day on.

Four years later I wrote a story about him for an airline magazine, which came out the morning of September 11, 2001. I woke up to the phone ringing. It was Ernie Harwell, calling to thank me for the article. Who does that?

The day soon turned tragic, but Harwell's little act of humanity will always stand in my mind as a poignant counter to everything that followed that day.

A few times over the years I invited him to call in to a talk show I was hosting.

"Just ask," he always said, "and I'll come running."

And he always did.

Harwell's passion for the national pastime, and all the people connected to it, never waned. So when he announced in September that he had contracted an incurable form of cancer, and would not seek treatment, it hit all of us who knew him, or felt like we did—which, really, is just about all of us. We were losing our baseball buddy, our grandfather, our friend.

The only person who didn't seem shaken by the news was Ernie Harwell. He said, "Whatever's in store, I'm ready for a new adventure. That's the way I look at it."

Harwell was a profoundly religious man, but he never wore it on his sleeve. He simply lived it. He was, truly, at peace.

But I was not. Like just about every sports writer who knew him, I felt compelled to write about him. In that piece I told a lot of the stories above, then closed by saying, "I wish there was something I could do for him now. If he just asked, I'd come running. And you would too."

I had to deliver that line in the studio a few times before I got through it without getting too choked up. The next morning, after the piece ran, an old friend called to thank me.

Who does that? Ernie Harwell, that's who.

It's a strange sensation, knowing you're probably having the last conversation with someone you love so much. I could have talked all day with him, but I didn't want to be greedy with his time so I kept it short. I had to tell him, though, how much I appreciated hearing from him.

"Well, John, we go back a loooong way," he said. "Thanks for the wonderful story. God bless you. Good bye."

After we hung up, I sat there for a few minutes. We went back about 13 years—not really that long for a man who had friends going back more than a half-century—and I'm sure he had read better stories about his life and career than mine that week alone. But he still took the time to call.

So, thank you, Mr. Harwell, for a lifetime of wonderful stories.

God bless you.

Good bye.

WILLIAM CLAY FORD: MISUNDERSTOOD MAN

March 12, 2014
The Wall Street Journal

In the course of his eighty-eight years, William Clay Ford, who died Sunday, captained Yale's tennis team, earned an engineering degree, and chaired Ford Motor Co.'s finance committee, which is enough for any lifetime.

But he will likely be remembered mainly as the owner of the Detroit Lions, during five woefully unsuccessful decades. Since he took over the franchise in 1964, the Lions have won exactly one playoff game, and remain the only NFL team to miss out on all forty-eight Super Bowls. Ford's critics claim he was a snob who didn't care about the average fan, a fat cat who was more focused on profits than the playoffs.

False, and false.

Bill Ford Sr. was a humble and competitive owner who made the mistake of hiring nice guys who finished last.

It is impossible to understand the Lions organization without first understanding the man who owned them. The sibling rivalries within the Ford family shaped the psyche of William Clay Ford Sr., which in turn determined his selection of coaches, his generous treatment of them, and his inability to win a Super Bowl before his time was done.

The decisions that seemed so mysterious to the average fan aren't so mysterious when you understand the man who made them. Bill Ford Sr.'s family history suggests it was because he resolved to be the opposite of his cantankerous older brother, Henry II.

"Hank the Deuce" was an autocratic leader who traded on his family loyalties when convenient, drank too much, married three times, and often behaved in a cold, calculating fashion.

Bill Sr. was the antithesis of all that, by design.

Much the way Henry I manipulated, humiliated, and dominated his only son, Edsel, Henry II tried to do the same to his brothers Benson and

186

Bill. For a time it looked as though Henry II's blind ambition would grind up Bill the same way it had chewed up Benson.

In 1954, Henry II put his twenty-nine-year-old brother Bill in charge of the Continental Mark II, the second coming of their father's trademark car, the Mark I. Henry II gave Bill all the tools he needed to succeed, including a generous budget, a good team, and complete creative autonomy. Bill, a graduate of Yale's engineering school, had the same knack for design Edsel I did. He and his staff worked incredible hours to create a new standard in luxury driving.

As the landmark car was nearing completion, however, Henry II took Ford Motor Company's stock public. Henry II feared telling potential stockholders their newest model would lose money, so they hiked the price, stripped Bill's car of its best features, and pirated them for the new Thunderbird—which was a great success.

After Henry II sabotaged the Mark II, Bill was demoralized. He took to calling his oldest brother "Lard Ass" and drinking hot gin at noon.

"The trouble is," Bill observed, "there is only room for one Ford at a time."

According to Peter Collier's classic book *The Fords*, Bill's drinking continued from 1955 to 1965, resulting in a "a ten-year lost weekend."

"What I needed most of all," Bill said later, "was something to do."

For $4.5 million, he found it: the Detroit Lions.

"I always wanted something that was all mine and mine to do," he said. "This was it."

Bill Ford entered a clinic, quit drinking cold turkey, and devoted himself to his wife, his four children, and his new football team. By the late sixties, it was clear Bill Sr. had triumphed where Edsel and Benson had failed. He had managed to get off the fast track with his sanity and family intact, and soon earned a reputation around Detroit and the NFL as a sincere, humble, and loyal man.

The contrast between the two brothers came into sharp focus on Thursday, March 13, 1980. According to Robert Lacey's book *Ford: The Men and the Machine*, Bill Sr. sat in his office at Ford World Headquarters, waiting to be named chairman by his oldest brother. Without any warning, however, Henry II came in to tell Bill that Philip Caldwell, not he, was about to be named chairman.

Bill finally let him have it. "You treat your staff like that, you treat your wives like that, and your children like that," he spat, "and now you treat your brother in the same way."

"I made a choice," Henry II later acknowledged. "I married the company."

Bill Sr., didn't. He remained happily married to his wife, and headed the only close-knit Ford household since the turn of the century.

The only place where Bill Sr. kept failing was on the football field—but contrary to his critics, it wasn't because he was an out-of-touch snob who cared more about cash than competition.

Quite the opposite. For a man born into the greatest business dynasty in U.S. history, you wouldn't know it if you worked for him.

"Let me tell you something: he's very down to earth," former head coach Rick Forzano told me, echoing the comments of a dozen people interviewed on the subject. "Mr. Ford always used to get upset with me because I would never call him Bill—but he finally he gave up. He isn't a snob by *any* stretch of the imagination."

When Bill Ford came home from Yale for the summers, he worked on the River Rouge assembly line—and loved it. He married Martha Firestone, a Vassar student and heiress to the tire fortune, who was initially against "dynastic marriages" but couldn't help falling for Bill. While Anne McDonnell married Henry II because he was a Ford, Martha Firestone married Bill in spite of it. They were genuinely crazy about each other.

"She is so unpretentious it's scary," Forzano said of Martha Ford, who is now in charge of the Lions franchise. "My wife used to say, 'The way she treats me, I think *I'm* the one who has all the money.'"

The couple worked hard to raise their children as normally as possible, and by all accounts they succeeded. Bill Ford Jr., for example, sent his two boys to Ann Arbor Huron, a public high school.

Bill Sr. found the perfect blend of informality and meritocracy in competitive athletics. As he said, "I always liked sports because they involved a democracy of talent."

Nowhere was that more true than in naval preflight school during World War II. As part of their training, hundreds of cadets—identified only by a number slapped on their backs—raced through a rigorous obstacle course designed by former heavyweight champion Gene Tunney.

Bill Ford finished first.

"Without anyone knowing my name or who I was or whether I had a dime," he recalled years ago. "I did it on my own." To the day he died, it was one of his proudest achievements.

According to the late Bill Talbert, a professional tennis star, "He was an excellent [tennis] player."

Ford's Yale teammates elected him captain of both the tennis and soccer teams, and he was also a fearless skier, occasionally courting serious injury.

After he snapped his Achilles tendon twice in the mid-fifties, he turned his attention to the links, where he soon became a scratch golfer, scoring over a half-dozen hole-in-ones.

When Ford bought the Lions in 1964, his competitive fires were easily transferred to their Sunday games. Joe Schmidt, the Hall of Fame linebacker who coached the Lions from 1967 to 1972, recalled a December game in Buffalo.

"It was a nasty day, rainy and muddy and cold," he said. "We dropped two balls in the end zone, and our kicker missed three field goals within twenty yards.

"Well, Ford came walking in the dressing room and kicked a water bucket clear across the room. I said, 'Too bad you weren't kicking for us today.' He shot me a look, but a few seconds later he had a little twinkle in his eye. That shows his sense of humor, but also his competitiveness."

Those who knew Ford well said the same thing: he was a pleasant, unassuming man with a fierce desire to win.

"I've told people Mr. Ford would give up a lot of the money he has to win," Forzano said. "When we won up at Minnesota [in 1974] for the first time in eight years, we gave him the game ball. He'll probably deny it, but this guy was crying. It excited me to no end, because I like emotional people, and Mr. Ford is an emotional person. If he's not a competitor, then I'm a laundryman."

"Mr. Ford can have anything he wants," said Bill Keenist, the Lions' longtime PR man, several years ago. "And what he wants is a Super Bowl."

It leads to the question: if Mr. Ford wanted to win as badly as the fans, and was willing to spend his money to do it, why did the Lombardi Trophy elude him?

In a nutshell, Ford was attracted to nice guys who finished third—or worse. And the reason for that was just as simple: he saw himself as one of them.

Since 1964, seventeen different coaches have guided the Lions. Only five of them had been NFL head coaches prior, and only Dick Jauron was hired as an NFL head coach afterward. Most of those seventeen coaches were Lions assistants who took over when the head coach was fired or resigned. In other words, serious national searches for proven talent rarely happened under Ford.

The former Lions leaders have more in common than just a lack of experience and success. In a business where egos run rampant, conflict is constant, and obsessiveness is the norm, the people Ford hired were generally likable, admirable men with bedrock values and a sense of perspective—with the notable exceptions of longtime right-hand man Russ Thomas and former president Matt Millen.

The chorus of respect for Mr. Ford within the organization and around the league is as uniform as is the disregard for Mr. Thomas and Mr. Millen. Not one person I interviewed offered a single kind word about either man.

Thomas was as meddlesome as he was underqualified—sort of like Henry II, without the smarts. When Thomas retired after forty-three years with the Lions, he was sufficiently disliked that the organization didn't even attempt to hold his retirement ceremony at the Silverdome. Instead, they waited for their last away game in Atlanta, where Thomas was given an official send-off before ten thousand puzzled Georgians.

The most common theory is that, during Mr. Ford's ten-year battle with alcoholism, Russ Thomas was the guy who made sure Ford got back safely to his home or office without incident. When Ford bought the Lions in 1964, his legendary loyalty prompted him to pledge to Thomas he would always have a job with the team—and as usual, Ford meant it.

As for Millen's seven-year reign as president and CEO of the organization, the Lions posted a record of 31 wins against 84 losses—an average of 12 a year—the very worst in the league. Millen wasn't a nice guy who finished last. He was an incompetent office bully who said so many stupid things he spawned websites devoted to his ill-advised comments. Even the secretaries, who almost never talk to the press, felt compelled to complain to reporters about Millen's conduct.

But those two exceptions prove the rule of the hundreds of genuinely nice people Bill Ford Sr. hired over his five decades at the helm, including the vast majority of his coaches. Bill Sr. tried to give men like Monte Clark, Wayne Fontes, and Marty Mornhinweg the chance Henry II never gave him. Bill Sr. fostered the kind of trusting, caring atmosphere in the Lions organization that Henry II could only dream of. Even those coaches and administrators who were let go by Ford speak very highly of him.

"Mr. Ford is as honest and generous a man as you can find anywhere," Forzano said. "I feel so strongly about him, I'd go back and coach tomorrow for Mr. Ford if he asked me."

"He is a very loyal and honest person," Joe Schmidt said. "I think he gives you the opportunity to do your job, he doesn't interfere, and he lets you follow through with your philosophy and what you think needs to be done—which is very unusual in the NFL these days."

The Fords have never threatened to move the team, nor hijacked the taxpayers for a new stadium. They paid most of the bill for Ford Field themselves, they successfully fought to keep their traditional Thanksgiving Day game in Detroit, and they've done it all very quietly.

Bill Sr.'s determination to be the anti–Henry II came with a price. Hiring and retaining nice guys who finished last was part of it.

But in the end, the abiding respect and affection for Bill Ford Sr. might have been worth more than a Lombardi Trophy.

Money and Madness

Having explored what I love about sports, from kid games to the stars, leaders, and legends, here I address what threatens all this: money, and the madness it too often generates.

I don't buy the arguments that it's inevitable that what we love is going to be steamrolled by the money men, and there's no stopping "progress." If we accept that lazy line of reasoning, then we shouldn't bother protecting our national parks either, since we have no choice but to surrender them to the next Niagara Falls-style tourist trap that wants to make a buck.

The good news is that we have the power to fight these forces and protect our little paradise, whether it's by scaling back "second tier" football programs like Eastern Michigan or instituting systemic reforms in college football and basketball, which I lay out in these pages.

As you already know from my pieces above, I feel sports are worth fighting for.

HOW TITLE IX CHANGED THE NATION

May 11, 2012
The Ann Arbor Chronicle

This week, the University of Michigan celebrated the fortieth anniversary of Title IX, with a host of speakers and panels discussing the historic legislation and its impact on girls, women, and the United States itself.

It all started pretty quietly. Just a sentence buried in the back of the Education Amendments Act of 1972.

"No person in the United States shall, on the basis of sex, be excluded from participation in, be denied the benefits of, or be subjected to discrimination under any educational program or activity receiving federal financial assistance."

Just a sentence—one that seems pretty straightforward to us, even self-evident. But that little line changed our nation more dramatically than any other piece of legislation the past century this side of the Civil Rights Acts.

But nowhere in that powerful paragraph do the authors say one word about sports. Title IX is not really about sports, but educational opportunities. It says a lot about Americans' unequaled belief in the value of school sports that we now consider them essential to a comprehensive education—something we never would have claimed a century ago.

Unlike the civil rights acts, which most Americans knew would have an immediate impact on daily life, the import of Title IX barely made the national radar when it passed. The NCAA's leaders, however, instantly saw the legislation as a threat to their hegemony, and did everything they could to stop it. They were joined by congressmen, school presidents, principals, athletic directors, and coaches coast to coast, all trying to limit Title IX, or kill it altogether. But the durable Title IX has survived the many attempts to cut it down.

Still, when Title IX passed it seemed like just an arcane legal issue to most Americans until a year later, when a seemingly meaningless tennis match between a 55-year-old man named Bobby Riggs and a woman twenty-six years his junior made it very real, very fast. Riggs was a Hall of

Fame player who had won six major championships in his career, and swept Wimbledon's singles, doubles, and mixed doubles titles—in 1939.

Riggs was also an incorrigible hustler. When he first challenged Billie Jean King, who would win thirty-nine major titles in her career, to an exhibition match, she declined. But after Riggs crushed Margaret Court, who was the top-ranked women's player, and half his age, to earn a *Sports Illustrated* cover story, King felt she had to accept.

They would play the "Battle of the Sexes" for the biggest payday in the history of the sport, and bragging rights that would be shared by half the country's population for years.

King had no illusions about the stakes. They weren't playing for a major title or even a sanctioned match, but something intangible—yet much bigger.

"I accepted the challenge," King said, "so that girls and women could feel positive about participating in athletics."

On September 20, 1973, in front of a Houston Astrodome crowd of thirty thousand spectators and fifty million Americans watching on TV— both still American tennis records—King stayed strong and focused, and won emphatically. In the process, so did millions of American girls, most of whom had not yet been born.

"There should be nothing," King said, "to stop them from pursuing and fulfilling their dreams."

Before Title IX and the Battle of the Sexes, one in thirty girls played high school sports. Today, more than half do.

Contrary to urban myth, the highly competitive Riggs wanted to win that match, and badly—but his theatrics were mostly for promotional purposes. He had been taught the game by a woman, won many titles with female partners, and fervently believed women should be allowed to play all sports—progressive views for his era. For this match, he was putting on an act—but it was a hell of an act.

Over the years Riggs and King became close friends, and talked often. The night before Riggs died of cancer, King called him to say, "I love you."

Title IX started with a single, dry sentence, written by legislators who could not have imagined its impact—and it ended with a short, emotional one, between the two people who made it come to life.

In between, everything changed.

THE UN-COLLECTOR

January 11, 1999
Sports Illustrated

It turns out your mom was right after all. You can get almost anything you want if you just ask nicely.

That's the whole of autograph collector Jack Krasula's strategy, if you can call it a strategy. Over the past twenty-five years Krasula, forty-nine, has amassed more than one hundred thousand autographs, signed photos, and personal letters—including the signatures of every living Hall of Famer in baseball, football, basketball, hockey, golf, track and field, swimming, bowling, and even softball—simply by writing gracious letters to the athletes, asking for their help. About 90 percent of the time, he's gotten it.

You might think this would make Krasula a big name himself, at least in collecting circles—but he's not even on the radar.

"Jack's collection is the best one I've seen," says John Stommen, who founded *Sports Collector Digest*. "But if you were to go to a sports show and ask who Jack Krasula was, I'd be surprised if anybody knew him. He's not in it for the publicity, and he's certainly not in it for the money."

Unassuming as he is, Krasula is outspoken on one point: "I've never sold *one dollar* worth of stuff," he says. "I do it for the love—and the journey."

In 1976, the young Krasula boldly launched his own company, Decision Consultants, Inc., a temp service for computer programmers. DCI started slowly, but it caught the eighties boom and now has eighteen hundred full-time employees, offices in twelve cities, and annual revenues of $160 million.

In the hallway of DCI's headquarters in suburban Detroit, Krasula has posted a personal letter from Zig Ziglar, the evangelical sales guru. "You can have everything in life you want," Ziglar wrote, "if you will just help enough other people get what they want."

What Krasula thinks his employees want, above all, is appreciation. So, twice a month, he sits down to write a personal thank-you note on every employee's paycheck. It takes him four hours.

Krasula's office feels more like a rec room than a corporate nerve center. He has a dozen baseball caps on his bookshelf, a train engine made of clarinet parts on the coffee table, and a framed doodle of Mickey Mouse drawn by Walt Disney himself on the wall. On another wall, he has a crucifix, a letter from Norman Vincent Peale, and a motivational speech by Vince Lombardi.

"Everything in his office is ultimately about success," says Lee Tonnies, one of Krasula's key lieutenants for eighteen years. "That is the core of Jack. He likes to talk about why people are successful, and compliment those who are."

That's what drew Krasula to his first NFL Hall of Fame induction ceremony in 1972. At the time he only had a handful of autographs, but as he sat there, it hit him: Why not collect them all?

Here's his modus operandi: Krasula picks a theme—Hall of Fame quarterbacks, say, or the NHL's greatest goalies—then sends three blank sheets to the first athlete on his list. The athlete signs all three and sends them back to Krasula, who then mails them out to the next person on the list. Krasula keeps a couple dozen envelopes criss-crossing the country at all times.

Even with everyone doing their part, it can take Krasula several years to round up all the usual suspects on one page, but when he's done, it's something to see. Krasula puts the finished pages in red, three-ring binders. (He now stores hundreds of these in bank vaults, but he still keeps a few around to show visitors.) He pulls one down, slowly opens it up, and then slides his finger down the lists, affectionately reading off every name, one by one, as if remembering old friends in a high school yearbook.

They're just signatures, but seeing them all together evokes something that seeing a single autograph by itself does not. Take the five-hundred-home-run club. As you study the artfully drawn autographs of Ted Williams, Willie Mays, Hank Aaron, and Mike Schmidt, you're forced to reflect less on each individual name, and more on the only thing they have in common: at one time in their lives, they were all the very best in the world at what they did. Perhaps recognizing this, the athletes who sign at the bottom of each page invariably do so with just a little more care than those at the top.

Krasula pulls down another red binder, and flips to a page devoted to World Series MVPs, then turns to the Superbowl MVPs, followed by a third sheet filled with *SI*'s Sportsmen of the Year. He even has a page reserved for the sultans of speed, an eclectic club that includes runner Frank Shorter, jockey Willie Shoemaker, and race car driver Parnelli Jones.

While most of the athletes have responded enthusiastically to Krasula's requests, some guys just don't budge.

"Mantle never signed outside of the shows, and Bill Russell wouldn't sign anything for anybody for twenty-five years," Krasula says. "Now he charges $300 [per autograph]. It's the bastards who reap the most benefit."

But for every Bill Russell there's a Joe Paterno, who always signs for free, or an Ozzie Smith, who was so moved when he signed his name under those of great infielders like Buck Leonard, Charlie Gehringer, and Brooks Robinson, that he enclosed a small, sincere note in the return envelope.

"Could I please have one of these sheets?" he asked.

Krasula happily returned the favor.

After Krasula had collected most of the autographs he wanted, he decided to ask his heroes two questions: What were the highlights of your career, and how do you think sports have changed since you played?

Former Red Sox pitcher Waite Hoyt cited his first big league win in 1919, a twelve-inning, 2–1 victory over the Tigers followed by a fight under the stands between Ty Cobb and umpire George Moriarty.

Swimmer Buster Crabbe recalled seeing the Hawaiian swim team compete at the 1924 Olympic tryouts in Indianapolis. "It was that day, without a shadow of a doubt, that I decided to become a swimmer," he wrote. "Swimming has done everything for me."

Reading Krasula's letters makes you feel like you've got a hundred grandfathers, all sharing their favorite memories with you alone.

Sometimes the former stars' answers reveal less about their careers than about themselves. Michigan Heisman trophy winner Tom Harmon claimed he succeeded only because he had great teammates and coaches. "With these talented individuals around me—I couldn't miss."

Kentucky coaching legend Adolph Rupp wasn't quite so humble. "I am very hesitant about writing about the headlines of my career because that would take hours and hours indeed. They are being published in book form and should be out in September."

"In other words," Krasula says with a wink, "I've done too much to mention, so buy my book."

Track star Billy Mills was brief, but poignant: "I ran track for fifteen years, a total of 40,000 miles, not [for] what I accomplished but to better understand . . . who I am."

While most of the retired athletes believe that money has spoiled sports, they feel less resentment toward the modern athlete than pity.

Buster Crabbe's response was typical. "In the old days it was a *sport*, and *fun*," he wrote. "And we were amateurs. Not so today! I sometimes wonder if it wasn't better years ago."

Although Krasula rarely asks for autographs in person, when you hear his stories from those encounters, you wish he did it more often.

When the Red Sox visited the Detroit Tigers in the early eighties, Krasula approached Johnny Pesky, the former Boston infielder turned assistant coach.

"He's walking around in front of the visitors' dugout when I show him a photo of himself from the 1940s," Krasula recalls. "Well, he looks at that picture, smiles, and calls the whole team over. 'Hey, c'mere!' he says. 'I wanna show you guys what a handsome cuss I was! I was better lookin' than all'a ya's!'"

During Krasula's twenty-five-year collecting career, the sports collecting business has changed as dramatically as sports themselves, and for the same reason: money.

"Ten years ago, you could get 95 percent of these [autographs] through the mail, and your only expense was postage," Krasula says. "You did it like some people do antiquing, just something fun to do. Now you have to get about 95 percent of these signatures through the autograph shows."

What used to be one of life's simple pleasures—the affectionate interaction between hero and fan—has become just another grubby financial transaction. As a result, Krasula has had to spend thousands of dollars tying up the loose ends of his collection.

Adding insult to injury, when Krasula's new bride moved in five years ago, his collection moved out. "I used to have these things all over the house," he says, chuckling, "But when I got married, nothing made the cut. Nothing!

"To any other guys out there collecting autographs, all I can tell you is, before the wedding, she'll think they're great, but the second that ring goes on, don't even *wait* for her to tell you to move the stuff out of there. It's going."

Of course, one day Krasula will have to decide what to do with his collection for good, after he's gone. With no children of his own, Krasula has a problem Willy Wonka would appreciate.

"I have a brother with a six-year-old son who's crazy about baseball," Krasula says. "He might be a candidate."

In the meantime, Krasula has fun making unexpected gifts of his treasures.

A decade ago, Krasula's employee, Lee Tonnies, stopped by his office with her eight-year-old nephew Bill, who told anyone who would listen that his hero was Jose Canseco. The kid had no ulterior motives—he didn't even know Krasula had an autograph collection—but when it got back to Krasula, he slipped out, drove home, and dug up a Canseco autograph. When Krasula got back to the office, however, Bill and his mom had just left for the airport, so Tonnies rushed off to catch them at the gate.

"Well, you should've have seen the look in Bill's eyes!" Tonnies says. "He couldn't *believe* someone would give him something like that, especially someone he didn't even know. He started to cry."

Bill is in college now, but he still has that autograph. It's in a frame, up on the wall, safe in his room at home.

ANN ARBOR NEWS' DEATH RULED SUICIDE

January 15, 2016
Michigan Radio

Last week, MLive.com, which covers ten cities in Michigan, laid off another twenty-nine employees, which was hardly surprising. On Monday, Alabama beat Clemson to claim college football's national title. These might seem completely unrelated, but I see a pattern here—and a warning for college football, if it's smart enough to listen.

In 1835, local citizens who cared about Ann Arbor started a newspaper. It survived a civil war, two world wars, the Great Depression, radio, and TV. It was still going strong well into the nineties, producing a robust 20 percent annual profit.

Did they invest the windfall back into the product, or the future? Did they take advantage of their unparalleled access to high school and college students, by getting them hooked on newspapers with free samples the way Camel cigarettes and Budweiser would have killed to do, if they were allowed? Did they notice how Apple got its products into schools at great discounts, years ago, to get students into the habit?

No, the *Ann Arbor News* and its parent company cut reporters and travel budgets, and sucked out the profits for the owners and executives, while they scoffed at the Internet. In 1998—*1998*—the *Ann Arbor News* employees still didn't have email and were given exactly one computer with Internet access. Your home had more computer power than the newsroom.

When one of the corporate executives visited the chain's paper in Kalamazoo, he saw a friend of mine doing research on their only Internet computer. The executive joked, "Ooh, you're looking at porn!" He compared the Internet to the CB radio craze in the seventies, then pointed to the computer. "Exactly the same thing. The Internet's a fad."

The executive retired with a golden parachute, leaving my friends and their readers to suffer the consequences of his ignorance, arrogance, and greed.

The chain assigned publishers and editors to the *Ann Arbor News* who weren't from Ann Arbor, didn't like Ann Arbor, and didn't move to Ann Arbor, either. The paper they produced reflected that. They didn't care as much about their employees, their readers, or their product as they did about their profits. They never seemed to grasp that those things are all connected.

They folded the *Ann Arbor News* in 2009, after 174 years. They brought the name back a few years later, with a fraction of the staff, and a smidgen of the quality. I know plenty of good, smart, hard-working people at MLive. com, but they're not the people running it.

So what's this have to do with Monday's college football game? Last year, college football set up the first four-team playoff in the sport's 146-year history. The games were great, the ratings spectacular, the profits enormous.

This year, they held the two semifinal games on New Year's Eve—and the ratings plummeted by 40 percent. Okay, the games were blow-outs, so they blamed that. But on Monday night, Alabama beat Clemson in a 45–40 thriller—and the ratings still dropped 23 percent. Now what do you blame?

I can answer that. They used to play the best bowl games on New Year's Day, from noon to night, when everyone could watch. This year they started the title game at 8:30 p.m., on Monday, January 11, a school night. The game ended after midnight. How many kids saw the finish?

You can trade tradition for novelty exactly once—and you can never swap them back, because tradition disappears as soon as you swap it. Just ask Major League Baseball, which started interleague play in 1997 to great fanfare, and now nobody seems to care. It's been done.

College football is also losing future fans by playing their regular season games at noon, or 3:30, or at night—or on Monday, Tuesday or Wednesday. The networks don't move around your favorite shows like that, for a reason: they'd lose their audience. Guess what's happening to college football? Habits take a lifetime to form, and a weekend to break. I see thousands of fans breaking the college football habit every week, the same way they broke the newspaper habit.

Ten years from now, the people running college football will be shocked—shocked!—to discover its audience is dying off, younger people are not replacing them, and attendance and ratings are falling. They will blame it on cell phones or the Internet or "kids today!" or just about anything but themselves—just like the former newspaper executives do now.

But when that happens, please don't tell me it was inevitable, or unavoidable. The *Ann Arbor Observer*, a great monthly magazine, faced the same problems the *Ann Arbor News* did, but made the opposite decisions, including sticking mainly to its print version, and most important, actually caring about its employees, its readers, and its mission. The *Observer* continues to climb back from the low point of the recession, and just gave out employee bonuses again at the end of the year.

On the electronic side, the *Ann Arbor Chronicle* did a great job, mainly by providing first-rate reporting and analysis of local government. The founders, Mary Morgan and Dave Askins, made money, too, but stopped publishing after six years simply because they decided it was time to do something else. Both publications have shown that it can be done, but only when someone is serious about doing it right.

So, when college football willfully creates the same problems newspapers have today, remember what the great Molly Ivins said about the demise of newspapers: "I don't so much mind that newspapers are dying—it's watching them commit suicide that pisses me off."

And that's exactly how I feel about the people ruining college football.

EASTERN MICHIGAN FOOTBALL
STILL NOT WORTH THE COST

A few months after I wrote this piece in August of 2016, the Eastern Michigan Eagles went on a historic run, finishing the season with a league record of 4–4 and an overall mark of 7–6, the Eagles' first winning record and bowl appearance since 1987. Athletic director Heather Lyke and football coach Chris Creighton did an amazing job rebuilding the program and attendance (both reported and actual), but the next year the Eagles slipped back to 5–7, and the attendance dropped with it. The exception seems to have proven the rule: Even at its best, EMU football's modest success does not justify the incredible costs.

August 31, 2016
National Public Radio

Last week, HBO's *Real Sports with Bryant Gumbel* investigated the arms race in college sports. It focused on three schools, including Eastern Michigan University. Gumbel asked why EMU still spends so much money to compete in Division I football.

I've been asking the same question for a decade.

The state government started "Michigan State Normal School," now Eastern Michigan University, in 1849—before Michigan State and every other state school except the University of Michigan was born. The school was created to teach teachers, always a vital mission. The University now offers everything you need to pursue a career in just about anything.

Eastern started playing football in 1879, and began competing in the Mid-American Conference in 1973. The Eagles have since won 134 conference titles in 20 sports. They excel in track, cross-country, and swimming—men's and women's—and they've had some great baseball and basketball teams, too.

But the football team is—well, bad. Very bad. The Eagles have taken home exactly one MAC title in forty-three years—and that was back in 1987. In 1995, the Eagles went 6–5, which is only notable because that was their last winning season. Under current head coach Chris Creighton, they're 3–21.

That's one problem. Here's another: last year, EMU's athletic department spent $24 million, according to the department, or almost $34 million, according to a Faculty Senate report, whose figure includes indirect expenditures like cleaning, human resources, building depreciation, and the like. But with either figure, both sides agree, most of the athletic department's money went to the football program.

Further, 80 percent of the department's budget comes from the University's general fund. (By comparison, Michigan and Michigan State get less than 1 percent of their athletic budgets from their universities' general funds.) As a result, almost $1,000 of the $10,000 in-state tuition the average EMU student pays each year goes to support the athletic department—whether they care about it or not.

And that's the next problem: Most EMU students, faculty, and alumni do not care about the football team. That's why the Eagles attract fewer than 10,000 paying fans per game—the lowest in all of Division I. Only a few thousand fans actually show up for most games, fewer than you'd see at a Friday night high school game in Ohio or Texas. Most Eastern students and alumni I know who follow college football watch the Wolverines or the Spartans, not the Eagles.

Of course, universities need to do a lot of things that don't make money, like teach Latin. That's why most universities work for the public, not for profits. It's also true that a football program can help an academic community stay connected, and keep applications and donations rolling in, too. Further, dozens of schools have leveraged football success to become academic powerhouses, including Notre Dame, Michigan State, and Penn State, among many others.

If the Eagles' football program did any of these things—raise EMU's profile, enhance its academics, or unify the community—you could have a fair debate over the cost-benefit of funding the team. But in addition to EMU's lack of success and interest in football, the program is siphoning badly needed resources from the rest of the University. Over the past decade, EMU's athletic department added twenty-one full-time positions, and doubled department staff salaries from $3.2 million to $6.4 million. Over that same span, the rest of the entire university added a total of only sixteen full-time employees.

When you see that, you have to ask some serious questions. What's the purpose of a state university? If it's to provide advanced education and research to benefit the public—which Eastern clearly does—what's the point of spending millions on a football program your students and faculty don't even care about?

These questions become more poignant when you consider most EMU students aren't from wealthy families. Typical EMU students live at home, take out expensive loans, and work their way through school. They're not looking for a rah-rah experience. They're looking to get a degree in Eastern's strong programs in business, health, and education. They get excited about the school's new $90 million science complex, not tailgating.

The most celebrated Eastern Michigan graduate at last week's ceremony was Ramone Williams, who gained headlines when it was discovered he was homeless. To save enough money to pay his tuition, he slept in the library. To EMU's credit, the school supported him and a handful of other homeless students through a unique program called MAGIC, for which Williams is grateful. Think how much more good EMU could do if it took the football coach's $450,000 annual salary and gave that money to more homeless students who are serious about making a better life.

Eastern actually has a lot of options, including dropping down to a Division II league like the Great Lakes Intercollegiate Athletic Conference. They'd swap playing Central Michigan for Grand Valley State, and save millions. They'd probably win more games, too. They'd *have* to, wouldn't they?

Or they could just drop football altogether, and spend all that money on something else—like scholarships and professors' salaries, things that students notice and care about. University of Chicago, a charter member of the Big Ten back in 1895, dropped football in 1939, and doesn't seem to have suffered for it. If football's not working and it's not helping, there doesn't seem to be any reason to keep throwing money down that particular drain.

True, the athletic department has recently generated more donations, season ticket buyers, and other revenue streams. So, perhaps the current athletic director and football coach—probably the best Eastern's had in years—deserve a chance to right the ship.

But when the EMU regents came out last week with an open letter, pledging their unwavering commitment to keeping the football team in the MAC, you have to wonder whom, exactly, EMU's regents are representing: the students, the faculty, the alumni, the state taxpayers, or the voters? Or are Eastern's regents speaking for Eastern's regents, and nobody else?

If the regents have their way, the Eagles will keep finishing last—in wins, in revenue, and in attendance. Or EMU could be a leader, and become one of the first Division I schools to say, "Enough!"

Now would be a good time to be a leader.

TRAVEL TEAM MADNESS

November 16, 2016
National Public Radio

Why do we do this? Why do spend countless hours, week in and week out, on endless road trips, transporting our child athletes across the state, even the country, while sacrificing everything else, including other sports, family dinners, and even family vacations?

Because the coaches tell us we must. If we don't, our kids won't have a chance at going pro, or getting a college scholarship, or even making their high school team.

Now, let's back that up a bit, and start with some cold facts: forget the astronomical odds of going pro. Nationally, less than 2 percent of high school athletes get college scholarships.

That's true at my alma mater, the University of Michigan, where only 2 percent of students receive *athletic* scholarships. But a whopping 70 percent receive *academic* scholarships.

That adds up to $23 million in athletic scholarships, compared to $915 million in academic scholarships—*forty times more!*

You don't have to be an AP Calculus whiz to figure out where to spend your time. You want a scholarship? Forget the fields. *Hit the books.*

The athletic scholarship racket is fool's gold, people. But they keep selling it, and we keep buying it.

Travel teams are also counterproductive. You don't get better at your sport by sitting in a van, traveling the country. You get burned out.

Legendary Yankees catcher Yogi Berra was amazed to see his grandchildren traveling the country just to take a few at-bats, then get back in the van and go home. When he was growing up in St. Louis, playing stickball with his buddy Joe Garagiola, they'd take forty at-bats by *dinner*. Berra learned to hit *by hitting*.

And what about playing one sport all year? Even the Great One, Wayne Gretzky, thinks that's crazy. "I was absolutely ecstatic to see the end of the hockey season," he said. "One of the worst things to happen to the game, in my opinion, has been year-round hockey." Gretzky spent *his* springs playing lacrosse.

I've coached eighteen seasons of baseball, hockey, and soccer. When I was an assistant coach at Culver Academies, we had two world-class players, Kevin Dean and Barry Richter, who both became captain of their college teams, and had good runs in the NHL. But at Culver, both captained the golf team. Swapping their hockey sticks for their golf clubs a few months a year didn't seem to hold them back.

In the U.S., hot-shot tennis players are pushed to enter junior tournaments year-round, and enroll in Florida's "tennis academies." But instead of ushering in a golden era of American tennis, it's ruined our most promising players. Since 2003, American men have not won a single major title.

On the women's side, the Williams sisters have been *dominant*. Why? Instead of entering them in endless tournaments across the country, their father, Richard, coached them himself on the public courts of South Central L.A., with a grocery cart full of tennis balls. The Williams sisters have won twenty-nine major titles. Their American peers have won just five—and none since 2002.

You want to succeed in sports? Go outside and play.

You want to succeed in life? Come inside and do your homework—just like always.

HOW MICHIGAN'S GREED ALIENATED FANS

By the spring of 2014, I was becoming increasingly concerned that the Michigan athletic department was committing a slow form of suicide by alienating its fans, old and young, mainly through greed. I felt compelled to write a column about this for the Bacon Blog, which runs on my website most Fridays. In other words, no media outlet had pitched me to write it, and I hadn't pitched any of them, either. This was just for me, and my blog readers.

I finished it on a Thursday night in my hotel room in Guatemala City, Guatemala, before giving a speech the next day. The next morning, my wife called me from home to tell me my site was crashing due to all the clicks the story was getting. I had apparently hit a nerve, rather unexpectedly. I wrote a follow-up column the next week, then put them together to run on PostGame. All told, among my blog readers, Michigan Radio, and PostGame, the piece got more than a million clicks, a record for me—and this was three months before the beginning of the 2014 season, which experts believed would be a good one for the Wolverines.

But after the Wolverines lost to Minnesota in the infamous "concussion game," they stood at 2–3. That's when a New York editor asked if I wanted to write another book on Michigan football. I replied that not only did I not want to write that book, I wouldn't want to read it. No, he said, we want a book about all the off-field issues you've been writing about, which he'd been following.

I said I'd think about it. By the time I finished my book proposal six weeks later, athletic director Dave Brandon had resigned, head coach Brady Hoke had been fired, interim athletic director Jim Hackett had taken over, and I knew he was hot on the heels of one James Joseph Harbaugh, no matter what the media was saying. A few days before Harbaugh was named Michigan's next coach, I signed a book deal for "Endzone: The Rise, Fall, and Return of Michigan Football." And it all started with a concern I first expressed in a hotel room in Central America.

June 23, 2014
The PostGame

This spring, the Michigan athletic department admitted what many had long suspected: Student football ticket sales are down, way down, from about 21,000 in 2012 to a projected 13,000–14,000 this season.

The department has blamed cell phones, high-definition TV, and student apathy sweeping the nation. All real problems, to be sure, but they don't explain how Michigan alienated 40 percent of its students in just two years—and their parents, too.

How did Michigan do it? By forgetting why we love college football.

The Students Are the Future

Dave Brandon, the former Domino's Pizza CEO-turned-Michigan athletic director, has often cited the difficulty of using cell phones at Michigan Stadium as "the biggest challenge we have." But when Michigan students were asked in a recent survey to rank seven factors that would influence their decision to buy season tickets, cell-phone coverage finished seventh—dead last.

What did they rank first? Being able to sit with their friends.

But Brandon did away with that last year, with a new student seating policy. Instead of seating the students by class—with the freshmen in the end zone and the seniors toward the 50, as Michigan had done for decades—last year it was first come, first served. If you wanted to sit together, you had to walk in together. (Michigan also raised the price from $195 for six games in 2013 to $295 for seven games.)

The idea was to encourage students to come early, and come often. Thousands of students responded by not coming at all.

Since the mid-70s, TV networks have loved showing blimp shots of the sold-out Big House—one of college football's iconic sights. Now, with the student section still half empty at kickoff, they don't show any.

Working with student government leaders, the athletic department revised the policy for the 2014 season, giving the best 6,000 seats to the most "frequent fliers" from 2013, and allotting the rest by class. But it was apparently too little, too late, as some 6,000 Michigan students decided to drop their tickets for 2014 anyway. Insult to injury: Michigan, like most college teams, now plays its biggest rival on Thanksgiving weekend, when most students have gone home.

If the students don't love college football now, when it's half-price, will they love it more when they're paying twice that?

Television

"We know who our competitor is," Brandon often says. "Your 60-inch, high-definition TV."

If that's true, maybe Michigan shouldn't have increased seat prices by an average of $100 each since Brandon took over in 2010. Perhaps they should stop charging six bucks for a hot dog, five bucks for popcorn, and four dollars for water. Maybe they shouldn't make their paying customers wait 20 minutes to get to their seats, another 20 to buy that six-dollar hot dog, and 20 more to visit a bathroom—marking an hour waiting in line for things fans at home can get in a minute.

Of course, every college football season ticket holder's most hated delay is TV timeouts. Because just about every major college game is televised, ticket holders have to endure about twenty commercial breaks per game, plus halftime. That adds up to more than 30 minutes of TV timeouts—about three times more than the 11 minutes the ball is actually in play.

To loyal fans, who sit in stadiums that are often too hot in September and too cold in November and too rainy in between, this is as galling as taking the time, money, and effort to drive downtown to a local store, only to have to wait while the clerk talks on the phone with someone who didn't bother to do any of those things.

I'm amazed how eagerly universities have sold their souls to TV. It wasn't always this way. Michigan's legendary coach, Bo Schembechler, often said, "Toe meets leather at 1:05. If you want to televise it, fine. If you don't, that's fine too."

Bo's boss, Don Canham, backed him. For years, TV was dying for a night game at the Big House. Canham wasn't. So, they compromised—and didn't have one.

If season-ticket holders want night games, give 'em what they want. But nobody likes waiting for TV to decide when your favorite team is going to play that week, especially fans flying in from far away.

Why do the people who run college football let TV spoil your day at the stadium? TV doesn't make spectators at the Indy 500, the Masters, or the World Cup wait for their ads—yet those events still make billions. If the TV whizzes can't figure out how to make a buck on football without ruining the experience for paying customers, those fans will figure it out for themselves, and stay home.

While TV is running ads for fans at home, college football stadiums too often give their loyal season-ticket holders not the marching band or—heaven forbid—time to talk to their family and friends, but rock music and, yes, ads! To its credit, Michigan doesn't show paid advertisements, but the ads it does show—to get fans to host their weddings at the 50-yard line, starting at $6,000, and hold their corporate receptions in the skyboxes, starting at $9,000—Michigan fans find just as annoying.

Yes, advertising in the Big House does matter. Americans are bombarded by ads, about 5,000 a day. Michigan Stadium used to be a sanctuary from modern marketing, an urban version of a national park. Now it's just another stop on the sales train.

Everything the ticket holders spend hundreds of dollars to wait for and pay for, they can get at home for next to nothing—including the ads—plus better replays. They can only get the marching band at the Big House.

Survey after survey points the finger for lower attendance not at cell phone service or HDTV, but squarely at the decisions of athletic departments nationwide. Fans are fed up paying steakhouse prices for junk food opponents, while enduring endless promotions. The more college football indulges the TV audience, the more fans paying to sit in those seats feel like suckers.

The Scandal Is Greed

Yes, Michigan's athletic department has always followed basic business practices, but it has never been run strictly as a business—until now. The proof is the wait list, which former athletic director Don Canham grew by the thousands. Canham was a multimillionaire businessman in his own right. If he wanted to "maximize revenue," he knew he could increase the price to meet demand, just like hotels do. But he didn't, because he believed that would dispel the magic of Michigan Stadium.

Brandon's predecessor, Bill Martin, introduced Personal Seat Licenses to the Big House, but only after the nation's next 19-biggest stadiums had already done so. Even then, Martin's PSL program was relatively moderate, he spared the fans in the endzones, and he lowered ticket prices after the 2008 recession.

"Just because you *can* charge them more," Martin told me, "doesn't mean you *should*. You're not there to ring up the cash to the *n*th degree. It's a nonprofit model!"

Michigan fans rewarded Martin's approach with loyalty. Even after the team finished 3–9 in 2008 and 5–7 in 2009, the wait list remained robust.

In Brandon's first four years, he has increased the operating budget from $107 million to $147 million. That does not include the building program, most recently estimated at $340 million. In Brandon's defense, he has generated a $5 million surplus (down from $9 million a year ago) and the buildings will benefit all Michigan's teams, not just football and basketball. But his budget also includes his $1 million salary, almost three times what Bill Martin paid himself—and yes, the AD *does* pay himself—plus Brandon's $300,000 annual bonus, which contributes to a 72 percent increase in administrator compensation; not to mention an 80 percent increase in "marketing, promotions and ticketing"; and a 340 percent increase in the department's budget for "Hosting, Food, and Special Events."

Okay, you start dictating terms to TV networks, they might cut back on the cash—though I doubt it. But even if they did, what would that mean? Perhaps Michigan's rowing team would have to make do with a $20 million training facility, instead of a $25 million one. Maybe Michigan head coach Brady Hoke would have to get by on $2 million a year, instead of $4 million. Perhaps Brandon might just have to feed his family on $300,000 a year, instead of $1.15 million.

I think Michigan could somehow survive these deprivations. It would be worth it if, in the bargain, the university got its soul back.

I've come to believe it's not scandal that will bring down college athletics, but greed. How long can these numbers, held up by increasingly unhappy fans, continue to skyrocket before they come crashing down to earth?

All that money comes from someone—and that someone is you, the fans. Michigan football tickets used to be underpriced, and you knew that when you scalped them for more than you paid. Now they're overpriced, and you know that when you try to sell them through Michigan's Official Scalper, StubHub, and get far less.

The wait list is long gone. The department has been sending wave after wave of emails to former ticket holders, retired faculty members, and even rival fans to assure them, "The deadline has been extended!" Beg your former customers to come back five times, and you don't have a deadline, and you don't have a wait list.

This fall Michigan is in danger of breaking its string of 251 consecutive games with 100,000-plus paid attendance, which started in 1975. Michigan boasts the most living alumni in the world, roughly 500,000, and the second biggest fan base, of 2.9 million, behind only Ohio State's.

Michigan fans are not the canaries in the coal mine. They are the coal miners. The people who run college football should take note.

Who the Fans Are, and What They Want

Michigan's biggest problem is not knowing who its customers are, what they're like, and what they want.

Brandon often says, "We all think of every home Michigan football game like a miniature Super Bowl."

I don't know any Michigan fans who think that. Quite the opposite, they think Michigan football games are the *antidote* for the artificial excess of the Super Bowl—as do most college football fans.

In 2005, then-athletic director Bill Martin commissioned a survey that revealed more than 50 percent of Michigan season-ticket holders had been buying them for more than two decades, but only 9 percent of them also bought season tickets to *any* professional team. This tells us a basic truth: Michigan football fans don't just love football. They love *Michigan* football—the history, the traditions, the rituals—the timeless elements that have grown organically over decades. They are attracted to the belief that Michigan football is based on ideals that go beyond the field, do not fade with time, and are passed down to the next generation—the very qualities that separate a game at the Big House from the Super Bowl.

After the 2013 Notre Dame night game, Brandon said, "You're a 17-year old kid watching the largest crowd in the history of college football with airplanes flying over and Beyonce introducing your halftime show? That's a pretty powerful message about what Michigan is all about, and that's our job to send that message."

Is that really what Michigan is all about? Fly-overs, blaring rock music, and Beyonce? Beyonce is to Michigan football what Bo Schembechler is to—well, Beyonce. No, Michigan football is all about lifelong fans who've been coming together for decades to leave a bit of the modern world behind—and the incessant marketing that comes with it—and share an authentic experience fueled by the passion of the team, the band, and the students. That's it.

In his speeches, Brandon often mentions he's served as the CEO for three Fortune 500 companies—the apotheosis of a recent trend among major programs such as Oregon, Notre Dame, and Penn State, who've passed over experienced athletic directors to hire outside business gurus.

But if Brandon knows so much about business, why does he know so little about the people who've been filling the Big House for decades?

When the late Michigan broadcaster Bob Ufer said, "Michigan football is a religion, and Saturday is the holy day of obligation," he was on to something.

If the people running college football see their universities as just brands, and the athletic departments as merely businesses, they will turn off the very people who've been coming to their temples for decades. Athletic directors need to remember the people in the stands are not customers. They're believers. Break faith with your flock, and you will not get them back with fancier wine.

If you treat your fans like customers long enough, eventually they'll start behaving that way, reducing their irrational love for their team to a cool-headed, dollars-and-cents decision to buy tickets or not, with no more emotional investment than deciding whether to go to the movies or buy new tires.

After a friend of mine took his kids to a game, he told me, "Michigan athletics used to feel like something we shared. Now it's something they hoard. Anything of value they put a price tag on. Anything that appeals to anyone is kept locked away—literally, in some cases—and only brought out if you pay for it. And what's been permanently banished is any sense of generosity."

After Brandon became Michigan's 11th athletic director in 2010, he often repeated one of his favorite lines: "If it ain't broke . . . *break it!*"

You have to give him credit: He has delivered on his promise.

HOW TO FIX COLLEGE SPORTS

October 9, 2013
The PostGame

Big Ten Commissioner Jim Delany—who might be the smartest man in college sports—stood outside the Big Ten's brand-new offices recently, telling a group of reporters, "Maybe in football and basketball, it would work better if more kids had a chance to go directly into the professional ranks. If they're not comfortable and want to monetize, let the minor leagues flourish."

It isn't clear if Delany's comments reflected his deeply held beliefs, an offhand comment, or just a daring bluff. But if it's the latter, it isn't as daring as it seems. By challenging the NFL and NBA to start their own minor leagues, Delany doesn't have much to lose. He knows they won't, because they have every reason not to. They've used the college leagues to develop their players from the day the pro leagues started. Why would they stop the gravy train now? And even if they did, it wouldn't cost the Big Ten much, if anything.

But if we call Delany's bluff and play it out, we'll see it leads to one idea that could actually save what we love most about college football: the passion no other sport can match.

The Unexamined Root of the Problem

I came to the same conclusion Delany did several years ago, though for different reasons.

Working on a book proposal a decade ago, I was struck by the essential difference between American football and basketball on the one hand, and just about every sport in the world on the other: football and basketball developed primarily as college games. When the NFL and NBA started decades later, they simply hired the best college players and coaches available, but it still took the pro leagues decades to challenge the popularity of college football and basketball. The NFL didn't get a permanent foothold until the classic 1958 title game between the New York Giants and the Baltimore Colts, and the NBA Finals were still on tape-delay until Magic and Bird joined the league in 1979.

Why does this matter? Because by starting after college football and basketball were already established, the NFL and NBA were freed from having to develop viable minor leagues of their own, making them virtually the only sports in the world that don't have them. Roughly a century ago, Major League Baseball and the NHL could not rely on the nascent college programs to fill their rosters, so they had to create their own minor leagues. And that's why almost every high school football and basketball star today has just one path to the big leagues: the NCAA.

This makes no sense. Athletes and universities *can* benefit each other, but they shouldn't *need* to. Pelé never had to worry about passing twelve credits before playing in his first World Cup, and the University of Chicago figured out it didn't need a football team to be a world-class university. As former University of Chicago president Robert Maynard Hutchins liked to say, "Football is to education as bullfighting is to agriculture." He backed it up in 1939, when he pulled the Maroons out of the Big Ten. Today, Chicago's admissions department is the fourth most selective in the country, behind only Harvard, Yale, and Princeton.

When a committed student-athlete enrolls in a four-year college, everyone involved receives at least some benefit. The athlete gets a free education, an enduring asset no matter what he does on the field, and the college enjoys reflected glory from his performance. But when we *require* a gifted athlete with little or no interest in higher education to enroll in a four-year college to get to the NFL or NBA, he is more likely to fail in the classroom, which may actually prevent him from pursuing a promising athletic career—something that happens only in America—and the school's academic reputation will take a very public hit. Nobody wins.

So, how do we fix this?

The Pro and Cons of Paying Players

Everyone agrees it's increasingly difficult to support the farce that the NCAA is foisting upon us, but we can't agree on how to fix it. In recent years we've seen proposals ranging from school-sponsored minor league teams to ending big-time college sports altogether.

The most popular idea sits between those two extremes: give up the ruse, and pay the players. After all, everyone seems to be making millions off the athletes, except the athletes.

Consider the skyrocketing salaries of Division I football coaches, which now average more than $2 million a year, an increase of 750 percent (adjusted for inflation) since 1984, about twenty times more than professors' salaries increased over the same period. In 2012, the highest-paid state employee in twenty-seven states was a football coach, and in thirteen it was a basketball coach. The number of states whose highest-paid public employee was a university president? Four. The explosion in CEO pay, and the rationales that go with it, would be a fair comparison.

This chasm between the value of the players' scholarships and their coaches' salaries will only become more obscene with the arrival of the four-team playoff this season, whose TV rights alone will be worth $5.64 billion over twelve years, or about $470 million a year—all for three games. In the NCAA basketball tournament this past spring, March Madness generated $1 billion *in TV ad revenue alone*.

As I wrote in my book, *Fourth and Long*:

They will tell you it's the cost of doing business—but what's the business, exactly? When *60 Minutes* interviewed [former Domino's Pizza CEO-turned-Michigan athletic director] Dave Brandon that fall, he said the "business model is broken." What he failed to grasp was that it is not supposed to be a business in the first place. After all, what business doesn't have to pay shareholders, partners, owners, taxes, or the star attractions, the players and the band?

This mind-set seems particularly true of the contemporary CEOs-as-athletic directors, for whom no amount is enough.

"As one digs deeper into the national character of the Americans," Alexis de Tocqueville wrote, almost two hundred-years ago, "one sees that they have sought the value of everything in this world only in the answer to this single question: how much money will it bring in?"

More recently, Homer Simpson told his boss, Monty Burns, "You're the richest man I know."

"Yes," Burns replied. "But you know, I'd trade it all for just a little more."

And that's the problem. Like Asian carp invading your freshwater paradise, once the money-grubbers take over, their appetites are insatiable, and they are impossible to remove.

The most serious threat to big-time college athletics is not the endless scandals, which affect only those who get caught, but the rampant greed, which affects everybody. As Michael Kinsley has famously said, "The scandal isn't what's *illegal*. The scandal is what's *legal*."

With so many millions sloshing around the athletes, it's no surprise they're reaching their limits. And it's not just "Johnny Football" Manziel, a uniquely unsympathetic figure, either, but Kain Colter, Northwestern's premed quarterback, who has taken to wearing an armband with "A.P.U." on it, for All Players United, in support of those fighting to protect their rights, and their safety.

Certainly, the idea of giving the players a stipend of one or two thousand dollars a year—which the NCAA almost passed four decades ago—so they can pay for a dinner date, a winter coat, or a trip home, is long overdue. But even that modest proposal will cost more than its proponents imagine, since Title IX will dictate that all scholarship athletes receive the same stipend, be they the All-American quarterback or the second-string coxswain on the women's crew team.

Thus, when people talk about $20,000 "salaries" for college athletes, the cost at the biggest programs, which have some seven hundred student-athletes, will quickly exceed $10 million. And before you know it, you're talking real money.

If you think for a second these payments will be deducted from the coaches' bloated salaries, I have a "Johnny Football" autograph to sell you. No, these salaries will be piled on to the mountain of money that college athletic departments already spend every year. And they will pay for that pile, of course, by extracting still more millions from alternate jersey sales, rising seat license "donations," corporate partnerships, and the ads that come with them—the very things that are alienating lifelong fans.

If I'm right that the biggest threat to college football is not scandal but greed, paying the players will only exacerbate the sport's central problem, setting up the kind of tug-of-wars we see in pro sports that turn everybody off. Pouring more gasoline on a fire will not make it smaller. Paying players will not solve the problem it is intended to solve. The players will soon want more, just like the coaches, and not without reason. But it will create many new problems that will threaten the future of the sport.

Universities already have a difficult time controlling their athletic departments, and the pay-to-play plans will not make it any easier. They will turn the student-athletes into bona fide employees, which will open a Pandora's box of legal issues, including questions from the IRS.

The pay-to-play proposals also assume the current record TV ratings, sweetheart corporate deals, and sold-out stadiums will continue far into the future. But we've already seen plenty of signs that the fans are nearing their breaking point.

Penn State fans travel an average of four hours to see their Nittany Lions play—as hardcore as any fans in college football. But Penn State snapped its six-year streak of one hundred thousand-plus crowds more than a year before Jerry Sandusky was arrested, thanks to an aggressive seat-license program. Three thousand fans dropped their season tickets in 2010, when the seat-license program was introduced. Three thousand more did the next year, and the departures have only accelerated since. When I attended the University of Central Florida–Penn State game this fall, my friends estimated there were no more than eighty-five thousand fans in the stands that night—no matter what they announced as the "official paid attendance."

The cost for a family of four to attend a Michigan football game, with average seats and no hotel rooms or restaurant meals included, runs about $500—more than a day at Disneyworld. And Mickey never loses. While the Michigan athletic department claims the streak of one hundred thousand-plus crowds, dating back to 1975, has never been broken, the game against Akron revealed wide swaths of empty seats, particularly in the student section—your future season ticket holders.

If you crank up the seat licenses, the TV timeouts, and the endless ads another notch or two to pay players' salaries, you will risk losing a generation of fans, and the whole enterprise will collapse. The question of paying the players will become truly academic if there's no money to pay them.

When did you last attend a boxing match or a horse race? If the bottom can fall out of those once-robust sports, it can happen to college football, too. And if you like off-track betting parlors, and the empty stands they create, you're going to love the future of big-time college sports.

Creating Two Tracks to the Big Leagues

Despite the many good reasons to pay the players, I think there are better reasons not to—and a better way to fix the same problem that paying the players is intended to fix.

Delany might not be serious about his dare, but I am.

In my previous book, *Three and Out*, I wrote, "For those rare stars, I've always believed, the NFL and NBA should set up viable minor leagues to give such players a real choice—the same one high school hockey and baseball players have." That came out two years ago. The need for this change is much more urgent today.

What football and basketball players need is what baseball and hockey players have enjoyed for almost a century: a viable minor league, so players who don't want to be college students, and prefer to be paid in cash instead of scholarships, can do just that.

This would cut down on the majority of problems that beset both sports, almost overnight. Johnny Football? Sign all you want. "One and done" becomes "None and done." Go!

Delany's bold statement aside, you have to believe that if the NFL and NBA actually called his bluff, Delany might fear losing some of the NCAA's most exciting players to the new minor leagues—and with them, some of the appeal of college football and basketball.

Fret not. As I wrote in *Fourth and Long*:

College athletes are more passionate playing for a scholarship than pro athletes are playing for millions. And we admire the college athletes more for this very reason. It's the difference between citizen soldiers volunteering for the army and hired Hessians. Give us the doughboys, the G.I. Joes, and the grunts fighting for a cause.

And this is why we watch: not for perfection, but passion—the same reason over a million fans watch the Little League World Series every summer. This point is easily proven: the worst team in the NFL would crush the best team in college football, every year. Yet college football is the only sport in the world that draws more fans to its games than the big league teams it feeds. The attendance at Michigan, Ohio State, and Penn State typically averages 50 percent more than that of the NFL teams in those states—and often doubles it. No minor league baseball or hockey team comes close to matching the attendance of their parent clubs.

This basic truth escapes both the proponents of paying players and the NCAA executives who try to squelch minor leagues from starting: college football is selling romance, not prowess. If ability were the only appeal, we'd move NFL games to Saturday and watch those games instead. But if you lose the romance of college football, you will lose the fans of college football.

We don't have to wonder if creating a separate minor league system will work. We already know. Just check out college hockey. The players who would rather have a paycheck than a scholarship can jump straight to the minor leagues—and they do. Because the players who opt for college are not forced to do so by the NHL, the graduation rates tend to be much higher in college hockey, and the scandals much fewer. College hockey fans love them all the more because they know the guys they're cheering for have chosen to be college hockey players. They're the real deal.

In hockey, at least, both the minor leagues and the colleges deliver the players and the fans exactly what they promise. The only games they play are on the ice.

How to Make It Honest

OK, but why would the NFL and NBA ever go for this, and voluntarily invest their millions to create something they've been getting for free since they started? They wouldn't, of course, so you'd have to force them.

But forcing them can be accomplished in one step: bring back freshmen ineligibility. If you want to make it honest, that's how you do it.

In fact, freshmen ineligibility was the rule from 1905, the year the NCAA was founded, until 1972, and for a simple reason: colleges actually believed their athletes should be students first, and this is how they proved it. It gave all athletes a year to get their feet on the ground and catch up where needed. Dean Smith and Terry Holland argued before the Knight Commission about the merits of freshmen ineligibility—but that was nine years ago, and nothing has changed. Until the NCAA, the leagues, the presidents, and the athletic directors bring back freshmen ineligibility, you should not take them seriously when they speak of "student-athletes." They do not mean it.

By requiring *all* student-athletes to be actual student-athletes, many elite athletes will opt out—but there's no way the NFL or the NBA will let talented eighteen-year-olds wander off if they might be able to help their teams win games. So the NFL and NBA would almost certainly do what they should have done decades ago: Prepare players for their leagues, with their own money, by starting their own minor league teams.

Creating two paths to the pros will throw a bucket of cold water on the overheated facilities arms race, the soaring coaches' salaries, and the insane TV contracts. Yes, those things exist in college hockey and baseball, but not on the same scale. Reclaiming a sense of proportion is what we're seeking here.

We need other reforms, too, of course. We need to put an end to the NCAA's absurd charade of posing as the sheriff when it's really the saloonkeeper. Universities should hire athletic directors who've spent their working lives nurturing student-athletes, not "maximizing the revenue streams" of their "brands." And we should require all universities to reinstate true faculty oversight of their athletic programs.

"Without faculty control," Michigan's legendary athletic director Don

Canham wrote in an essay that came out after his death in 2005, "the presidents are running up to $70 million budget programs (Michigan, Ohio State, Stanford, Texas, etc.) with no oversight. What $70-million business could conduct business without a board of control?"

In the eight years since Canham warned of "unbridled expansion," Michigan's budget has more than doubled. Guess he knew something.

All these changes are needed, but creating a second path to the pros is the key. And—as Smith, Holland, and Canham urged—bringing back freshmen ineligibility is the way to do it.

No, this solution will not create a perfect world. There will still be athletes who aren't bona fide college students. There will still be coaches and boosters happy to break the rules. And there will still be an outsized mania for the sport.

The goal is not perfection, but restoring the sanity needed to protect the integrity of the universities the players are representing, to protect the players from being trapped, and to preserve the passion the players and fans still feel for their favorite sport.

The time to save this century-old game is now. And creating minor leagues to preserve college athletics, while giving all athletes a real choice, is the way to do it.

It's time to call Mr. Delany's bluff.

The Future

WHAT I WANT FOR MY SON

In the spring of 2017 my father turned eighty-five, and he started attending weekly geriatric exercise classes so he could continue walking without a cane. I was fifty-two, and started running again to keep up with my son, who was nineteen months old and just learning how to walk—a late starter, just like his dad.

I'm in a place few find themselves, between one generation near the end and another just beginning. But that's what happens when you have a kid at fifty-one—if you're lucky.

My wife and I are very lucky. She gave birth to a healthy boy, one as happy as any kid can be who still cries a few times a day over putting on his shirt, and taking it off.

Being an older dad is easier in some ways because I've already done all the things I wanted to do as a bachelor, from dating to skydiving to traveling the world. Being married and raising a son is what I want to do now, and it's wonderfully consuming. But it comes with a price: I have to get back in shape—thank you, book deadlines!—to ensure that I can keep up with Teddy for at least twenty years. I owe him that. My rule is simple: whenever he asks me to go play catch or hockey or climb a hill, I can never say no because I'm too old or too tired. My answer has to be, "Sure, let's go!"

I also have a goal: Whenever I pick him up from school, I never want to hear any of his little buddies say, "Hey, Teddy, your grandfather's here!"

So I've got some work to do.

But in most ways, raising a kid in my fifties doesn't seem all that different from what my friends did in their twenties and thirties. Teddy's first months were tiring for us, just like they are for all new parents, until he started sleeping through the night and rewarding us with smiles, then laughter, then actual jokes—jokes that he usually intends.

And now he is two-and-a-half, with all that comes with it—most of it good. Still, as one friend told me, "The reason they call them the Terrible Twos is because they haven't seen the Threes yet."

"You know about the Terrible Twos?" asked another friend, whose sons are in their forties. "They don't end."

We'll face the same challenges all parents do, including how to handle sports. For that, my father is a pretty good model.

My dad grew up in Scarsdale, New York, playing baseball and golf, and was decent at both. He was a passionate fan, too, shifting his loyalties to the Tigers, the Lions, and the Wolverines after my parents moved to Ann Arbor. When his sons started playing hockey, he started following that sport, too, and came to all our games. But he never pushed it, he never coached our teams, and he never criticized those who did—even when I was convinced a few of them richly deserved it.

None of his three kids became all-star athletes, but we were all respectable, hardworking players who earned varsity letters on competitive teams. Our dad took pride in this, though whenever he praised our play, he quickly added that schoolwork was what really mattered.

I plan to take a similar approach, though I suspect it's harder than my dad made it look. I know you shouldn't push your kid into sports. It can backfire, and even if Teddy goes along with it, it will suck all the joy out of the pursuit. But I admit I'd be disappointed if Teddy didn't take an interest in sports. Not because I expect him to achieve some greater glory, or to become some know-it-all winning bar bets, but to get from sports the lifelong lessons and pleasures they've given me.

What I want for Teddy is simple, but not easy: To be healthy, to be coordinated, to delight in what his body can do, and to develop the inner confidence those things can bring. I want him to stay in shape his entire life, and if he chooses to compete, to enjoy the games whether he wins or loses—something his dad hasn't always been able to do.

I want him to savor the simple fun of playing with his friends, far from adults, whether it's a game of shinny on a pond, pickle in the backyard, or H-O-R-S-E on a garage hoop. I want Teddy and his friends to learn how to make up their own rules, pick their own teams, and settle their own disputes.

I want him to know the value of being on a team—both tight-knit, successful squads, and disconnected, dysfunctional ones—because we spend more of our lives working together than alone. I want him to learn how to give more than he gets, how to help the lesser players with humility, and when he's one of those lesser players, to develop the resolve to hang in there and contribute what he can, and feel good about it. Of course, when you've been at both ends, you know better than to get too high or too low—a tenet of the mature person.

Part of me naturally wants to spare Teddy the pain of being picked last, of blowing the big play, of losing the game, or getting cut from the team—

all of which I experienced. I suspect watching those things happen to the person I love more than anyone will be more painful for me than for him. I hope to be strong enough to do what my dad did when I was the last man cut from the travel team for the third year in a row, a demonstrably unfair decision: Nothing. When I made my case to him, he agreed I had been screwed, so I didn't understand why he refused to do anything about it. But years later, when I stubbornly plowed through piles of editors' rejection letters until I could make a living doing this, I realized my dad had helped me develop the emotional muscle I need to keep going.

I know Teddy will have to face all of it, or he won't grow up.

Of course, I'm getting ahead of myself. The kid's just two. But I'm already watching him with the unequaled scrutiny of a loving parent, my emotions rising and falling with each little triumph and setback. Teddy was an early talker and a late walker—imagine that. The genes are strong with this one. Well, kid, welcome to sports writing! Don't worry about all those big, fast guys on the field. You'll be up there in the press box, clacking away.

Watching him learn to walk was my first experience cheering for him. He was a determined little practice-walker at home, constantly raising his hands for us to walk him around the house. But at his daycare it was hard watching Teddy stand up to try his "stumble walking." When his "walking friends" saw him wobble, he immediately plopped down on his butt and scooched across the room. I was stunned to see he was old enough to feel embarrassed, and I ached for him to catch up to his buddies. But as a parent, what can you do? The answer: not much.

When he finally learned the trick at 19 months, he took off, walking everywhere and climbing over everything, reveling in his mobility like a teenager with a driver's license. I saw him gain real confidence, the kind a kid can only give himself—and that was worth the heartache of watching him struggle to get there.

I'm sure we'll repeat that cycle many times.

I'm 5'-8", my wife is 5'-5", and we both got glasses before high school. This is not the breeding of a future Olympian, or even an average basketball player. But the good news is, there's no jumping in hockey, so if the kid likes my favorite sport, he has a fighting chance.

I've spent some twenty seasons coaching high school baseball, hockey, and soccer, but I'm not sure if I want to coach any of my son's teams. I do know I want to see his face after he gets his first hit or his first goal. From coaching, I learned that it's far more exciting than any hit or goal I ever got myself. I want to see the self-assurance that comes from doing something he didn't know he could do.

But whether I coach his teams or not, there is no avoiding that moment when you have to let go of his bicycle seat, watch him pedal off, and simply hope for the best—knowing that he's bound to wipe out, again and again, and it's his job to get himself up and hop back on the bike.

Bo Schembechler had it right: as a coach, it's your job to get your players to kick-off ready to play. After that, it's up to them, and if they come through, they get the credit, not you.

I also hope Teddy becomes a fan, because cheering your heroes is one of the best parts of being a kid. When I was a teenager, sports kept me connected to my dad when few other things did, and today they keep me connected to my friends, who still come over to watch the games. I hope Teddy sees in sports an expression of our values—good and bad—and is still able to find inspiration under all the commercialization.

In short, I hope sports give him a richer life, and make him a better person.

In the end, what counts is not what I want for Teddy, but what he wants for himself.

So I hope he gets what he wants—and perhaps a few things he doesn't. That's what sports have given me.

Acknowledgments

Producing any book requires lots of help, and therefore warrants lots of thank-yous. Because this book is a collection of pieces, it was not nearly as arduous to put together as my usual non-fiction narratives, but every book has been trickier than I expected.

The pieces in this book span a quarter-century and were drawn from a dozen media outlets. Credits are listed below each piece's title, but I want to thank the editors who worked on these stories the first time around. I was given my first column at the *Ann Arbor News* in 1992, under the always kind Anne Valentine Martino. At the *Detroit News* I was lucky to work under three journalistic stalwarts: publisher Bob Giles, a brave and wise man; editor-in-chief Mark Lett, who brought great vision to our work; and Sunday sports editor Jim Russ, simply one of the best I've ever worked for, anywhere. For the seven-part series on Jackie Robinson, which included the piece on Branch Rickey, I worked with Alan Whitt, first class "on and off the field."

I've free-lanced for probably two dozen media outlets, including *Sports Illustrated*, where the legendary Myra Gelband practiced her craft; the *Wall Street Journal*, where Sam Walker and Darren Everson invited me to write more than a few pieces; and ThePostgame.com, where Victor Chi runs a half-dozen a year. At National Public Radio, David McGuffin has guided my work with aplomb and good cheer, a classic Canuck to the core.

I owe a special thanks to Steve Schram, Executive Director of Michigan Radio, for asking me more than a decade ago to provide weekly sports commentaries, and assigning Vince Duffy the unenviable task of editing my work. Vince has wielded his scalpel with skill and precision, usually on short notice.

I also want to thank the wonderful Mary Morgan at the *Ann Arbor Chronicle*, which enjoyed a short but brilliant run, and my friends at *Traverse Magazine* and *Michigan History*.

John Lofy not only did pioneering work leading *Michigan Today* into the digital age, he has edited my stories—officially and otherwise—for almost as long as I've known him, including most of these pieces. James Tobin, another close friend, has provided his editorial help from my try-out with the *Detroit News* in 1995—including the story on the Big House—right up to *The Great Halifax Explosion*. Speaking of which, a number of these stories either inspired books or were drawn from them, including *Blue Ice, Bo's Lasting Lessons, Three and Out, Fourth and Long,* and *Endzone,* for which I need to thank Kelly Sippell, Rick Wolff, Thomas Lebien (who's edited five of my books, because he's that good), Marc Resnick, and Peter Hubbard. I cannot thank them enough.

At the University of Michigan Press, Kelly Sippell edited my first book, *Blue Ice: The Story of Michigan Hockey,* with incredible skill, dedication, and care, back in 2001. If she hadn't, I'm not sure I would have been able to write another book, let alone nine more. Kelly's disciple Scott Ham edited this book, for which I'm equally grateful. A rising star, Scott has lent his talents, judgment, and good humor to a surprisingly dicey enterprise, then turned it over to the designers, who have transformed a stack of words into a truly attractive package.

Although my wife Christie didn't start reading my stories until 2013, she has given her advice on just about all of my work since, to great effect, not to mention her boundless support during the many late nights and early mornings needed to finish all these assignments under often crushing deadlines. She has been a great teammate in more ways than I could imagine five years ago.

Our two-and-a-half year old son Teddy has yet to get his fingers on my manuscripts—except to toss them on the floor and spread peanut butter on them—but that's only because he can't read yet. I sincerely hope he'll join the family business soon enough, but even if he doesn't, he has already provided the best inspiration for this collection: My desire for him to have some idea what captured his dad's imagination all those years before he showed up. I have no illusions that my work will last forever, but I hope it lasts long enough for Teddy to enjoy it, because he will surely outlive everything else I do.

Last but not least I want to express my deep gratitude to you, the readers. Without your quarter century of support, I would not be able to do what I love for a living.

Thank you!